# DECODING
# THE CHURCH

# DECODING THE CHURCH

## MAPPING THE DNA OF CHRIST'S BODY

HOWARD A. SNYDER

WITH

DANIEL V. RUNYON

**BakerBooks**

A Division of Baker Book House Co
Grand Rapids, Michigan 49516

Published by Baker Books
a division of Baker Book House Company
P.O. Box 6287, Grand Rapids, MI 49516-6287

Printed in the United States of America

**Library of Congress Cataloging-in-Publication Data**

Snyder, Howard A.
    Decoding the church : mapping the DNA of Christ's body / Howard A. Snyder with Daniel V. Runyon.
        p.     cm.
    Includes bibliographical references.
    ISBN 0-8010-9142-X (pbk.)
    1. Church renewal.  I. Runyon, Daniel V.  II. Title.
    BV600.3 .S67 2002
    262′ .77—dc21                                                          2002004991

For current information about all releases from Baker Book House, visit our web site:
http://www.bakerbooks.com

To our students
at Spring Arbor University
and Asbury Theological Seminary
Bearers of the church's DNA

Jesus said, "The rest of the seeds fell on good ground where they grew and produced a hundred times as many seeds." When Jesus had finished speaking, he said, "If you have ears, pay attention!"

Luke 8:8 CEV

# Contents

# Acknowledgments

Some of the material by Howard A. Snyder contained in this book was published previously in different form and is used here by permission, with considerable revision.

Chapter 2 was first published as "The Complexity of the Church," *Great Commission Quarterly* (May 1994): 22, 27–30.

Chapter 3 is adapted from "The Trinitarian Nature of the Missional Church," *The Gospel and Our Culture* 10:1 (March 1998): 4–5.

Chapters 4, 5, and 6 are adapted and expanded from "New Wineskins: With What Materials? A Theology of New Wineskins for the Twenty-First Century," *Journal of the American Society for Church Growth* 12 (winter 2001): 15–40.

Chapter 5 includes material from "The Work of the Holy Spirit," *Decision*, January 2000, 11–12.

Chapter 6 includes material from "By All Possible Means," *Light and Life*, August 1996, 15–17, 25.

Chapters 7, 8, and 9 first appeared as *Coherence in Christ: The Larger Meaning of Ecology*, Mission Evangelism Series, no. 4 (New York: General Board of Global Ministries, United Methodist Church, 2000). Some of this material is adapted also from *EarthCurrents: The Struggle for the World's Soul* (Nashville: Abingdon, 1995), chapters 16–17.

Chapters 10 and 11 are based upon "Globalization: Challenge and Opportunity for Christian Mission," an address given at the Mission Korea 2000 Conference, Seoul, Korea, August, 2000; not previously published in English.

Chapter 12 incorporates the following previously published articles: "Speaking Words of Grace," *Light and Life*, July/August 2001, 23; "Is God's Love Unconditional?" *Christianity Today*, 17 July 1995, 30; "Why We Love the Earth," editorial in *Christianity Today*, 15 May 1995, 15; "Prayer in Community," *Light and Life*, May/June 1999, 52.

# PREFACE

Behold, a pastor who enjoyed gardening went forth to plant a tiny tree in his yard. It was a weeping willow seedling that, with time, might grow into a graceful, rounded tree higher than his house. For the tiny seedling's genetic code carried everything needed to produce a magnificent tree.

The pastor cared for the tree and watered it. Sunlight and nourishing rain fell upon the tree, and it began to grow. Before long it sent up a fair shoot more than a foot tall, sprouting beautiful, narrow leaves along its length.

But one day the pastor went out, and behold, the little tree was broken. Maybe an animal had nipped it, or a bird had tried to land on it, or a falling branch had crushed it. The pastor saw how vulnerable this little tree was, despite its great potential. So he put a fence around the tree until it could grow stronger.

The pastor recalled that thrice before he had tried to start a weeping willow tree, and each time he had failed. One time he had been away for three weeks during a very dry season, and when he returned home, behold, the tree was withered, smitten by hot August winds. He watered it profusely, but it was too late; the tree died.

Yet the pastor knew that this time, with proper care and protection, his little tree might still grow into a mighty, beautiful weeping willow in which the birds might find shelter and under which happy children might play.

The pastor thought much about this, and he realized that all living things are vulnerable when they are very young. A child might snap off an oak seedling, and it would die. But if the seedling grew into a mighty tree, it would be stronger than a man and would survive through many human generations.

Then the pastor began to understand Jesus' parables about trees and vines and branches. This is the way it is with the church. A new, little church is very vulnerable. A small force can break, warp, or kill it. But if the church survives and grows, it becomes a mighty living presence in the earth, constantly reproducing and renewing itself, spreading out to bless the whole world. It is fruitful and multiplies, becoming not just one tree, but many. And yet every new seedling from the great tree must pass through that same wondrous period of vulnerability.

*Yes,* the pastor thought, *so it is with the church. It is a living thing, like a tree or a vine. It has all the vulnerability and yet all the potential, promise, and reproducibility of living things.*

And he thought, *God has put his own life into the life of the church. He has given it a unique genetic code, so that it may grow up into the full potential he built into it. I wonder,* he thought, *what would change if we meditated on the church as a living thing, an organism with its own special DNA, created by God?*

# INTRODUCTION

This is a book about the DNA of Christ's body, the church. According to the New Testament, Jesus is the head of the church and the church is his body.

Have you ever wondered about Jesus' own DNA? Jesus Christ was the son of Mary—and the Son of God! Certainly Jesus had DNA, since he was fully human. But it couldn't have been exactly the same as Mary's, or Jesus would have been her clone.

Did Jesus have the DNA of Adam? Or was it more nearly that of David, the "man after God's own heart"? Clearly it couldn't have been that of Joseph, his earthly father, for from him Jesus inherited nothing genetically, though much culturally and spiritually.

Such questions may sound frivolous—even blasphemous—to Christians who, heavily accenting Christ's deity, easily forget that Jesus Christ was fully human. If Jesus was human, he had human DNA. So in these days of genetic revolution, the question of Jesus' DNA naturally arises. What does it mean that Jesus was made like us in every way, except without sin (Heb. 2:17; 4:15)? Surely it says something about his full humanity—including his DNA.

These are questions about the physical body of Christ. Amazingly, the New Testament calls the *church* the body of Christ! (See Rom. 12:4–5; 1 Cor. 12:27; Eph. 1:22–23; 4:15–16; 5:23, 30; Col. 1:24.) How can this be? Is this merely a spiritual metaphor, or is it more?

Clearly the church, Christ's body, does not have the same physical DNA of Jesus—even though the church is in some sense physical, made up of flesh-and-blood Christians living on earth. The church is the body of Christ spiritually. Yet it is to bear the image of Christ, just as surely as if it had inherited his physical DNA. The church, as individual persons and as a social organism on earth, is to be conformed to the likeness of Jesus Christ (Rom. 8:29). There must be a family resemblance. Whatever Jesus' *physical* DNA, his DNA as head of the church—what we might call ecclesial DNA—is to be carried through into every part of his body, into every branch of the vine, out to the last leaf and the last grape.

13

In this age of genetic awareness, it is helpful to ask what it would mean to view the church genetically and organically. We use the image of DNA here deliberately, not incidentally. It is more than an illustration. The DNA analogy fits, for the primary biblical images of the church are organic, not static or institutional. Searching for the church's "genetic code" can help us understand the mystery of the church.

Though genetics and DNA are modern concepts, they are rooted in creation as it comes from the hand of God. So we are actually closer to Scripture, and to the way God works in nature and in society, when we think genetically about the church than when we think organizationally.

Beginning with this genetic model, then, this book ponders some key questions:

- How can our knowledge of genetics and DNA help us understand the essential nature of the church?
- What does a genetic understanding of the church say about its mission?
- If we view the church and its mission genetically, what insights does this give us about church structure?
- Given a genetic view of the church's nature, mission, and structure, how should the church live its daily life? If the body of Christ shares in some significant way the DNA of its head, Jesus Christ, what does this say about practical public discipleship?

## Introducing Heartland Evangelical Church

This book about the DNA of Christ's body is also the story of Heartland Evangelical Church. Heartland is a fictional congregation that passes through a long, sometimes painful but finally fruitful search to discover its own unique DNA and to live faithfully as Christ's body. Heartland Evangelical is a church of mostly middle-class folk firmly committed to the authority of Scripture and to sincere Christian living.

In each chapter, we see how the Heartland church faces the issue discussed in that chapter. In trying to live faithfully as Christ's body, Heartland discovers that when it adopts methods, structures, or concepts that clash with its own fundamental nature as Christ's body, the result is either frustration or failure—even betrayal of the gospel itself. It becomes like a rabbit that tries to fly or like a bird that never uses its wings, supposing its calling is merely to walk.

Heartland is a composite of many churches we have known. It is not an actual church but in many ways is typical of theologically conservative Protestant churches in the United States. Most of the more dramatic things we narrate in this book really happened, however, though not all in the same church or the same time and place.

The members of the body at Heartland struggle to discover the central lesson of this book: *Churches that would be faithful to Jesus Christ and effective ministers of the Good News must understand what they are and live consistently with the way God made them.* Heartland is a church that has learned some priceless lessons about the DNA it inherited from Christ.

1

---

# Do Churches Have DNA?

For several years now, news reports have been full of startling breakthroughs in genetic research. Scientists are mapping the human genome, seeking answers to the mystery of life. Some kinds of cloning have become a reality. Specific disease-causing genes have been isolated. We are in the first stages of a history-shaking genetic revolution.

What does this mean for the church—for its nature and mission? Thinking of the church genetically raises fascinating and fruitful questions about the nature of the church—the church as a living organism with its own genetic structure, its unique DNA.

What is the church's DNA? Can it be decoded? Can it help us better understand what the church is essentially—how it lives, grows, reproduces, and fulfills God's purposes?

Understanding the church genetically is *not* the way it has been understood for many generations. In this chapter we examine the genetic traits of the DNA we have inherited from Christ and what these inherited traits mean for the church. This is one way of viewing the church genetically. In later chapters we will explore other dimensions of the church's rich and complex genetic inheritance.[1]

Theology can be thought of as a kind of genetic typing. Creeds are declarations about the church's perceived DNA. The Nicene Creed (A.D. 325) was an especially seminal declaration that shaped the way Christians have thought of the church ever since.

The Council of Nicea declared that the church is *one, holy, catholic,* and *apostolic*. This classic Nicene formula *(una, sancta, catholica, apostolica)* continues to shape the way we think about the church today.

Christians of varied traditions accept these four classic characteristics of the church as fundamental components of its DNA. Whatever else we may say about the church, it is one, holy, catholic, and apostolic, or it is not the true church of Jesus Christ.[2]

These four classic characteristics, often referred to as the "marks" of the church, have been almost universally accepted through the centuries. "Within the Reformation there was much difference of opinion about the number of *notae*," or marks, G. C. Berkouwer wrote, and yet

> the four words themselves were never disputed, since the Reformers did not opt for other "attributes." There is a common attachment everywhere to the description of the Church in the Nicene Creed: one, holy, catholic, and apostolic. Even after the Reformation, in spite of all the differences in interpretation which appeared with respect to the four words, this usage remained the same. . . . The striking thing here is that the general question about whether the Church is truly one and catholic, apostolic and holy, is not asked; rather, a number of [additional] marks are mentioned [such as] the pure preaching of the gospel, the pure administration of the sacraments, and the exercise of church discipline.[3]

## The Marks as the Church's DNA

Two things stand out when we examine the classic marks in the light of history. First, they arose in a particular context and were in fact used as a test to exclude Christians who understood the church differently. Second, at various points in history, earnest Christians have argued plausibly that *other* traits more truly define the essence of the church.

Consider an example from the nineteenth century. Benjamin T. Roberts (1823–93), principal founder of the Free Methodist Church, took a different route in describing the essential character of the church. Writing in 1860, Roberts affirmed that the "provisions of the gospel are for all." He then asked,

> *But for whose benefit are special efforts to be put forth?* Who must be *particularly* cared for? Jesus settles this question. . . . When John sent to know who he was, Christ charged the messengers to return and show John the things which they had seen and heard. "The blind receive their sight, and the lame walk, the lepers are cleansed, and the deaf hear, the dead are raised up," and as if all this would be insufficient to satisfy John of the validity of his claims, he adds, *"and the poor have the gospel preached to them."* This was the crowning proof that He was the *One that should come.* . . . He that thus cared for the poor must be from God. In this respect the Church must follow in the footsteps of Jesus. She must see to it, that the

gospel is preached to the poor. . . . This was the view taken by the first heralds of the cross.[4]

Roberts then quotes the apostle Paul:

Brothers, think of what you were when you were called. Not many of you were wise by human standards; not many were influential; not many were of noble birth. But God chose the foolish things of the world to shame the wise; God chose the weak things of the world to shame the strong. He chose the lowly things of this world and the despised things—and the things that are not—to nullify the things that are, so that no one may boast before him (1 Cor. 1:26–29).

Roberts notes, "Similar statements in regard to the rich are not to be found in the Bible." He concludes, "Thus the duty of preaching the gospel to the poor is enjoined, by the plainest precepts and examples. This is the standing proof of the Divine mission of the Church."[5]

Roberts is making a claim about the nature of the church itself, about its DNA, not just about evangelism. This is even clearer as he goes on to quote Stephen Olin (1797–1851), president of Wesleyan University and one of Roberts' theological mentors. In his sermon "The Adaptation of the Gospel to the Poor," Olin said:

There are hot controversies about the true Church. What constitutes it—what is essential to it—what vitiates it? These may be important questions, but there are more important ones. It may be that there can not be a Church without a bishop, or that there can. There can be none without a Gospel, and a Gospel for the poor. Does a Church preach the Gospel to the poor—preach it effectively? Does it convert and sanctify the people? Are its preaching, its forms, its doctrines adapted *specially* to these results? If not, we need not take the trouble of asking any more questions about it. It has missed the main matter. It does not do what Jesus did—what the apostles did. Is there a Church—a ministry—that converts, reforms, sanctifies the people? Do the poor really learn to love Christ? Do they live purely and die happy? I hope that Church conforms to the New Testament in its government and forms as far as may be. . . . I wish its ministers may be men of the best training, and eloquent. I hope they worship in goodly temples, and all that; but [much more important:] They preach a saving Gospel to the poor, and that is enough. It is an apostolic Church. Christ is the corner-stone. The main thing is secured, thank God.[6]

B. T. Roberts wrote similarly in an 1864 article, "Gospel to the Poor":

*The preaching of the Gospel to the poor is the standing miracle which attests to its Divine origin.* It is placed by our Saviour in the same class

with raising the dead, and cleansing lepers—something which no man
acting from the mere promptings of nature ever did, or ever will do. . . .
To go out, without purse or scrip, among the poor and the outcast, and
proclaim the Gospel of God in all fidelity, having no dependence for support but the promise, "Lo, I am with you always," is a course of life, which
one will not be very likely to pursue until the end of his days, unless he
has been sent by God. He who does this, is in the true succession. He walks
as Christ walked.[7]

Roberts makes both a sociological and a theological argument about
the priority of the poor—or perhaps more accurately, a sociotheologi-
cal argument. "Wesley and Whitefield, going to the collieries and com-
mons, and into the streets and lanes of the cities, proclaiming the Gospel
to the neglected masses, . . . did more to rescue England from infidelity
than all the learned divines who wrote essays upon 'the evidences of
Christianity,'"[8] he said. Roberts believed that "in all ages" the poor are
most ready to respond to the gospel. He added,

> If it is the duty of the Church of Jesus Christ to preach the Gospel to
> the poor, then all the arrangements of the Church must be made with a
> view to the accomplishment of this end. . . . It must be aimed at directly.
> Every thing . . . that has a tendency . . . to defeat this, must be thrown out.
> If the Gospel is placed within the reach of the poor it is placed within the
> reach of all. . . . Preaching that awakens the attention of the poor, and
> leads them to Jesus, will interest all classes.[9]

Roberts concluded his article with a Jubilee appeal to Isaiah 61 and
Luke 4:

> Let us come back to the spirit of the Gospel. Let us get down so low at
> the feet of Jesus as to forget all our pride and dignity, and be willing to
> worship with the lowest of our kind, remembering that we are the fol-
> lowers of Him "who had not where to lay his head." "THE SPIRIT OF THE
> LORD IS UPON ME, BECAUSE HE HATH ANOINTED ME TO PREACH THE GOSPEL TO
> THE POOR; *he hath sent me to heal the broken-hearted, to preach deliverance
> to the captives, and recovering of sight to the blind, to set at liberty them that
> are bruised, to preach the acceptable year of the Lord.*"[10]

Two fundamental claims about the nature of the true church are made
here: First, that preaching the gospel to the poor is an identifying mark
of the church—part of its essential DNA. Second, that this mark is a test
of whether the church is genuinely *apostolic*—is the church walking in
the steps of Jesus? Whoever ministers the gospel among the poor "is in
the true succession. He walks as Christ walked," Roberts observed. The

church that preaches the gospel to the poor "is an apostolic Church," Olin said. Note that these authors appeal to Scripture, particularly to the teaching and example of Jesus Christ, not to particular creeds. They are digging deep, looking for the church's real DNA.

## A Broader Perspective

If we go back to Scripture in search of the church's DNA, we discover that preaching the gospel to the poor as an essential mark of the church has at least as much biblical support as do the four classic marks.[11] There is actually more direct biblical basis for ministry to and among the poor than for universality or catholicity, for example, as a mark of the church.

In fact, Jesus' example of and teaching about the gospel for the poor raises pointed questions about the four classic marks. How biblical are they? How *comprehensive* are they, in terms of the full mystery of the body of Christ? How completely do they reflect the church's DNA?

The four classic marks are, in fact, highly ambiguous. They don't give a clear enough picture of the church's DNA. Through the centuries, theologians have debated just what these marks mean and how to read them. Frequently the marks have been interpreted, or reinterpreted, to harmonize with some other schema. For example, someone concerned about the spiritual vitality and evangelistic vigor of the church will interpret these marks in a way consistent with that concern—as did John Wesley.[12] Someone concerned with authority in the church might emphasize unity in doctrinal teaching and apostolic authority and succession, as in classic (pre–Vatican II) Roman Catholic ecclesiology. Someone concerned primarily with church growth may reinterpret these marks to undergird a theology of church growth, as does Charles Van Engen in his book *God's Missionary People*.[13]

Often, Ephesians 4:3–6 is assumed to be the key text for the classic marks:

> Make every effort to keep the unity of the Spirit through the bond of peace. There is one body and one Spirit—just as you were called to one hope when you were called—one Lord, one faith, one baptism; one God and Father of all, who is over all and through all and in all.

This important passage highlights particularly the unity (and by implication, catholicity) of the church—"one Lord, one faith, one baptism." A number of other New Testament passages—especially John 17—also speak of the unity of the church. Other passages in Ephesians point to the church's holiness (especially 5:25–27) and apostolicity (note 2:20, "built on the foundation of the apostles and prophets," and 3:5, "revealed by the Spirit to God's holy apostles and prophets"; cf. 4:11).

But is this approach inductive or deductive? Discerning the church's true DNA requires an inductive approach, starting with all the biblical evidence. Ephesians 4:7, for example—the very next verse after the key declaration of the church's unity—says, "But to each one of us grace has been given as Christ apportioned it." This clearly introduces the contrasting element of charismatic diversity.

When we look carefully at the New Testament, we discover that the four classic marks really tell only half the story. They highlight but one side of the church's DNA. We need a fuller picture. It would be more biblically accurate to say that the church is:

DIVERSE as well as ONE
CHARISMATIC as well as HOLY
LOCAL as well as CATHOLIC or UNIVERSAL
PROPHETIC as well as APOSTOLIC

Classic theology has tended to speak of *one holy catholic* and *apostolic* church. Less frequently has it spoken of the church as *diverse, charismatic, local,* and *prophetic.* Yet if we take our ecclesiological cues from the Book of Acts, or even the Gospels, we see it is the second set of qualities that often is emphasized. In Acts, for example, the *diversity* of the church is clear in the stories of the early Christian communities, such as those at Jerusalem, Antioch, Philippi, and Corinth. The *charismatic* nature of the early church is obvious in the many "miraculous signs and wonders" that the apostles performed (Acts 4:30; 5:12; 14:3; and 15:12; for example). The *local* nature of the church is evident precisely in the fact that the church had to be planted and contextualized in specific local social environments. The *prophetic* character of the early church is seen in the church's formation of a contrast society (note Acts 2:42–47) whose values and worldview clashed with those of the dominant society (Acts 19). Of course, one can also find evidence in Acts of the unity, holiness, catholicity, and apostolicity of the church.

How do we reconcile these two sets of contrasting marks? Genetics can help us find the balance. DNA is always made up of four base pairs of compounds. The components of each pair are not opposites but are complementary. Likewise, the contrasting sets of marks of the church that we have discussed are not in opposition to each other but are instead *complementary.* They are essential truths that are at some level in tension with yet necessary to each other. The genetic counterpart of *unity* is not division but *diversity.* The genetic match of *holiness* is not sinfulness but *charismatic giftedness.* The counterpart of *catholic* is not locally confined but *contextual*. And *apostolic* pairs not with heretical but with *prophetic*, a characteristic that focuses on justice as well as truth and on being an alternative society as well as a winsome evangelistic community. No one under biblical authority would claim that the true church is divided, sinful, heretical, and locally confined! But many sincere Christians have in fact denied that the true church is essentially diverse, charismatic, contextual, and prophetic.

The genetic pairing of these sets of traits comes into sharp relief when we see how they imply differing models of the church. When the church is a dynamic movement, it tends to be prophetic, charismatically empowered, diverse (perhaps contrasting with the larger church), and contextualized to its immediate social environment.[14] But when the church transitions into a more settled institution or organization, it tends to celebrate (and perhaps enforce) its oneness, holiness (that is, sacredness as institution!), universality, and apostolic authority.[15]

In chart form, we see two contrasting models:

| Organic Movement | Organized Institution |
| --- | --- |
| Diverse, Varied | One, Uniform |
| Charismatic | Holy (sacred) |
| Local, Contextual | Catholic, Universal |
| Prophetic Word | Apostolic Authority |

## Completing the Church's DNA

Have our churches been operating with only half of their DNA? Have we reduced the mystery of the church to a neat but incomplete package, thus setting the stage for splits and new movements that sense intuitively that something is missing? For example, this dynamic helps explain the emergence in the second century of the New Prophecy Movement (so-called Montanism), which emphasized charismatic gifts that the larger church was beginning to ignore.[16]

As we have seen, the contrasting marks of the church are not in opposition to each other. They are like the left and right sides of the human brain; they balance each other. Faithful churches live in dynamic tension with these pairs of character traits, or genetic predispositions. The church is the multifaceted emblem of the kingdom of God, and these contrasting qualities present complementary, corollary truths about the complex mystery that is the body of Christ. When churches operate with their full DNA, they become, in effect, stem cells of the kingdom of God.

If we view this second set of marks as the missing half of the church's DNA, a more complete yet complex picture of the true church emerges. The church is *simultaneously* one and diverse, holy and charismatic, catholic and local, apostolic and prophetic.

We may ask some pointed questions about this contrasting, often neglected second set of marks—questions that in fact reach beyond ecclesiology to the whole Christian theological enterprise.

- Is there not at least as much biblical basis for the second set as for the first?
- Would not a proper Trinitarian ecclesiology stress both sets in mutual interdependence, like genetic pairs?
- Is the first set (taken alone) biased against the proper work of the Holy Spirit?

If we base our churches on the full range of biblical revelation rather than only on particular creeds, we have a fuller, more potent, and truer image of the mystery that is the body of Christ. These two contrasting sets of characteristics *together* make up the complex reality of the church. Each pair represents complementary facets of the church's life that are essential to its genetic makeup.

## The Biblical Roots of the Missing Half

Scripture shows that the "missing half" of the church's genetic code is just as firmly grounded in divine revelation as are the traditional marks.

1. *The church is not only **one**; it is also **many**.* It is manifold and diverse. Consider the diversity of the first Christian congregations (Jerusalem, Antioch, Ephesus, Corinth, for example). Note the biblical passages celebrating the ethnic, socioeconomic, and class diversity of the church (for example, 1 Cor. 12:13; Gal. 3:23–29; Col. 3:11). The New Testament highlights not only the unity we have in Christ but also the diversity that makes this unity so miraculous. Unity in spite of great diversity is one of the most amazing things about the early church.

Further, it seems legitimate to apply the "one body, many members" teaching of 1 Corinthians 12 and Romans 12 to the universal as well as the local church. The church, locally and globally, is *both* one and many.

2. *The church is **charismatic** as well as **holy**.* The same Holy Spirit who sanctifies the church invests it with diverse gifts (1 Cor. 12; Eph. 4:7–16; Heb. 2:4). It is the *Holy* Spirit who gives gifts. The church func-

tions best with both the fruit and the gifts of the Spirit, incarnating both the character and the charisma of Jesus. Several Scriptures directly link the holy (or sacred or set-apart) character of the church with its being a gift-endowed community of the Spirit (for example, Acts 1:8; 2:4–38; Heb. 2:4; 1 Peter 2:9). Also, the church is often described in Scripture as holy and charismatic, though in different passages.

Historically, however, the church has found it hard to hold these two characteristics together, both in theology and in practice. Church history offers varied examples of tensions at this point, including the early-twentieth-century split in the Holiness Movement that produced modern-day Pentecostalism.[17] Strangely, churches have difficulty holding the fruit and the gifts of the Spirit together in creative balance.

3. *The church is both **local** and **universal***. It exists simultaneously as the worldwide body of Christ (in this world and beyond) and as very diverse, particular local communities, each with its own special flavor, style, and culture. The church both transcends culture and immerses itself in particular cultures.

Here again, the church has trouble maintaining a balance. In its mainline forms the church has tended to value uniformity over particularity, universality over locality, cultural transcendence over cultural incarnation, and stability and predictability over innovation. Sometimes it has gone to the opposite extreme.

Biblically, the church is both local and universal. The New Testament use of the word "church" shows this (for example, Matt. 16:18; 18:17; Acts 8:1; 9:31; 11:22–26; 13:1; 15:22; 20:17; 1 Cor. 12:28; Eph. 1:22; 3:10; 5:29–32; Rev. 2–3). Further evidence is the history of early Christian communities (pictured especially in the Book of Acts) and apostolic teaching about adapting to local customs regarding food and dress (note Rom. 14:21; 1 Cor. 8:9–13).

The New Testament puts at least as much stress on the local character of the church as it does on its universality. We miss the richness of the church's DNA if we fail to see this.

4. *The church is just as truly **prophetic** as it is **apostolic***. The church is built, after all, "on the foundation of the apostles and prophets, with Christ Jesus himself as the chief cornerstone" (Eph. 2:20; also note Eph. 3:4–5; Rev. 18:20). Jesus is both the Apostle and the Prophet who establishes the church (Luke 1:76; 13:33; 24:19; Heb. 3:1). The biblical pairing of "apostles and prophets" signals that the two belong together.[18]

The church is apostolic in the sense that it is sent into the world as the Father sent Jesus, sent to continue the works he began (John 14:12; 20:21). Jesus first commissioned his twelve apostles, then Paul and an expanding corps of apostolic witnesses (Rom. 16:7; Eph. 4:11). Faithfulness to both the words and the works of Jesus Christ—both his life and his teaching—is necessary for true apostolicity. This is why B. T. Roberts and others are right to insist that genuine apostolicity means preaching the gospel to the poor. But apostolicity also means faithful witness to who Jesus really is in truth—fidelity to the gospel *of* Jesus and the gospel *about* Jesus. Faithfulness to the words, works, and life of Jesus Christ together define the real meaning of apostolic succession.

But the church is prophetic as well as apostolic. This is true in two ways. First, the church is an actual community that visibly incarnates the prophetic messages of justice, mercy, and truth found in the Old Testament prophetic books and in the life of Jesus. Second, the church is prophetic in proclaiming the good news of the reign of God within the present world. This will mean different things in different historical contexts, but it always means being salt and light in the present world (Matt. 5:13–14; John 8:12; Phil. 2:15). It always means holding up before people the joy, promise, and cost of the kingdom of God.

Being "built on the foundation of the apostles and prophets" means the church is an apostolic *people*, not just a church with apostles; it means being a prophetic *people*, not just a church with prophets. There is the apostleship and prophethood of all believers as surely as there is the priesthood of all believers. Churches demonstrate this reality when all the gifts, functioning corporately, constitute the church a prophetic people (1 Cor. 12–14; Eph. 4:7–16; Rom. 12:4–10).

The full range of Scripture reveals that the church is *both* one and diverse, *both* holy and charismatic, *both* universal and local, *both* apostolic and prophetic.[19] The church becomes powerfully dynamic in any context when these paired marks become its experience. When they don't, Christians are robbed of essential parts of their genetic endowment.

## The Gospel to the Poor

Where, then, does the gospel to the poor fit into the church's DNA? Is it an essential mark of the church or only secondary? If it is essential, how does it connect with the eight marks discussed above?

The answer is found in Luke 4:16–21 and related passages.[20] The truly apostolic church continues in the world the works that Jesus began. This is why Jesus sent word to John the Baptist, "Go back and report to John what you hear and see" (Matt. 11:4). The key point: "Good news is preached to the poor." Translation: Here is the true church! The gospel for the poor is the test that shows whether the church is apostolic. More exactly, preaching Jesus Christ to and faithfully incarnating the body of

Christ among the poor is a key sign that the church is apostolic—that it really is sent by Jesus.[21]

Preaching the gospel to the poor is powerful precisely because it *combines in one* the apostolic and prophetic notes, holding them together. This is no doubt what B. T. Roberts had in mind when he said "preaching the Gospel to the poor is the standing miracle which attests to its Divine origin," and what John Wesley meant when he called preaching the gospel to the poor "the greatest miracle of all."[22] It is a miracle because it won't happen unless the church is empowered by the Spirit and captivated by the character of Christ. For a church to preach the gospel to the poor is more of a miracle than are physical healings. Of all the "miraculous signs and wonders" in the church, this is the greatest. It is more miraculous for the church to transcend in this way the laws of sociological dynamics than for the laws of physics or physiology to be transcended in a healing or physical miracle.

The church is uniquely, divinely both apostolic and prophetic when it ministers the gospel to and among the poor in fidelity to the words, work, and life of Jesus Christ. This requires being empowered by the Holy Spirit, the one through whom the Son "made himself nothing, taking the very nature of a servant," humbling himself, becoming "obedient to death" (Phil. 2:7–8).

*Preaching the gospel to the poor is essential to the church's faithfulness.* It is a test of the church's apostolic mark. It is a sign that, spiritually speaking, the church is genetically related to Jesus and is being conformed to his likeness. Apostolicity is rather abstract and easily loses its tie to the actual life and ministry of Jesus Christ. Ministering to and with the poor is concrete action, not abstract concept. It is done or not done. Claims of apostolicity ring hollow if the church is not in fact good news for the poor. Whatever else apostolicity may mean, it certainly means incarnating the gospel among the poor. Here, then, is a key test of the church's apostolicity.[23]

In faithfully ministering the gospel to and among the poor, the church is both apostolic and prophetic. It is both holy and charismatic, because it demonstrates God's holy love powered by the Spirit.[24] It is both catholic and local, because ministry to and among the poor is always a universal, global concern even while it is always a matter of specific places. Similarly, preaching the gospel to the poor combines the unity and diversity of the church. It unites the church in a common gospel mission while it also affirms the world's cultural mosaic as the church incarnates Jesus' love among the diverse populations of the world's poor.

## The Great Confession and the Great Identification

The question is not just *what* we confess but also *who*—and *whose*—we are. It is not enough simply to say that the church must minister among the poor, powerful as this is. In the Gospels, we see not only what Jesus did but also who he is. We find Peter saying, "You are the Christ, the Son of the living God," and Jesus responding, "Blessed are you, Simon son of Jonah, for this was not revealed to you by man, but by my Father in heaven. . . . and on this rock I will build my church, and the gates of Hades will not overcome it" (Matt. 16:16–18). Again, the issue is not just what Jesus did but also who he is. Jesus is himself the "chief cornerstone" of the church (Eph. 2:20), and the church is based on the confession of him as "the Christ, the Son of the living God." The church is based on who Jesus Christ is and on what he provides for us in his life, death, resurrection, and continuing reign. The purpose of the church is not to help people be religious; it is to help them live like Jesus Christ seven days a week.

And so the question of the true identity of the church comes back to the identity of Jesus Christ. The meaning of being the body of Christ depends on who Jesus Christ is. If the church truly is the body of Christ, it has Jesus' DNA. Our ecclesiology (how we understand the church) depends totally on our Christology (how we understand the person and work of Jesus Christ).

In other words, the true church combines *the great confession* ("You are the Christ . . .") and *the great identification* ("As the Father has sent me, so I am sending you" [John 20:21]). The great confession is that Jesus Christ is Lord, Savior, and Liberator of the world. The great identification is that we are his body, share his spiritual DNA, and must follow in his steps (1 Peter 2:21). We, the church, are his disciples, servants, and priests. Think of the many "as" passages ("Love each other as I have loved you" [John 15:12], for example). Or, in the words of the apostle John, "Whoever claims to live in him must walk as Jesus did" (1 John 2:6).

The church is born in the great confession of, and great identification with, Jesus Christ. So Jesus said, "Where two or three come together in my name, there am I with them" (Matt. 18:20). Jesus spoke of his disciples "abiding" or "remaining" in him and of our finding our life in him (John 15:4–7). This is the great identification. And if the Spirit of the Lord is upon us, our identification with Jesus will lead us to do what Jesus did: preach the gospel to the poor. It runs in the genes of the true church. Ministry to and with the poor runs in the family.

The great confession and the great identification constitute biblical ecclesiology, the meaning of Christ's body. The church is born out of this *koinōnia* of the Spirit, this identification with Jesus Christ. Identification with Jesus through the Spirit issues in the *great communion* or community—the church (*koinōnia* the communion of saints)—and the *great commission*, identification with the disciple-making mission of Christ as given in Luke 4:18–19, Matthew 28:19–20, and 1 Peter 2:9.

## The Pavement Test

Does the understanding of the church's DNA presented in this chapter stand up to the pavement test? Does it work on the streets—in the homes and offices, schools and factories, prisons and hospitals, where the church is called to minister? Or is this just theory?

As a reality check, we sent a draft of this chapter to Mark Van Valin, a friend who for a dozen years has faithfully pastored an urban church in Indianapolis. His response accented especially the church's identification with Jesus Christ and his coming kingdom. His words capture much of the thrust of this book:

> The creeds, Acts, and the epistles give guidance in determining the "marks" of the church. I have found great help, however, in simply seeing Jesus' person and work as the compass by which all other things become clear. Jesus' intimate life with the Father and the Spirit, and his invitation to graft us "in," will forever stretch our vision of the *unity* of the body. His cross, with its sacrificial, self-denying posture before the Father will call us ever deeper into *holiness.* His resurrection, the proof of his lordship, will continue to birth confidence in the victorious *catholicity* of the church. His incarnation, his "Emmanuel" presence that continually seeks out the margins of a sinful race, will forever direct our sense of *apostolic* mission.
>
> The sociological implications of these marks challenge me as I try to lead the people at West Morris Street. I also think they hold the key to a peculiar witness that would capture the world's imagination and whet its appetite for God.
>
> Another mark of the church strikes me as vital to our self-understanding and our mission. This is the *apocalyptic* nature of the church. [Genuine Christians] are in earnest to get to heaven. If we are convinced of a coming Kingdom, we should be set free to live courageous and sacrificial lives here and now.

Yes! The body of Christ, united to Jesus, stretching forward toward that day when the kingdom comes in fullness. It is this intimate connection with Jesus, our head and forerunner, that prompts the church to flesh out in today's world the meaning of being one and diverse, holy and grace-filled, universal yet local, apostolic and prophetic.

## Conclusion

What, then, can we say about the church's DNA? Three things, in particular:

- By themselves, the four classic marks of the church are inadequate and one-sided. A fuller appeal to Scripture reveals the necessary key complements to the traditional marks.
- A fuller understanding of the marks of the church that stresses the necessary complements to one, holy, catholic, and apostolic, yields an understanding of the church that is both theologically richer and missiologically more powerful, affirming that the church is also diverse, charismatic, local, and prophetic.
- A biblical ecclesiology will emphasize that the church is the body of which Jesus alone is head. The faithful church will radically identify with the life, works, and words of Jesus Christ, because Jesus is its progenitor. A key sign of faithfulness is taking the gospel to the poor through the power of the Holy Spirit, as Jesus did.

Our endeavor to decode the church's DNA must conclude with a warning: There will always be a tendency for the church to drift away from the more radical marks to the more manageable ones. There will always be the tendency to over-objectify the marks, making them abstract attributes of the church as institution or invisible reality rather than as flesh-and-blood community. Therefore, the church must always be alert to its biblical DNA—especially the more "radical" components—staying close to Scripture and to radical expressions of Christian community.

Obviously, this look at the church's genetic structure only begins to decode the church. Fully decoding the church's DNA is a task that is no doubt beyond us. Mapping the spiritual genome of the church will require more than one brief survey. But perhaps this introduction will prove useful in understanding more fully the church's life and mission. It gives a broader picture of the *mystery* and *complexity* of the church and will also help us decode other issues that we will examine in this book.

*Mystery*. The church is a mystery because it participates in the mystery of the incarnation, the mystery of the Trinity, and the mystery of the kingdom of God (Matt. 13:11; Mark 4:11; John 17:23; Eph. 1:9–10;

3:6–10; 5:32; Col. 1:26–27). But God has revealed to us "the plan [*oikono-mia*] of the mystery" as it centers in Jesus Christ (Eph. 3:9, NRSV). The church has the high calling to live out the Good News within society so that we may see God's kingdom come and his will done "on earth as in heaven."

*Complexity.* The church is a complex organism, partly because it *is* a living organism. It is simultaneously a spiritual, a social, and a physical organism. (Christians have bodies and live in time and space.) Our next move, then, is to ask: What more can we learn about the church by exploring the concept of *complexity?* This will be the focus of the next chapter.

———

## Heartland Church Discovers the Body

Pastor Darrell Dorset had been serving Heartland Evangelical Church for three years. Things were going well. He had come to love the people, and they appreciated his open spirit, his love, and his biblical preaching. The church was growing not only in number but also, many felt, in spiritual depth.

In the spring, sometime after Easter, Pastor Dorset began a series of sermons on the nature of the church. He had never preached on this subject before, so it was a learning experience for him. He knew that the Book of Ephesians was the a good place to find rich material on the church, so he decided to base his sermon series on the first four chapters of that book.

Several years earlier, Pastor Dorset had read a seminary textbook that talked about the "marks" of the church. He found his old textbook and reviewed the passage about the "four marks": one, holy, catholic, apostolic. With this in mind, Pastor Dorset began a careful study of Ephesians. *Why not build my sermons around these four marks?* he thought.

Along with the sermon series, Pastor Dorset decided to try something he'd heard about from another pastor. It was risky, but he thought the people would buy it. He proposed replacing the usual Wednesday night prayer meeting for six weeks with small groups that would meet in members' homes. Each group would study Ephesians, the same passages he would preach on.

A few people weren't happy about the change in routine, but the church agreed to try it. They trusted their pastor, and they could hardly object to some extra Bible study.

To give the congregation a chance to warm up to the topic, Pastor Dorset decided to begin the small groups three weeks before the sermon series started. He gave each group an outline with several discussion questions and appointed two leaders for each group, one to guide the discussion and one to jot down comments and questions that came up. He asked the scribes to give him copies of their notes to help him make the sermons practical.

Things went well the first three weeks. Pastor Dorset was surprised that attendance at the small groups was greater than that at the usual Wednesday prayer meetings. People were talking about what "church" means and what the New Testament church was like. The response to his first sermon, on the unity of the church, was encouraging.

Monday night after the first sermon, Pastor Dorset got a call from Ray Schilling, one of the group leaders. "Our group discussions have been really good," Ray said. "Questions have come up I never thought about. And we've been having some great prayer and sharing times.

"We had an interesting discussion on unity and oneness. You know, Roberto and Leda are in our group, and they're fairly new to the church. We're getting more diverse. How do we have unity and diversity at the same time? And Roberto wanted to know what the gifts of the Spirit are all about.

"But actually I have a different question, pastor," Ray continued. "We had a big discussion last week about Ephesians 1:23, where it says the church is 'his body, the fullness of him who fills everything in every way.' What in the world does that mean?"

Pastor Dorset knew better than to be the answer man and give a learned response. So he replied, "Well, what do the people in the group think?"

"Some say it is referring to the risen Christ, not the church," Ray said. "Others think it must mean the church triumphant, when we all get to heaven. I don't know."

The pastor had an idea. "Let's try this," he said to Ray. "What key words do you see in that verse?"

"Well," Ray replied, "certainly 'body,' and I guess 'fullness.' And maybe 'everything.' And of course, 'church' from the previous verse."

"Right," said the pastor. "Now, we've got three more weeks. As you're working through the rest of the passages, look at other verses where those words occur and compare them. See what you find and let me know."

Ray agreed, and the key words from Ephesians 1:23 helped spark the discussions over the next weeks. Ray liked to study on his own, and in a commentary he discovered that the phrase "members together of one body" in Ephesians 3:6 is actually one word in the Greek, *syssōma*, "joined in one body" or "one-bodied together." He reported his finding to the group. Debbie Smithson, one group member, pointed out how often Paul used the word "together." "Are we really 'one body together'?" she asked. "What does that mean? Is it like we all have the same genetic code or something?"

That kicked off some lively discussion. Jim Richards, another group member, said, "You know, I saw something on the news last night about DNA and genetic research. If the church is the body of Christ, do you suppose it has some kind of spiritual DNA?" Jim liked the idea, and since he was the scribe, he stuck that in his notes. Pastor Dorset was intrigued when Jim's notes landed on his desk.

Meanwhile, Pastor Dorset continued his sermon preparation. As he went back and forth in Ephesians and other Scriptures, Jim's question kept popping up in his mind. Does the church have DNA? He worked the idea into his fourth sermon, in which his theme was the church as apostolic.

The sermon series ended, and so did the small-group discussions. Wednesday night prayer meeting resumed. Everyone felt that the sermons and the groups had deepened the church's life.

But the question kept percolating in Darrell Dorset's mind: Does the church have DNA? If so, what is it? What does it *really* mean that the church is the body of Christ, that Jesus is its head? He decided to read up on genetics a bit as he continued to study the Bible.

A couple of weeks later Pastor Dorset ran into Ray Schilling at a local restaurant. They were both alone, so they shared lunch together and soon were talking about the church.

"I kind of miss our small group," Ray said. "We should do that again." The pastor had thought about that, too, but summer was coming on, and it didn't seem like a good time to start something new. He discovered, though, that Ray was beginning to think in similar ways about the church. The two decided to meet for an early breakfast once a week to discuss these things and to pray and study the Bible together. Pastor Dorset thought it was a good discipling opportunity. Besides, he found he actually learned things about what the church is and what it could be through his talks with Ray. They developed a deeper bond in Jesus Christ.

It was only months later that Pastor Dorset realized that a shift had occurred in his thinking and even in his preaching. He was beginning to think and talk of the church as a living organism—as something alive, not just as an organization or program or building. He discussed his thoughts with Ray. Ray understood. "I guess I've been thinking that way, too," he said.

As it turned out, this was only the beginning of the story.

# Questions
## for Group Discussion or Personal Reflection

1. The creeds define the church as "one, holy, catholic, and apostolic." This chapter identifies Scriptures that suggest the church is also diverse, charismatic, local, and prophetic. Why is it that often only some of the church's genetic traits are emphasized and others are slighted?
2. Try to imagine how history might have developed differently over the past two thousand years if the church had defined itself as "diverse, charismatic, local, and prophetic" rather than as "one, holy, catholic, and apostolic."
3. What social dynamics or other factors cause the church to ignore the mandate in Scripture to preach the gospel to the poor?
4. If your local congregation began to think more in organic terms, defining the church as a body instead of as an organization or building, what changes might occur?
5. Of the Scriptures or marks (genetic traits) of the church mentioned in this chapter, which ones seem especially important to you right now? To your church? Why?
6. What do you think of Heartland Evangelical Church's attempt to reach a deeper understanding of what the church really is?
7. Do you see any signs that Heartland Evangelical Church is *one, holy, catholic,* and *apostolic?* Is there any evidence that it is *diverse, charismatic, local* (rooted in its locality), and *prophetic?*

# 2

---

# THE CHURCH

## *A Complex Organism*

*Complexity* is another word for *diversity*. Only it's much more complex!

The church of Jesus Christ is a mystery. It partakes of the mystery of Jesus' redemptive work. It experiences the wonder of new community and new humanity that is the body of Christ. The DNA of the church is wondrously complex.

A number of New Testament passages speak of the church or the gospel using the Greek word *mystērion* (found twenty-seven times in the New Testament, for example, Eph. 3:3–4; 5:32; Col. 1:26–27; 2:2–3). And Jesus spoke of the "secret" or "mystery" *(mystērion)* of the kingdom of God (Matt. 13:11; Mark 4:11; Luke 8:10).[1]

The church is a mystery partly because of its unique spiritual-physical genetic structure. Yet throughout history, church leaders and theologians have often reduced the wondrous mystery of the church to more easily grasped human-size models—the church as a building, a hierarchy, an institution, or even a political force. The New Testament sense of the church gets lost in such approaches. Historically, whenever the church has failed to make a culturally transforming impact, one reason has been an insufficiently biblical model of the church. We do better when we stay closer to biblical models, even if they leave us with questions.

Part of the mystery of the church is, in fact, its complexity. Since the church is complex, we use images and models to help us understand it.[2] Which models help us the most? The primary biblical models for the church are clear: body of Christ, community of the Spirit, people and family of God, and bride of Christ. Only if the church knows what it really is can it have the redemptive impact on society that God intends. This means, in part, that we must embrace the mystery and complexity of the church's being.

## Order versus Chaos

Most nonbiblical models of the church are *reductionistic* in some harmful way. That is, they reduce the church to only one part, or a few parts, of its reality, then blow those parts out of proportion. We saw examples of this in the previous chapter. Such reductionism distorts the church and hampers it from being and doing what God intends.

A new branch of science called *complexity theory*—the study of complex systems—can be useful here. Complexity theory is described as "the emerging science at the edge of order and chaos." It studies the way order sometimes arises from seemingly chaotic systems. It looks at the highly complex interaction of the many factors involved in weather, economics, living cells, and other systems.

A *complex system* is one in which "a great many independent agents are interacting with each other in a great many ways." Mitchell Waldrop writes, "Think of the quadrillions of chemically reacting proteins, lipids, and nucleic acids that make up a living cell, or the billions of interconnected neurons that make up the brain, or the millions of mutually interdependent individuals who make up a human society."[3] Related to chaos theory (the systematic study of disorder), complexity theory studies systems that were previously thought to be complex beyond comprehension, or perhaps totally chaotic, having no order at all.[4]

What has this to do with the church? Well, if we look at the church as a complex system, perhaps we can avoid reducing it to simply a social service agency, a church-growth machine, or a religious entertainment center. By understanding the complexity of the church, we can stay closer to the church's real DNA—which by definition is highly complex.

Complexity theory grows in part out of the study of life itself and the complex systems that make up our environment. It may be thought of as the merging of ecology, economics, cybernetics, and the life sciences. Modern computer power makes the study of complexity possible.

We are not proposing a new model for the church when we speak of the church as a complex system. That could simply be a new form of reductionism. After all, most complexity theorists don't understand the importance of the reality of God. Rather, we are suggesting that complexity theory may give us some insights into the deep dynamics of biblical models of the church. If anything, the discoveries of complexity theory reaffirm the nature of the church as the body of Christ and the community of God's people. The genetic model and the complexity perspective shed light on each other.

## Six Insights for the Church

If we apply complexity theory to the church, whether a local congregation like Heartland Evangelical Church or the church in a larger sense, we discover some helpful surprises. Six insights about the nature of the church arise from complexity theory and can help us understand the church's DNA.

1. *The church is a totality of complex factors, not a linear cause-and-effect system.* Since the rise of modern science, we have been taught to think in a linear cause-and-effect fashion. *This* happens because of *that.* Everything has its cause, and we can trace back (or maybe even forward) the chain of causes and effects. Modern society is built largely on cause-and-effect rationality, from the ideologies underlying both classical capitalism and Marxist communism to the logic that led to the development of the computer and the space rocket.

But this bias toward linear cause-and-effect thinking is changing as our culture shifts from modernity to postmodernity.[5] It is changing even in computer science, as people begin to study "nonlinear systems" and to develop "fuzzy logic."[6]

Here is an important lesson for the church, as well. Far too much church programming assumes that the church is a linear cause-and-effect system: Just adopt this or that program, and the church will thrive. It may be a program in evangelism, Christian education, worship style, small groups, or anything else. Behind these proposals is the faulty assumption that the church is like a machine and that churches are pretty much the same everywhere, with interchangeable parts. Plug in the right program, and off it goes!

Many of us have felt intuitively for years that this approach is wrong. Complexity theory helps us see why. The life of the church—*any* church—is made up of too many factors to give us any confidence that a method or program developed in one context will work in another. The church's DNA is just too complex—and too unique in each local embodiment—for that to be true.

The church is a complex system, a living organism. Stop and think of the complexity of a church composed of only fifty people. There is, first of all, the complexity of the interaction of all these people (multiply fifty by fifty by fifty . . . !). Second, there is the relation of each person to God, with no two relationships being quite the same. Throw in the complexity of personality types, cultural backgrounds, family experiences, job involvements, physical health or illness, denominational traditions, aesthetic tastes, and the multitude of choices each person makes daily, and you begin to get some sense of the church's real complexity! The church is a complex ecology of spiritual, physical, social, political, psychological, and economic dimensions.

We should rejoice in this! We should celebrate the church's complexity and allow the church to be the church, not try to squeeze it into some ill-fitting framework. We should concentrate on the basics, which means carefully and closely following biblical instruction concerning the church and its life.

The church is a *body,* not a machine or a corporation. The church is not an army of Christian soldiers. An army functions by forcibly restricting the complexity of human interaction and programming it into a strict chain of command. An army is an unnatural community—very effective for one purpose, but not for building a healthy community.[7] The church is a body, and the body is a complex system with unique DNA.

This view can help us appreciate the church in all its complex beauty—even the strange mix of faithfulness and unfaithfulness that so often marks it. This view seems, in fact, to be the biblical perspective. We get into trouble when we try to program the church, just as we do when we try to program a teenager, or the love between two people, or the life of a family. Human relationships are too dynamic for that.

2. *Complexity theory illuminates the long-range significance of small actions.* As an Amish farmer in Pennsylvania used to say, "Remember the importance of small things done at the right time." We need to understand what that means. The church is a complex network of many little things: times of secret prayer, a word aptly spoken, an unexpected hug, a telling sermon illustration, a fight and reconciliation between two church members, the quiet testimony of Christian example. These are the things authentic church life is made of.

A preacher gave a sermon illustration about a revival meeting in England. No one was converted, he said, except for one small boy who came forward the last night of the meeting. That child turned out to be Charles Spurgeon, later a great preacher and evangelist. The story was meant to illustrate how we should not judge success by immediate, visible results. Equally significant, however, is that the story illustrates the complexity of the church and the unpredictability of its life.

So in our church life, we should remember the importance of small actions and events. The *long-range* effect of small and seemingly chance actions is often great. Why is Brother Brown a fine Christian and church member today? Because when he was six, a caring Sunday school teacher noticed him and showed him Christ. That simple action had lifelong results. Yet from a complexity perspective, we understand that this was but one of many influences over many years. Other people, other events, and other influences joined in. None of us can know the whole story. Often we can identify critical events and turning points but not how they fit into the complexity of the larger story.

What does this mean practically? We should recognize and celebrate the many small things that constitute the church's vitality—as well as watch for the small things that destroy that vitality, whether a lying tongue, an unkind word, an unresolved conflict, or a seemingly innocent outdated tradition. It means, especially, that we should understand the vital importance of Christian *character* and *community* in the life of the church. Character is built from a myriad of small choices and events. Behavior flows from character more than character flows from behavior. Yet too often in the church we focus on getting people to *do* things rather than on helping them to *become* the disciples God intends.[8]

Vital churches and ministries focus on the many small actions that collectively give visible expression to the life of Jesus in the world. When planning and programming, vital churches will ask, How will this affect people's real growth? Will it provide an environment for them to come to know Jesus Christ more deeply and serve him more surely?

3. *The complexity perspective underscores the vital role of interrelationships and structure in the church.* Complexity theorists are fascinated by the way complex systems appear to be self-organizing. Out of seeming chaos, order emerges. Life itself seems "poised between order and chaos."[9] This suggests that certain structures are natural and organic to complex systems—and that such structures arise out of a web of interrelationships.

Perhaps we have always known intuitively the importance of interrelationships among people and their relationships with God. These relationships should be basic to all our structuring. In practice we often put structure ahead of relationships, or we over-structure and thereby over-complicate our relationships. The history of the church and its mission abounds with examples. Take, for instance, small groups in the church. It is clear that any vital church will have some kind of cellular or small-group life. No church can really be lively without it. But there is no magic formula for small groups, and they should not be over-programmed.

Later in this book we will look briefly at the small-group structure of early Methodism. The system thrived, producing accountable, nurturing relationships. But it was not nearly as highly structured as many have assumed. It was highly disciplined in the sense of the level of commitment required, but within that context, the groups were very flexible and relational. This was their genius for one hundred years. The system was simple, but it nurtured relationships that were healthily complex.

Structure is important in the church, as in all life. Every creature has some kind of framework. Even a tiny cell has highly complex structure. But structure must be compatible with the system in which it is found. There has to be harmony between the system and its structure. Structure is both a *functional* question—What structures help the church really be the church?—and an *emergence* question—What structures seem to emerge naturally from the nature or character of the church?

The question of church structure—what we call the wineskins issue—will be discussed more fully in later chapters. However, it is clear from the nature of the church as the body of Christ and the community of God's people that vital church structure will be highly relational, will provide the context for growth and discipleship, and will be adaptable to different contexts and changing circumstances.

4. *Viewing the church as a complex system teaches us that size is always a function of other factors.* Size is never a question in itself; therefore growth is never an end in itself. There is no perfect size for a church in any abstract sense, and a large church is not necessarily better than a small one (or vice versa). Size is purely and completely a question of deeper issues such as purpose, vitality, mission, and what we might call a healthy *homeostasis* (dynamic internal balance).

We know this from nature. There is a kind of natural, functional proportionality in all of earth's living creatures. If a housefly was ten times larger, it would have to be structured differently. An elephant could not, in fact, be as small as a mouse; it wouldn't work. There is a normal size range for every living creature. Maybe the same thing holds true for the church.

We are pleased to see our children grow up and become adults, but we would be worried if they didn't stop growing when they reached adult stature. A human being twenty feet tall, or one hundred feet tall, would be hopelessly ungainly—a monster. Such things make good movie plots, but not livable reality.[10]

This is an important point today because of all the attention being given to megachurches. A common assumption, sometimes stated but more often simply assumed, holds that the bigger a church is, the better. Yet nothing in the Bible suggests this. And nothing in the church's

DNA supports this idea. Conversely, a church is not necessarily better for being smaller. Size is simply the wrong question. It's like asking how big a building or a tree should be. For the church, the only valid answer to the question of size is that the church should be whatever size best enables it to fulfill its mission and "grow up into Christ."

Here again genetics can help us. A certain growth potential and proportionality is built into our DNA. A living organism grows to its proper size and then, if it is healthy, stops getting larger. It's all there in the genes.

Perhaps there is a natural proportionality to church size. It is intriguing that throughout history, most vital congregations have ranged somewhere between fifty and perhaps three hundred people. Maybe there is a natural spiritual and social ecology to church size. Perhaps our goal should be to have churches that number on average, around one hundred to two hundred people but that are committed to missions and evangelism as well to inner spiritual development. The goal would be to spin off new daughter churches from time to time rather than growing beyond a healthy size. The optimum size would probably vary according to a church's cultural context, but the principle would be the same: find and maintain the optimum size for continued growth in missions, discipleship, and church multiplication.

Maybe the natural ecology of church life means there will always be a great number of small- to medium-size churches and a scattering of very large churches. It seems that the dynamics here are mainly inner spiritual factors relating to the life of the church more than they are dynamics of the surrounding culture. If so, megachurches will always be the exception, though they may play a significant role within the larger church. (We will return to this topic in chapter four.)

The practical lesson here: We should not be preoccupied with size! We should not use size as a sign of success, but neither should we let small size be an excuse for not being involved in effective mission. We are called to faithful discipleship, not numerical growth. But faithful discipleship will, in most cases, inevitably lead to growth in numbers as well.

5. *Complexity theory underscores the uniqueness of each church's particular DNA.* In important ways, each congregation is unique, because its particular combination of complex events and relationships is unique. This uniqueness is consistent with what we know of DNA. While we can speak of an overall ecclesial DNA—the basic, essential marks of the church discussed in chapter 1—we need to be reminded that each congregation's DNA is special.

Genetic models and complexity theory can be useful here. How can a congregation discern its own special DNA? This happens by a Spirit-guided discernment process. It happens not so much by looking at and studying *other* churches, though that may help at times, but by asking questions such as: How has God led us in the past? What "charism" or genetic endowment have we received from our forebears (including, perhaps, from our particular denominational tradition)? What special gifts and callings has God given our congregation? What does the Holy Spirit want to do through us that he will not do through any other church?

Complexity theory and genetic models together help us understand that each local congregation is unique and important. This should give us hope! My church is not called to be a clone or a weak imitation of some other church. It is called to live according to its own DNA and to fulfill its own God-given mission for the sake of God's kingdom. It is to live a life worthy of the calling it has received (Eph. 4:1).

6. Finally, complexity theory suggests that *"emergent structures" arise from the church's complex vitality as they are needed.* That is, the church's growth itself—in vitality, ministry, and numbers—will often give rise to the necessary structures. Thus the key issue may be one more of discernment than of structural cleverness or planning.

This does not mean we should shun wise planning or ignore future needs. Complexity theory stresses, however, that it is simply *impossible* to predict very far into the future. The multiplied number of variables increases exponentially as time passes. The handiest illustration of this is the weather report, which generally misses the mark if projected more than two or three days into the future.

Complexity theory is thus suspicious of long-range planning. We think the church should be, too. Vital systems, and vital churches, are marked more by flexibility and adaptability to changing circumstances than by long-range plans. They are marked more by vision than by detailed strategies. How many churches have brilliant long-range plans gathering dust on shelves because of unforeseen circumstances? From a complexity and organic perspective, such an outcome is no surprise.

Of course, God has given us the ability to think and plan and analyze, and we should use it. Churches and mission structures should be alert to demographic trends and other factors that will affect their life and ministry in years to come. They should plan accordingly. But such alertness and planning can never take the place of present vitality, faithfulness, and discipleship—and Spirit-led intuition. The ecclesiastical landscape is littered with the skeletons of churches that had exciting long-range plans but no power to carry them out.

In a vital church, functional structures emerge naturally out of the church's life, provided there is alert, sensitive leadership. Probably the best biblical example of this is the selection of the seven helpers in Acts

6. The apostles, led by the Spirit, guided the church to make a wise response to a new crisis.[11] This is an excellent example both of leadership and of naturally emerging structural changes.

## Practical Implications

The church should focus on what it does best. What is that? When empowered by the Holy Spirit, what the church does best is to love God with all its heart, soul, strength, and mind and to love its neighbor as itself. What it does best, based on this love, is to build a faithful community of Jesus' disciples. The calling of the church is to really *be* the body of Christ and allow the Holy Spirit to work through all the diverse complexity of the body.

The complexity perspective yields four lessons that help the church live out its DNA.

1. *The church should focus on the genuine worship of God.* Only God fully understands the church's complexity. In worship the church opens itself to God's power and perspective. It puts itself at God's disposal so that divine energy can guide its complexity to the fulfillment of kingdom purposes. Genuine worship is openness to God's direction.

2. *The church should focus on building vital, accountable community.* Community *(koinōnia)* is central to the church's essence as the body of Christ. It is an essential part of the church's DNA. Accountable community energizes the church to develop creative, effective, redemptive responses to the challenges of its growth and mission. In community the church learns to employ all its gifts, not just the gifts of professional ministers.

3. *The church must visibly show the compassion of Christ in the world.* As Jesus was in the world, so the church is to be (1 John 2:6). An incarnational model of church life and witness is very complex and sometimes chaotic. But it is powerful when truly centered in Jesus Christ. Showing Christ's love in hundreds of little and big ways, the church represents the kingdom of God—often without even realizing it.

4. *The church must provide people with a functional, livable worldview.* Unlike the complex system of the weather or a colony of ants, the church's complexity includes the reason, reflection, and imagination of all its members. In part, the church responds to complex challenges according to its view of reality, of the world. Faithful responses to these challenges require that the church think in a Christianlike manner. Effective mission, therefore, will be concerned with the formation of a Chris-

tian worldview as well as Christian community and character. We will return to this topic when we discuss the church's role in the world.

Nothing in the world is more revolutionary than the church of Jesus Christ. The gospel of Jesus is still the power of God bringing salvation to all who believe. We can still say: "Where sin abounded, grace did much more abound" (Rom. 5:20).

How can this become real in new and fresh ways today? One key is perceiving the complexity of the church and carrying out our mission with great sensitivity to the uniqueness of this wonderful spiritual-personal-social organism called the church.

――――――

## Heartland Uncovers Complexity

As Darrell Dorset continued his ministry at Heartland Evangelical Church, things got more complicated. Not bad, just complex.

The church was growing. During the summer several new families and some singles had been added. There was, for example, Larry Troublemeier. Always had questions but never seemed to want answers.

The new people included single moms and a recently divorced father who had his two teenage kids with him every other weekend. Pastor Dorset read an article in the paper about how their city had grown much more ethnically diverse over the past decade and wondered what this would mean for the Heartland church.

Darrell Dorset continued meeting Ray Schilling weekly for breakfast. One day in September, Ray said, "Would it be all right if a couple of other guys started meeting with us? I'm thinking of Bill and Jim. You remember Jim Richards, he was the scribe for our small group. And Bill Silver teaches at the same high school I do. I've talked with both of these guys recently about our church and about their spiritual walk. They're doing okay, but I think they'd gain a lot from joining us in our breakfast get-togethers."

Darrell Dorset thought a minute. He hadn't planned to turn his informal chats with Ray into a small group—but why not? "Sure," he said, "that's fine, if they're open to it."

They were. Jim and Bill weren't sure what to expect, but as the days shortened and fall came on, the four men began to meet early each Thursday morning for breakfast. The discussion was lively, and prayers were answered. Pastor Dorset found himself looking forward to these times; they had become a high point in his week.

One Thursday morning Bill Silver surprised the pastor by asking, "Would you mind if Angie started coming with me?" Bill's wife was an alert, thoughtful person, and she was always interested in what the guys had discussed at their breakfast get-togethers. She had been bold enough to ask Bill if he thought the pastor would let her attend the breakfast meetings.

Darrell Dorset thought about it. This was a new wrinkle! He had no objection to Angie's joining the breakfast group, but he realized it would no longer be a "guy thing." The dynamics would change. But the breakfasts were an informal time of conversation and sharing, not a covenant group, and the pastor really had no objection. Soon Bill and Angie were attending together. Angie suggested they also invite Linda Hartsell, an older single woman with a heart for God and the church, to attend as well, and everyone agreed.

Yes, the dynamics of the group changed. Angie and Linda brought up questions and perspectives the guys wouldn't have thought of. Darrell felt the discussions were actually getting better.

One Thursday morning, a couple of weeks before Thanksgiving, the group's conversation turned to the sermon series on the church that Pastor Dorset had preached some months earlier, and to the six-week small group experiment. Everyone agreed that meeting in small groups had been a very good experience. Angie said, "You know, I got closer to the people in our group than I ever had before. I think I began to *feel* what church really is. I could understand better what the Bible says about the church, like in Acts and 1 Corinthians."

"Couldn't we do something like that again?" Ray asked. "Or maybe we could start some ongoing small groups for people who are interested."

This wasn't a new idea for Darrell Dorset, of course. He had thought several times that it would be good if the church had a network of small groups. But he wasn't quite sure how to start them. Besides, people were busier now that the church was growing; more people were involved in teaching Sunday school, leading youth and music activities, and serving on committees. It would complicate things to add another program. And nobody had expressed much interest in small groups. The matter had come up only a couple of times, mainly because of the small-group experience in the spring.

But Pastor Dorset welcomed Ray's suggestion. Bill, Angie, and Jim were interested, too. Linda said, "If we did start some small groups, I'd certainly want to be in one." Bill said he was interested, but finding time might be a problem.

The Thursday breakfast group pondered the idea of small groups for a couple of weeks. Then one Thursday Angie said, "You know, it hit me this week while I was having my devotions and praying for the church. We already have a small group! Our breakfast time together really is a sort of small group. And it's been an encouragement to me."

Pastor Dorset could see this was true. He hadn't planned it, but the breakfast group had become a new experience of church for all six of them.

"I guess we sort of discovered a small group by accident!" Jim said.

"Yeah," Ray said, "but what about the rest of the church? We don't want to be selfish or to seem like a clique."

"Well," Darrell Dorset said, "let's think and pray about this and see where it leads. God will guide us. Maybe we can start several groups." This sounded good, but he was talking off the top of his head. He had no idea how it might be done. Whenever he had thought about this before, he had always wondered where they would get small-group leaders. He hadn't gotten much further than that.

Christmas came and went, with its swirl of activities. The Thursday breakfast group stopped meeting for three weeks but picked up again early in January. The discussion, the Bible reading, and the prayer times continued and deepened.

By early February two ideas had emerged from these group discussions. Everyone agreed that, first, they should continue this group, because they felt it was helping them personally and that it was actually good for the church. But second, Pastor Dorset should propose to the church board that a Vision and Planning committee be formed to consider whether and how the church should form small groups. The group thought it would be good for the committee to address not only the question of small groups but also several other issues facing the church. How would small groups relate to other church activities, like the Wednesday night prayer meeting and the church's committee structure? What long-term challenges did the church's growth present? How should the church respond to its growing diversity and to its opportunities for evangelism and service?

Pastor Dorset took the proposal to the church board early in March. The board approved it, though some of the members weren't sure it was really necessary. Angie Silver and Ray Schilling would be on the Vision and Planning Committee, along with the pastor and several other people. Soon the committee was formed and began meeting twice a month.

The Thursday breakfast group continued as well. Pastor Dorset wondered whether anyone in the church would criticize the Thursday morning group, but so far he'd heard no complaints. His wife, Beth, applauded the group because she saw it was an encouragement to her husband.

And this wasn't the only group in the church; Beth and a couple of other women got together twice a month for coffee, Bible study, and prayer, and there were a couple of similar groups that had started more or less spontaneously.

One April morning Pastor Dorset asked the Thursday group how they thought the church was doing overall. The feedback was generally positive.

Ray Schilling said, "I think we're making progress. There's a good spirit in the church, and people feel they're being fed by the sermons."

Jim Richards agreed. "Also, I think there's more of a sense of God's presence in the worship services," he said.

"True," Bill said. "I like some of the more contemporary songs we're singing along with the traditional hymns. I know some people would like us to have more of a 'contemporary worship style,' as they say. Others probably don't like the newer songs. Overall, I think the mix is about right. Is the Vision and Planning Committee going to discuss this?"

"Worship format?" asked Pastor Dorset. "Well, it has come up once or twice in our meetings. I think we will discuss it further."

Angie said, "We need to do more in outreach. I'm concerned about some of our own kids' friends. They really need to know the Lord. And there are a lot of hurting people around that we could be ministering to."

"Yes," Ray said. "We're having a problem with drugs in the high school. And we're getting more diverse. I saw a report the other day that we now have eleven different languages spoken in our school system. I couldn't believe it. I mean, we're not Chicago or Cleveland."

"These are all challenges we should pray about," Pastor Dorset said. "We can be thankful God has guided us so far."

This led the group to reminisce about the history of the church and their own personal journeys of faith. Each shared how they had come to know Jesus Christ. They were surprised to find that most of them had come to faith when they were young, through the influence of a friend or parent or Sunday school teacher—though Bill was converted through an InterVarsity group when he was at the university.

Ray Schilling said, "When I was in high school, my Sunday school teacher once quoted Jim Elliott, the missionary martyr: 'He is no fool who gives up what he cannot keep to gain what he cannot lose.' That nailed down my commitment and has stuck with me."

Pastor Dorset also shared his story. This was the first time Bill, Angie, Ray, Jim, and Linda had heard about the pastor's faith journey and his early struggles.

The next day, as Darrell Dorset was completing his Sunday preparation, he thought back over the last few weeks in the church. He remembered a couple of difficult counseling sessions that had shown him some of his people had deep-seated issues to deal with. One couple, he was afraid, was headed for divorce.

And Pastor Dorset said, half to himself and half to God, "You know, this thing of 'church' is a lot more complex and complicated than I ever realized! But I think God is helping us."

Just then the phone rang. It was Beth, with a message: Old Sister Daggett, Heartland's only remaining charter member, had just died. She was ninety-six—a saint, if ever there was one. Pastor Dorset began thinking about her family, and about funeral arrangements.

# Questions
## for Group Discussion or Personal Reflection

1. Drawing from your personal experience, tell the story of one seemingly inconsequential action that had a tremendous ripple effect for good in God's kingdom.
2. On a blank sheet of paper, try to draw a picture of the church as a complex organism. Where is God in your picture? Where would you place the pastor and other leaders? Where do all the members of the body fit in? Where does this organism fit in the larger society in which you live?
3. Think of a time when you were involved in delivering good news to the poor. What was the response from the poor? What was your own response?
4. This chapter makes many suggestions about the nature of the church. From all the information presented, pick one thing that you think ought to be changed (and could be changed) in your church to make it more mission focused.
5. In what ways could Heartland Evangelical Church be described as a "complex organism"? What evidence of complexity do you see?
6. Do you see any new structures emerging in the Heartland church?
7. Can you see anything else in the story of Heartland Evangelical Church that illustrates the main points of this chapter?
8. Do you think it was a good idea to form the Vision and Planning Committee? Why or why not?

# 3

## CHURCH, TRINITY, AND MISSION

Orthodox Christians profess to believe the doctrine of the Trinity. Yet it would seem that most believers make little or no practical connection between this fundamental doctrine and the day-to-day life and witness of the church. For most, the doctrine of the Trinity is theologically essential but practically irrelevant.

There are, however, important genetic links between God as Trinity and the missional nature of the church. This chapter will explore these links.[1]

Clearly, a faithful church—one that is born of God and lives by the Spirit—is committed to God's mission. Such a church must be structured so that it can live out that mission in the world. But the issue here goes deeper than structure. The church's fundamental DNA makes the church the sign, foretaste, and initial embodiment of the reign of God and a reflection or echo of the Trinity. In this sense, the church may be described as a community that is *missional, alternative, covenantal,* and *Trinitarian.*[2]

### A Missional Community

The church is genetically missionary because it is the community of Jesus Christ, God's great missionary. It is the body of Christ, the community called into existence by the mission of God. This is the starting point for all ecclesiology. A vital understanding of the church begins here, not with the traditional structures of culture Christianity that rise from two millennia of Christendom.

At its deepest level, the church is a missional community. As the body of Christ, mission is in the church's DNA, even if mission often gets suppressed in practice. This means three things:

1. *The church has a mission **to** God as well as **from** God.* The church is called "to represent God's reign as its community, its servant, and its messenger." The body of Christ is a "community spawned by the mission of God and gathered up into that mission."[3] Its mission is Trinitarian in that it is "a temporal echo of the eternal community that God is."[4] But there is a reciprocal action of mission that might be termed the church's mission *to* God—that is, the church's calling to worship and serve God, giving him preeminence in all things.

The church's fundamental mission to God is worship. This truth, however, can become a cliché that actually subverts mission. Worship, so-called, can become a diversion from mission, especially in postmodern North America, where "worship" may mask considerable self-centeredness. Too often worship is more consumer-centered than God-centered.

But this danger doesn't blunt the fact that the church is called and privileged to worship God. Worship undergirds and prompts the church's witness, both in equipping believers for mission and as itself a form of witness to the world. The Christian community is called to live "to the praise of [God's] glorious grace" (Eph. 1:6), to sing exultantly, "to [God] be glory in the church" (Eph. 3:21). That is our doxological purpose, and it is based in the church's fundamental DNA.[5]

Sometimes the church and its mission are defined by three words found in the New Testament: *kērygma* (proclamation or witness), *diakonia* (service), and *koinōnia* (community). This definition is useful, but it is too narrow. It fails to fully represent the church's rich genetic inheritance. We believe the terms *worship, community,* and *witness* (*leitourgia, koinōnia,* and *martyria,* which includes *diakonia*) are both more holistic and more biblical. The church's mission is grounded in all three: genuine, God-focused worship; close, accountable community; and whole-bodied witness in all the church does.[6] (We will discuss this further in chapter six.)

2. *Evangelism has a special place in the church's mission.* Evangelism, in its broadest and basic sense, means announcing and embodying the reign of God.[7] It addresses particularly personal faith, the decision of the heart in response to God's call to follow Jesus Christ, be born again, and be his disciple. It is concerned with justification and regeneration as well as discipleship and sanctification. The *circumference* of evangelism may be thought of as all that is included in the good news of the

kingdom of God, but the *center* of the circle is the appeal to "turn and be converted" (see Mark 4:12).

Missional churches feel the urgency of winning people to personal faith in Jesus Christ. True, this is the work of the Holy Spirit, and the church's whole life should itself be witness of God's kingdom. Still, Jesus' commission to preach the Good News to everyone and to make disciples of all peoples remains the active commission given to every church.

But to whom, specifically, should the Good News be proclaimed? This question leads to a third affirmation.

3. *Preaching the gospel to the poor is a special priority of the church.* Jesus said he was anointed by the Spirit "to preach good news to the poor" (Luke 4:18). He pointed to the fact that "good news is preached to the poor" (Luke 7:22) as a sign of his messiahship. Liberation theology speaks of God's "preferential option" for the poor. John Wesley said the poor have a "peculiar right to have the gospel preached unto them."[8]

Since Jesus made these statements in the context of the Jubilee and the reign of God, they are deeply missional. Preaching the gospel to the poor, however, does not mean preaching *at* the poor, but incarnating the Good News among the poor as Jesus Christ did, through healing, teaching, touching, preaching, and forming kingdom communities. In this way the church visibly expresses the key mark of apostolicity.

## An Alternative Community

A missional church is an alternative community called to build its own culture, economy, and lifestyle in the world and among all peoples. A faithful church is a visible alternative to both neopagan society and to ecclesial models of Christendom that clash with the church's basic DNA.

*Alternative*, however, is a slippery word. It has no specific content. Alternative to what? And why? According to what principles? The issue becomes even more complex when we recognize that the church does not have *totally* different behaviors, allegiances, interests, or relationships from the dominant culture. People in all cultures must eat food, for example. Christians and non-Christians may share much the same behaviors, allegiances, and relationships regarding family life. Which behaviors are in view, and in what cultural context?

The church might legitimately have a vested interest in some aspects of the status quo but not others. Yet at those strategic points where Christian faithfulness is at stake, the church must indeed be an alternative community. Part of this alternativeness is in fact the strange phenomenon that true Christians are so much like and yet so much unlike the dominant culture.

The church as a missional community *is* an alternative community. But we should call it that only in contexts where the meaning is clear. Otherwise, people might think that the church must always and at every point be a counterculture—regardless of the "culture" to which the church is being "counter"! This raises the question, When and in what sense is the church a *culture,* a *subculture,* or a *counterculture?* When the church is true to its DNA, it creates a kingdom culture that will be countercultural at key points.

The church really is an alternative community when its mission is the kingdom of God. Its mission makes it countercultural. And it is an alternative reality when it exists as a covenant community.

## A Covenant Community

The church is the covenant community of God's reign. The covenant calls the church to ministry and mission, to "equip [God's people] for the work of ministry" (Eph. 4:12 NRSV), and to structure its life accordingly. A covenant community focused on ministry and mission must pay attention to several key points.

1. To be a covenant community, the church must have some form (probably a variety of forms) of small covenant groups. Precedents such as the early Methodist "class meetings," the "mission groups" of the Church of the Savior (Washington, D.C.), and the contemporary cell-church model are examples of this.[9]

2. The biblical meaning of *member* needs to be rethought. Today "member" has an exclusively organizational sense for most people. One "joins" an organization and thus becomes a "member." The New Testament, however, speaks of "members of the body," not of "membership."[10] We speak today of "membership" rather than "bodyship," which shows that most North American Christians are simply blind to the difference between the biblical and contemporary meanings of "member." With few exceptions, the original organic meaning of *member*—"a part of the body"—has completely disappeared, having been replaced by the words "limb" or "organ." Ironically, the main exception to this is the verb "dismember"! Someone has said the mission of the church is "to re-member the dis-membered."

Surprisingly, the New Testament says nothing about "joining the church." When the Bible speaks of being a part of Christ's body, the emphasis is not on the individual's action but on God's action as he joins us to Christ, makes us part of the body, and adopts us as his children. Once made a part of the body, Christians of course "join together" in worship, community, and witness as part of their response to the gospel. But they do not initially "join the church."[11]

3. The split between clergy and laity must be overcome in concept and practice. This division is deeply rooted in the consciousness and practice of most North American churches. Yet in the New Testament, the whole church is the *laos* (people) of God, and the whole people of God is called to *diakonia* (service) and other forms of ministry. This truth calls us to reform our language as well as our practice. We should cease to use "minister" and "ministry" exclusively as being equivalent to "clergy" and should stop using "layman" and probably even "laity" unless we can recover their biblical sense.

Five hundred years after the Protestant Reformation, a new reformation is now underway that is restoring ministry to the whole people of God and equipping the entire Christian community for mission.[12] This new reformation must reshape the way that pastors and other leaders are identified and trained—including a basic change in seminary curricula and structure (which is still based mainly on a professional model of ministry).

4. Healthy covenant communities teach and practice plural leadership. Spiritual gifts are taught and understood, and all members use their gifts to build up the entire body. Most of the New Testament Christian communities apparently had "elders" (plural), not a single, solo elder or pastor.

Various forms of team leadership should be explored. Whatever the particular form, it must be consistent with New Testament teachings about giftedness, universal priesthood, and non-hierarchical plural leadership.

5. The theology and practice of ordination needs to be rethought. The Old Testament priesthood did not carry over into the New Testament church. In the New Testament, apostles, prophets, and teachers are viewed in terms of charismatic endowment (giftedness), rather than in terms of ordination to office. Note how Paul speaks of the various equipping ministries in Ephesians 4:11–12 and 1 Corinthians 12:28. Such passages show that Paul intended to organize church leadership the same way God had in fact formed the church. Note that the order in these two passages ("first of all apostles, second prophets, third teachers . . ." in 1 Corinthians 12:28) is based on an organic image of the body, not on a static image of organizational hierarchy.

6. Church structure (wineskins) must be consistent with the organic nature of the church. The structure must be functional for mission. Bib-

lically, only four identifiable structures seem to be essential to the church: the congregation, some form of small group, charismatic or gift-based leadership, and some form of networking or connection beyond the local community. In contrast to many institutional structures, these four are cross-culturally valid.[13]

It is dangerous to view particular organizational structures as being of the *essence* of the church. When this happens, structure becomes sacred and may cease to be serviceable. Denominational and all other organizational structures periodically need to be renewed or re-formed in order to be thoroughly missional. But according to what model? Consistent with the church's fundamental DNA, connectional structures as well as local congregational structures should be organic in nature—in harmony with the nature of the church itself. This means, for example, using the model of the organic network rather than the vertical (hierarchical) institution.

This "wineskins" issue is of such practical importance that we will explore it in more depth in later chapters.

## A Trinitarian Community

Finally, we return to the Trinity and to the church as Trinitarian community. The church is not only a missional, alternative, and covenant community; in a fundamental sense, it is a Trinitarian community.

The Trinitarian nature of the church is an important area for investigation, provided it doesn't become too speculative or theoretical. The doctrine of the Trinity teaches us about ecclesiology and Christian mission. Because the church is Trinitarian—based on what God the Father has done and will do through Christ by the power of the Spirit—the church is at the same time *incarnational* and *eschatological.*

Viewed organically, three aspects of this Trinitarian emphasis help us grasp the missionary character of the church:

1. *The church is a Trinitarian worshiping community.* The church in its worship, and often most explicitly in its hymns, worships the Trinity: Father, Son, and Holy Spirit. Further, the Trinity forms the basis of the church's mission as the community responds to the call of the Trinity to participate in the *missio Dei,* the mission of God. In worship the community draws near to God and comes to understand the Father's creative love and care for all he has made, the Son's self-giving in becoming a servant for our salvation, and the Spirit's call and push to go into the world as the Father has sent the Son (John 5:26; 15:9; 20:21). Genuine worship impels us into mission.

Incidentally, the theological richness of the church's great Trinitarian hymns is one reason why vital churches need the church's historic hymnody as well as contemporary praise songs.

We noted at the beginning of this chapter that the church has a mission to God as well as a mission to the world. This reciprocal, back-and-forth action is grounded in the classic doctrine of *perichōrēsis* (literally, "dancing together"—mutual sharing of characteristics). We give ourselves to God (our mission to God), and he gives himself back to us with an overflow of love that impels us out of ourselves and into mission. This seems, in part, to be the point of John 17: "As you sent me into the world, I have sent them into the world. . . . I in them and you in me. May they be brought to complete unity to let the world know that you sent me and have loved them even as you have loved me" (John 17:18, 23).

Mission in Trinitarian perspective is never one-way. We do not simply go out in mission because the Trinity sends us. Rather, mission is reciprocal. In response to God's grace, we carry out our mission to God and thus are "carried" into mission in the world by the Holy Spirit, who in fact goes ahead of us. This happens not in a way that overwhelms us and turns us into zombies; rather, the Spirit empowers us to will to do God's will (John 7:17; Phil. 2:13; Gal. 5:23).[14]

The church is Trinitarian. Its mission is grounded in the Trinity. And in Trinitarian perspective, the church's mission includes its mission to God, to one another, and to the world.

2. *The Trinitarian community is sent especially to the poor.* Though "being in very nature God," Christ "made himself nothing, taking the very nature of a servant" (Phil. 2:6–7), and carried out his mission. This is literally a demonstration of the wisdom of God. For God

> chose the foolish things of the world to shame the wise; God chose the weak things of the world to shame the strong. He chose the lowly things of this world and the despised things—and the things that are not—to nullify the things that are, so that no one may boast before him. It is because of him that you are in Christ Jesus, who has become for us wisdom from God—that is, our righteousness, holiness and redemption.
>
> 1 Corinthians 1:27–30

God's special concern for the poor, and Jesus' explicit mission to the poor, is grounded in the Trinity—not in sociology or politics. That is why the gospel for the poor receives so much emphasis in this book. The Trinity is unbounded, self-giving love that always seeks the best for the other and receives love in return. Since the church's mission grows out of the overflow of this love, it is mission to all people. Amazingly, however, in the incarnation, Jesus Christ becomes the suffering Trinity, and thus the Father and the Spirit have particular compassion for him in his sufferings. This is mirrored in God's concern for "the widow, the orphan, and the alien" that is accentuated throughout Scripture. Thus it is mirrored also in the mission of the church.

*God loves everyone, but especially those who suffer.* It is as simple as that—and as profound. The mutual love of the Trinity impels God, and therefore the church, to incarnate the gospel among the poor. Thus Jesus can say, in words that echo the mystery of the Trinity, "The Spirit of the Lord is on me, because he has anointed me to preach good news to the poor" (Luke 4:18). The church's preference for ministry to the poor is grounded in the Trinity.

3. *The church's whole ministry is grounded in the Trinity.* All ministry—ordained or unordained, paid or unpaid—is rooted in the Trinitarian mystery. Its roots are in Spirit-empowered community, not in organizational hierarchy.

The Trinity is the opposite of hierarchy.[15] The church's ministry, including its leadership, is non-hierarchical. The deep theological grounding of this is the Trinity itself, not some philosophical egalitarianism. The Trinity and the very nature of the material creation God has made show us that we should conceive of the church and its ministry in organic, relational terms, not in mechanical-hierarchical ones. The church is not so much a rational organization or a social machine as it is a complex organism, as shown in earlier chapters. The Trinitarian nature of the church is built into the church's very DNA.

In sum, the church is essentially a community in mission and in movement. This is so because of who God is as Trinity and how he is manifesting himself in the world. Given this rich, profound reality, the church is missional, countercultural, covenantal, and Trinitarian. Mission goes deep into the church's DNA because it reflects the spiritual DNA of God himself (if we may so speak), our heavenly Parent.

———

## Are We Trinitarians?

One day Pastor Dorset was sitting in his study reading a new book, *The Mission-Driven Church.* He was about to underline a sentence when the phone rang. It was Debbie Smithson, one of the church's faithful

Sunday school teachers. Debbie was in charge of the junior high class this year, and she had a question.

"The Trinity came up last Sunday," she told Pastor Dorset. "Actually it was part of our lesson about God. The lesson book said the Trinity is a mystery like the mystery of water. Water can be solid or liquid or vapor, but it's still water. Is that a good way to think of the Trinity?" Debbie asked. "Seems kind of simplistic to me. What do you think?"

Darrell Dorset pondered a moment. "Well, I guess it's all right as an analogy or object lesson," he said, "but the Trinity is a whole lot more profound than that. We're talking about how three distinct spiritual persons, Father, Son, and Holy Spirit, can together be one God, not about water!"

They talked a little more, and Debbie seemed satisfied. After he hung up the phone, Darrell Dorset thought more about Debbie's questions. He had just been reading about the church. Somewhere (maybe in this book) he had read that the church was "a Trinitarian community." *What does that really mean?* he wondered.

Darrell Dorset had always been taught that the Trinity was an essential Christian doctrine. "That's what separates us from Unitarians," he'd been told. He once heard someone say, "The Trinity is a mystery. Try to explain it, and you'll lose your mind. Deny it, and you'll lose your soul." But actually he'd never given much thought to the doctrine. He had noted hints of it here and there in Scripture and, of course, knew the key reference in Matthew 28:19, ". . . baptizing them in the name of the Father and of the Son and of the Holy Spirit."

The very next day, in his own Bible study, Pastor Dorset came across these words in John 17:21–23: "As you, Father, are in me and I am in you, may they also be in us, . . . so that they may be one, as we are one, I in them and you in me, that they may become completely one . . ." (NRSV). He wasn't sure he knew what that meant, but obviously it had something to do with the church—and maybe with the Trinity as well.

Pastor Dorset began thinking and praying more about the Trinity. He was using a book of hymns in his devotions, and he began to notice how often the older hymns ended with a verse of praise to God as Trinity.

During the next breakfast discussion group Pastor Dorset brought up the topic of the Trinity. He decided to take a provocative approach. "Are we Trinitarians? Do we have a Trinitarian church?" he asked.

"Well, of course," Ray Schilling said. "We've always believed in the Trinity. It's even in our statement of faith, I think."

"I know," said Darrell, "but what does the Trinity really mean to you?"

They discussed this, and finally Angie Silver said, "Well, it's important to me that God is Father and Son and Holy Spirit. But I guess it's

not really very important as a *doctrine*. I mean, I hardly ever think of it."
Her comment seemed to sum up the consensus of the group.

Pastor Dorset then read the passage from John 17. "Let's think more
about this," he said. "What did Jesus really mean here?"

They left it at that for the time being. But the subject came up from
time to time on other Thursday mornings, and the group decided to
watch for signs of the Trinity in the Bible passages they studied.

At the breakfast meeting a few weeks later, the passage to be discussed
was Luke 4:16–30, where Jesus is rejected in the synagogue at Nazareth.
Jim said, "I noticed in verse 18 it says, 'The Spirit of the Lord is on me,
because he has anointed me to preach good news to the poor.' Now, this
is Jesus who is speaking, or reading. The verse says 'Spirit' and 'Lord.'
Is this a Trinitarian passage? I mean, the Lord being the Father, the
Spirit being the Holy Spirit, and then Jesus, the Son?"

"Interesting question," Pastor Dorset said. "Of course, 'Spirit of the
Lord' is a common Old Testament phrase. And notice how Luke mentions the Holy Spirit several times in this chapter. Luke seems to emphasize Jesus and the Holy Spirit, if not specifically the Trinity."

"Well," Ray said, "I've noticed that when the Holy Spirit is mentioned,
it often has something to do with witness or mission—especially in Luke
and Acts."

"Yes," Angie said. "I've noticed that, too."

Bill said, "Do you suppose that if we were really led by the Spirit, our
church would be doing more to 'preach good news to the poor,' like Jesus
did? Would we be more of a witness in our community? Would we do
more in missions?"

"Yes," Ray said. "And would the Spirit help us lead more holy lives—
be more different from the world around us?"

"Well, I think we *are* being led by the Spirit," Pastor Dorset replied.
"Look at the ways our ministries have expanded and the new people
who have been added to the church. And I know the Vision and Planning Committee is seeking God's guidance as we think about our future."

They closed with a prayer that God would continue to guide them
and that they would really understand what it meant for their church
to be a community of the Father, the Son, and the Holy Spirit.

# Questions
## for Group Discussion or Personal Reflection

1. Does your church have an organizational chart? If so, place every member within the chart and determine the extent to which your church structure is based on the hierarchy principle. If not, create a realistic diagram showing how every member in your church interacts with every other member.
2. Think about the mission of your church. Explain in your own words the difference between the church's mission *to* God and its mission *from* God. Do you agree that the church has a mission *to* God?
3. To what extent does your church reflect the spiritual DNA of God himself? How does the Trinity relate to this?
4. Is Heartland Evangelical a Trinitarian church? In what way or ways?
5. Is there a difference between a church's belief in the Trinity and its being Trinitarian?
6. What connection do you see between the Trinity and the DNA of the church?
7. In view of the points discussed in this chapter, how might the Heartland church become more fully Trinitarian?

# 4

---

## THE DNA OF CHURCH STRUCTURE

### *Dead Ends*

As far as we know, Jesus never heard of X and Y chromosomes, genetic engineering, or DNA. But he had a profound understanding of the church as a dynamic organism. He explained it to his listeners in terms they understood, and they understood wine. Some of them were planters and pruners and pickers of grapes. They had trod the winepress. And, of course, they had enjoyed the resulting beverage.

Let us dip back into Jesus' wineskin metaphor so that we can better understand the DNA of Christ's body—both what makes it work and what kills it.

Jesus once said, "People do not pour new wine into old wineskins. If they do, the skins burst, the wine runs out, and the wineskins are ruined. No, they pour new wine into new wineskins. That way both are preserved" (Matt. 9:17, authors' paraphrase).

Jesus was speaking at a time of joyful celebration. The summer fruits were harvested in August and September. Baskets of grapes were taken to small vats and trod to squeeze out the juice. It took forty days for the sediment to settle, and then the fermenting wine was stored in new goatskin bags.

Leatherwork was a major industry of the time, producing clothes, belts, footwear, and tents in addition to goatskin bags for wine. Tanners were expected to live outside the town because their work was smelly, but their products were highly desirable.

Paul, Aquila, and Priscilla were leatherworkers, not just tentmakers.[1] And perhaps Paul's ecclesiology—his understanding of the church—was partly shaped by the image of the goatskin bag. Wineskins were the ideal solution to the problem of storing, preserving, and transporting—indeed, exporting worldwide—a precious and highly desirable product. The church structures Paul fostered had appropriate and efficient delivery systems and a major focus on the elixir within.

History reveals a massive tendency in the church to confuse the wine with the wineskins. This confusion still exists, especially in the churches of North America but also globally because of North American influence. Christians continue to confuse the dynamic life of the gospel with the human-made structures that contain and often constrict it.

We seek to cut through that confusion. One essential point underlies everything else: God in his sovereignty, working through the Holy Spirit, powers the church and makes it dynamic. Church structures don't do that. In fact, in some instances they stifle the very life they seek to foster. Church structures have repeatedly imprisoned the church, just as containers that prevent fermentation can kill the life of the wine—and anyone can smell and taste the difference.

Wine producers of the New Testament era were careful to avoid using wrong packages for their product. And we must be careful how we "package" the church. We seek to decode its DNA and to know the workings of the Holy Spirit as thoroughly as wine producers understood the life of their product and knew how to package it appropriately.

The power of the gospel is in the wine, not the wineskins, but by recognizing the key role of wineskins, we begin to realize the possibilities for a healthier church.

In Jesus' day wineskins were made of leather. Fill an old, dried-out skin with new wine, and it will burst as the fresh beverage ferments. There is fresh ferment in the twenty-first-century church, causing the new wine to spill out as old church structures fail.

What is "church structure"? We think first of buildings and denominations, but church structure also means the forms and patterns the church uses to carry out its mission in the world. If these structures are not made of goatskin or bricks or organizational charts, then what are they made of? Where do we find the best material for new wineskins?

If we wish to be biblical Christians, we must answer this question in a way that is consistent with Scripture. If we put Scripture first, we will see that some popular resources for church structure are not very helpful. They may be useful in a secondary sense, but only secondarily.

It is helpful here to make a distinction between *fundamental* and *secondary* sources for new wineskins because the essential nature of the church is at stake. Too often questions of church structure are seen as merely pragmatic, organizational questions instead of as questions of basic theology. We want to challenge that approach. Unless we are biblically and theologically clear about what we mean by "church" at the most foundational level, we will end up doing what the church has always done at its worst: putting new wine into old wineskins.

When it comes to the church, the most obvious thing is not always the right thing. The obvious thing is to ask, "Where is the church growing?" Growing churches *must* be doing things right. Let us simply find out what they are doing, attend the latest "how-to" conference, and do the same things.[2]

Let's begin first with the negative, discussing three sources for church structure that are not fundamentally helpful, though they may be secondarily. Fundamentally, they are dead ends, or worse. The three places people generally look first for new wineskins are *megachurches, microchurches,* and *business models.*

## Megachurch Mania

Yes, we can learn from the experience of megachurches, both in the United States and around the world. This is particularly true if these churches are really apostolic—that is, if they are seeking and saving the lost, caring for the poor, and building genuine communities of disciples. Many megachurches, however, fail to do this.

Whatever good things we may learn from them, megachurches should not be a primary source for new wineskins for four reasons.

1. *Megachurches are too limited in cultural context* to be a primary source for wineskins. In part, wineskins are an issue of cross-cultural effectiveness. If we want churches that can be birthed and grow in diverse cultural contexts, then we need to look deeper than megachurch models.

True, not all megachurches are the same. But the models commonly lifted up today from such places as the United States, Korea, and Singapore are more alike than different. Most megachurches are composed primarily of middle-class, professional, young to middle-aged, upwardly mobile people who live either in suburbs or in relatively affluent urban neighborhoods. They are accustomed to commuting by private automobile or public transportation for employment, shopping, and entertainment. Though megachurches may be heterogeneous in other ways, they tend in this sense to be homogeneous. Around the world, these churches look much alike.

There are exceptions, of course—for instance, some urban mega-churches composed primarily of African Americans and megachurches of the poor located in major cities around the world or sometimes even in rural areas (in regions of Central Africa, for example). But when it comes to the question of new wineskins, these churches are little studied and are not the models that attract hordes of visiting pastors looking for success.

Is it possible that megachurches are in fact a historical aberration rather than the wave of the future? Is it possible that they function only within a rather narrow cultural range and that if taken as models can lead church leaders down a blind alley?

Today's Protestant megachurches are not unparalleled in history. As Michael Hamilton writes, "For a century now, self-confident preachers have been willing to reinvent church in order to appeal to the unchurched. They have used nonsacred architecture, innovative worship services, popular music, drama, and diverse programming to meet the needs of people who felt unwelcome in traditional churches. And a few of these churches—to the surprise and dismay of the traditionalists—grew really large."[3] This is true, although we should perhaps look back one thousand years, not just one hundred, to find historical examples, each unique to its time and social location.

Throughout history, megachurches have flourished (and then waned), especially since the time of the Roman Emperor Constantine in the fourth century. We know from church architecture and other sources that in most eras of Christian history, megachurches have existed and have sometimes had great impact. We can find examples from medieval Europe and from a variety of mission contexts throughout history.

Eighteenth-century England provides some examples. A number of Anglican pastors caught up in the great Evangelical Revival built strong congregations of two or three thousand members. In nineteenth-century America, we think of Charles Finney's Broadway Tabernacle in Manhattan, Henry Ward Beecher's affluent Plymouth Church in Brooklyn, or his brother Thomas Beecher's First Congregational Church in Elmira, New York. Then there were the urban gospel tabernacles of the 1920s and 1930s, such as Paul Rader's Chicago Gospel Tabernacle and Aimee Semple McPherson's Angelus Temple in Los Angeles.

Manhattan's Broadway Tabernacle in the 1830s was the nerve center of a nationwide social reform and benevolence network that helped reshape American society (though the use of the tabernacle for this purpose was as much a matter of convenience as an explicit expression of the church's ministry). Thomas Beecher's church in Elmira (a town of 38,000 in 1900) had a Sunday school of 1,000 people and a worshiping congregation of about 1,500. Sometimes called "the first institutional church" in the United States, Thomas Beecher's church boasted a gymnasium, a library, a theater, a variety of social rooms, and a basement pool table. Beecher called it "a family on a large scale."[4]

In fact, many such "institutional churches" dotted England and America in the late 1800s and early 1900s. Though apparently successful at the time (at least in terms of numbers), they left later generations with drafty buildings and huge maintenance bills that became a major drain on mission.

Rapid growth and congregations numbering into the thousands are thus nothing new. But these large churches reflect particular social contexts. Perhaps the most important thing to note about these megachurches is that while they had laudable ministries, they were not the most important thing happening in the larger church *even at that time.* Then as now, the church was growing and extending its witness, not primarily through megachurches, but through growing networks of smaller churches.

Elephants and dinosaurs are impressive, but they thrive only in certain environments.

2. A second reason megachurches are not a reliable source for new wineskins is simply a matter of *size and scale.* When viewed as a model, the megachurch can hardly avoid creating the impression that success is tied to numbers.

We rejoice in the growth of any church that, without compromising the gospel, is growing in numbers and ministry. And we are not opposed to large churches. We are actually speaking more of North American cultural values than the question of megachurches *per se.* North Americans place an inordinately high value on size, growth, and newness. *This is our worldview.* These are assumed values; seldom questioned, except in specialized areas like body weight and microtechnology.

Some literature on megachurches and "metachurches"[5] explicitly rejects this bigness bias, or at least stresses that megachurch principles can operate successfully in any size church. But generally this message is not heard. What most people hear is that *large churches are better than small churches* and "success" is a function of growth rate.

We question this at a theological and worldview level. Nowhere in the New Testament do we find even a hint that faithfulness to the gospel of the kingdom is related to size—unless it is to smallness, as in a mustard seed or a grain of wheat.[6] The numbers given in the first chapters of Acts clearly show that when the Holy Spirit is poured out, the church grows and expands. But Luke avoids measuring success with statistics.[7] Paul indicates (for example, in 1 Thessalonians 1) that the gospel spread into surrounding regions from the little churches he planted, but his point is extension through discipleship and church planting, not the growth of super-congregations.

The Bible has no theological bias toward largeness or rapid numerical growth. Nor does church history support any significant correlation between gospel fidelity and large congregations. We know that in the case of early British Methodism, John Wesley sometimes viewed large numerical increase as a sign of God's blessing and other times as a red flag signaling a breakdown in discipline and rigor. Growth and size were never factors by themselves; they had to be gauged by other criteria.[8]

Focusing on congregational size is too one-dimensional. Given the importance of other factors, we may question whether it is even an important consideration at all. We know that healthy things grow. If the church is a healthy organism, it will grow. But growth is not always a sign of health. Cancer and other diseases tell us that growth may signal serious illness. The question underlying this whole book is, What makes the church a healthy organism?

More research is needed here. What is the correlation between congregational size, numerical growth, and effective witness? This is researchable. Undoubtedly church size would vary according to sociocultural context, but is there an optimum size for a congregation? Given the sweep of Christian history, our hunch is that there *is* an optimal size, perhaps in the range of one hundred to two hundred people—more or less, depending on context. Christian Schwarz's research suggests that on average, smaller churches grow more rapidly than larger ones and reports, "On nearly all relevant quality factors, larger churches compare disfavorably with smaller ones." Sociological studies show that as the size of a congregation increases, usually the commitment level decreases.[9]

If this is true, megachurches are something of a historical anomaly. While there probably have always been and always will be megachurches, they are the exception, not the rule. They may fill a niche, but they are neither normative nor the wave of the future. More important, if the church functions best with medium-size congregations, what does this say about strategy? Should not many hundreds of churches that are now growing into the thousands actively be planning to "mutate" into networks of smaller congregations rather than simply growing larger? Certainly they should be planting new congregations, even as they (perhaps) experiment with creative ways to network these congregations in such a way as to gain the advantages of both smallness and largeness.

How do we know when a congregation is growing too large? Try the name-tag test. When you have to have name tags to know everyone, the church is too big—and probably community is too weak. In a vital congregation, everyone knows everyone else on a first-name basis. And that can happen only in a small- to medium-size church, or a larger one that is honeycombed with small groups. Megachurches that maintain strong community do so only through a vital network of subcommunities.

Face-to-face community at the local level is assumed in all the accounts of the New Testament church. The "one another" passages, such as "encourage one another" and "greet one another," imply it. So do the personal names found frequently in the letters to the churches. Of course, the church is broader than this; in some sense it is like the whole people of Israel in the Old Testament; it is "a holy nation," a new people. But unless this reality includes face-to-face community and covenant relationship, something essential is missing and the church easily begins conforming to the world.

Some may view these first two reasons for not using megachurches as fundamental resources for new wineskins (limited cultural context and excessive focus on size) as irrelevant. The argument often runs something like this: We live in a new context, a new, postmodern world in which the megachurch is the wave of the future. This view is naive and very limited both historically and theologically. It simply is not true.

3. Another substantial reason for not using megachurches as models is that many *megachurches fail to emphasize the gospel to and for the poor*. Here again we can find exceptions, particularly among African American and Roman Catholic city churches. But this generalization holds true for the bulk of middle-class Protestant megachurches that get the most media attention, as the literature from such churches shows.

The pastor of a megachurch was enthusiastically telling the story and philosophy of his growing church. He was full of tips on leadership, programming, and evangelism. But he spoke not one word on social justice or on reaching the poor. In fact, the whole ethos was just the opposite. The church was "seeker-sensitive," but it was clear that a particular class of "seekers" was desired. This church was being built, and *seeking* to be built, primarily of middle-class professionals. The whole mentality was success-oriented in a way calculated to appeal to young professionals. Poorer folk would find it alienating. And their rusting cars would look out of place in the parking lot. Totally lacking was the spirit of Jesus' manifesto in Luke 4: "The Spirit of the Lord is on me, because he has anointed me to preach good news to the poor."

We are not suggesting that all churches should make the poor their primary focus. Faithful churches will to some degree reflect their particular social context. But Scripture in both Testaments stresses God's particular concern for the poor. If this essential biblical note is missing from megachurch models, those models are dead ends as sources for new wineskins.

4. Finally, megachurches do not provide good material for new wineskins because *though some megachurches have good ecclesiologies, there is no good megachurch ecclesiology.* A megachurch ecclesiology would articulate theologically the basis for existing *as megachurches.* But that is generally not what we find. Granted, some megachurches have articulated excellent, Bible-centered models of the church. They have carefully thought through the "architecture" of their organizations. The churches of Willow Creek, Saddleback, and Ginghamsburg United Methodist are examples. But what is good about such ecclesiologies is not essential to their existence *as megachurches.* In fact, their existence as megachurches is in some tension with their articulated ecclesiologies. The larger a single congregation becomes, the harder it is to live out an ecclesiology that maintains biblical standards of vitality and discipleship.

Willow Creek Community Church has done a good job of addressing these issues and of maintaining vitality in the midst of rapid growth. Lynne and Bill Hybels' *Rediscovering Church: The Story and Vision of Willow Creek Community Church* is an inspiring and frank account, giving excellent insights on leadership and other issues. It does not, however, directly address the questions: What does it mean to be a megachurch, and to what degree should megachurches be seen as models for most churches?[10]

Because megachurches are large enterprises, the models they follow *as megachurches* tend to be business models. The problem is that models, concepts, and procedures taken from the business world are often not subjected to theological critique *based on a biblical ecclesiology.* And too often the result is a growing disconnect between stated ecclesiology and actual practice. This may be one reason why many people initially attracted to megachurches leave them by the hundreds to settle in smaller churches with deeper levels of community.[11]

It is very difficult for a congregation to grow beyond about one thousand people without developing a serious discipleship gap that eventually undermines vitality. A discipleship gap occurs when professions of faith outrun the actual living of the faith in costly discipleship. This is the difference between professing faith in Christ and living like Christ. Once the gap between evangelism and discipleship reaches a significant level (a kind of tipping point), the superficial adherents to the faith, not the serious disciples, set the tone and agenda for the church.

Where, then, can we find material for new wineskins? We have suggested that we *not* go to megachurches because their cultural context is too limited, they are too biased toward bigness, they tend to overlook the poor, and they lack a megachurch ecclesiology.

## The Microchurch Option

If megachurches are not a good source for wineskins, then why not microchurches? Some people, in reaction to megachurches or the so-called organized church, argue that house churches or other very small Christian communities are the true model of the church.

We might call this the microchurch option. Primarily, the microchurch option is the house-church model. There are other forms, however, including Roman Catholic "base communities" *(comunidads de base)*. Early Methodist class meetings and the Pietist *collegia pietatis* (spiritual nurture groups) also fit this model to some degree, though within the context of a larger structure and community.[12]

Most people in megachurches or denominational churches don't realize how many house churches dot the landscape. Often these groups are nearly invisible. They have no church buildings or elaborate organizations. They get no media attention. Anecdotal evidence suggests, however, that there are at least tens of thousands of house churches in the United States and Canada, often unknown even to each other outside of fairly limited networks. In this sense, one could make the case that microchurches deserve to be taken as seriously as megachurches.[13]

For the past two generations, house churches have provided the primary vehicle for church growth in China. Granted, a "house church" numbering into the hundreds of people, as sometimes happens in China, is no longer a house church in the traditional sense. But the Chinese church has grown primarily through the multiplication of small home-based units. With time, many of these have expanded beyond the simple house-church form. Such growth through house churches is not surprising. The New Testament church was essentially a network of house churches.[14]

Microchurches can teach us much about church vitality. In many places, the microchurch structure is the main way the church has grown for nearly two millennia.

There is a whole body of literature on microchurches that has argued over the past four centuries that the house church is the normative form of church life. Yet for some key reasons microchurches, like megachurches, do not offer the best material for new wineskins today. Here is why:

1. *Microchurches are too biased against "traditional" churches.* In too many house churches, the "organized" or "traditional" church is the enemy. This bias may take the form of a theological argument about the fall of the church and the "secret history" of a faithful remnant through the ages. More often, the argument takes a pragmatic and psychologi-

cal form. Thousands of people who have been wounded in traditional churches find comfort in intimate, relatively unstructured house churches and maintain a strong animus against denominational or other traditional churches.[15] Because of this bias against traditional churches, microchurches often miss some essential elements of a faithful and effective ecclesiology.

2. In many cases, *microchurches are ingrown and have little evangelistic witness.* Though there are happy exceptions, most microchurches we have encountered are so focused on creating and sustaining their own community that they have little evangelistic vision. Evangelism seems to be missing from their DNA. House churches expend tremendous energy restoring people to health and tending wounds received from "bad" church experiences. As a result, they often have little energy left for outreach. Microchurches can teach us much about community, but often their sense of community is not matched by apostolic vision.

3. *Microchurches often lack a theology of the "great assembly."* Healthy churches maintain a creative balance of small group and large group.[16] Microchurches often are good at *koinōnia* (redemptive small-group dynamics) but slight the large group. As we see especially from the Psalms, the church is not only *koinōnia;* it is also the "great assembly" (Ps. 22:25; 26:12; 35:18; 40:9–10; 68:26). It is people coming together in numbers for corporate worship and shared vision. There is an inherent dynamic, a synergy, in combining the small group and the large group in a church's life. This dynamic seems to be built into the church's very DNA. But microchurches often miss this. They see the great assembly as inescapably tied to dead formalism. Thus they miss some of the inherent dynamic of a biblical ecclesiology.

4. For these reasons, *microchurches generally have a one-sided theology of the kingdom of God.* The kingdom is too internalized and is divorced from sociopolitical and economic spheres. This is not always the case; some house churches do have a strong sense of kingdom values and of the church as a kingdom counterculture. But others (perhaps influenced by Watchman Nee) develop a spirituality that is essentially dualistic when it comes to the church's witness in the world.

In these and other ways, microchurches often exhibit a sociological naivete that fails to appreciate the importance and usefulness of traditional forms of the church and of the necessary structures of society. They tend to view traditional church structures as hopelessly compromised or apostate. Historically, however, these "dead" structures have often proved to be the incubators of fresh forms of renewal. Renewal movements do not spring from nowhere; they arise from within (though often at the periphery of) the "institutional church."

For all these reasons, we suggest that microchurches do not provide primary material for new wineskins today. We can, and should, learn from them. But we must go deeper.

## The Lure of Business Models

What about business models? What can we learn from the experience of successful businesses, particularly those that are most effective in achieving their goals? Do they provide raw material for new wineskins?

Business models are relevant to the church to the extent they are biblical. The church can learn many things from successful business enterprises. The importance of a clear mission and priorities consistent with that mission, approaches to organizational effectiveness, and insights about leadership and working with teams are often modeled by effective companies. But do we really need business models to learn these things? Most effective business principles are taught clearly, and with deeper rationale, in Scripture.[17] The church can learn from business models, but these models do not provide primary material for new wineskins for at least four reasons.

1. *Business enterprises operate on the basis of secular presuppositions.* The primary basis of business is the profit motive, though sometimes this is moderated by other considerations, such as the welfare of employees or (occasionally) social justice or environmental concern.

This is not a criticism of business enterprises *per se.* It is simply an observation about their nature. They are not the church. Therefore, at a fundamental level, we believe Eugene Peterson is right in saying that business has *nothing* to say to the church. Whatever we *do* learn from business, we must pass carefully through the filter of a biblical ecclesiology.

2. *The fundamental model of business is in tension with Scripture.* Business itself is not evil, for Scripture gives useful advice on how to act responsibly in business. But there are profound distinctions between business and the church.

If we take the New Testament seriously, we must conclude that business enterprises and commercial wisdom are part of "human tradition and the basic principles of this world" rather than of Christ (Col. 2:8). They are part of the passing world's "basic principles" to which Christians have "died" (Col. 2:20).

Christians are to function redemptively within the world's structures. If Christians are faithful to the kingdom of God, they act to humanize the realms of business, economics, and politics. But as citizens of God's new order, Christians are aware of a fundamental tension and must be careful not to confuse business with the church.

3. Like megachurches, *business models are too limited in cultural context* to provide fundamental material for wineskins. Commercial enterprises take different shapes in different times and cultures. Often the church imitates business (or other dominant social structures) in its life and forms. Due to the fundamental tension between business models and the essential nature of the church, such imitation has arguably done more harm than good.

True, we are in a new age of globalization. But it would be naive to think that this means churches should now mimic cutting-edge global corporations in order to be "successful." Quite the opposite. We should remember that there are many other forms of human organization effectively at work *right now* in the world, from various kinds of cooperatives and networks to the range of voluntary societies and nongovernment organizations. The church is to operate as salt, light, and leaven *within* the globalizing structures of this world, not simply to follow the examples of those structures.

4. Finally, *business enterprises do not make community a primary consideration.* Interestingly, some of the most effective, cutting-edge businesses today *have* discovered community as a means toward greater business effectiveness. But establishing community is not their reason for existence. Rather, they use community as a means to an economic end.

In contrast, community *(koinōnia)* is a *primary* consideration for the church. The church is the *"koinōnia* of the Holy Spirit"; it is "devoted to community" (2 Cor. 13:14; Acts 2:42).

In sum, business models have very little, if anything, to teach the church *as church.* It is important to note, however, that creative, effective business organizations *do* have a lot to teach about how Christian organizations can function—*as human organizations,* not as church. Church structures, from local and denominational to various mission and service organizations, can benefit from the careful analysis of a business perspective. But in all such analysis we must be clear about one thing: Such church structures are to serve the life and mission of the church—nothing else. Because we so seldom think theologically about the church, we tend to blur the distinction between church as body of Christ and our human-made structures. The result is predictable and perhaps inevitable: We "nullify the word of God for the sake of [our] tradition" (Matt. 15:6).

All this may sound negative, but the goal is positive. Our intention is to "deconstruct" popular thinking about church structure in order to answer the basic question with which we began: *With what materials are new wineskins to be constructed?* Where do we find the resources for new wineskins?

Our next step in this search will be to look at more promising sources, beginning with the Bible.

————

## Heartland Searches for Wineskins

Darrell Dorset usually devoted Wednesday mornings to going through his mail. Often there was quite a stack—a few letters but mostly brochures, magazines, and flyers about products and services available to churches. He might mark a couple magazine articles to read later, but most of the mail usually ended up in his recycle box.

One particular Wednesday morning as Darrell was leafing through a Christian magazine, he noticed a full-page ad for a "Creative Church Leadership Conference" to be held in early October. It caught his eye because it said, "Churches of all shapes and sizes will learn principles that will help them grow dramatically."

The conference was to be held at the Spring Harvest Church near Indianapolis. *That's not too far away,* Darrell thought. *Maybe I should go and take a couple of key leaders with me.* The ad suggested the two-day seminar was for "pastors and key lay leaders." Darrell thought he could probably interest Ray Schilling or Bill and Angie Silver in the conference. It might be good for them to attend; Ray and Angie were active on the Vision and Planning Committee.

Pastor Dorset brought the subject up at the Thursday breakfast group. A brochure had just arrived in the mail about the conference, so he had stuck it in his Bible and now showed it to the group. "What do you think?" he asked.

They all looked over the material and discussed it. "It's a little expensive," Ray said, "but it might be worth it. We'd probably learn a lot. I've heard that Spring Harvest Church is a real going concern."

"Yes," Pastor Dorset said, "they're pushing three thousand. The church has more than quadrupled in the past twelve years. They used to be a church of only a couple hundred, I think. And I understand they have some really creative ministries."

But Jim Richards was skeptical. "What do we need a conference or seminar for?" he asked. "Things are going well for us. We're growing. And we've got a committee looking at our future."

"Well," Pastor Dorset responded, "I think it would be good for the Vision and Planning Committee to get some outside input—you know, think outside the box. We don't have to buy everything, but we might get a few good ideas."

Eventually the church board decided to send Pastor Dorset and several other people to the conference. Even Jim went along.

The two days at the Spring Harvest Church were an uplifting time of inspiration. Pastor Dorset and the others enjoyed the music, the large crowd of other pastors and church leaders, and the slick presentations. "These people really believe in excellence," he thought. He was especially impressed by the presentations of the senior pastor, who was an inspiring speaker. He peppered his talks on church growth and successful administration with quotations and examples from leading technology companies like Cisco Systems and Dell Computer. Large video screens amplified his messages and illustrated them with well-chosen video clips.

Darrell, Bill and Angie, Ray, and Jim returned from the conference with fat notebooks, a couple of paperbacks, and a video. Driving back home in the van, they talked over what they had seen and heard.

"Well, that church certainly has its act together," said Bill.

"They do a lot of things well," Ray agreed. "I was impressed with their video setup."

"I'm not so sure," Jim said. "Could we really ever be like that? Do we *want* to?"

"Well, let's evaluate it," Pastor Dorset said. "What did you see that might be helpful for us at Heartland?"

"I like the emphasis on excellence," Bill said. "We do a lot of things well, but some of our programming is rather slipshod. We certainly have room for improvement."

Angie said, "I got some good ideas about children's ministries."

Jim wasn't convinced. "You know, I just read a book called *Going to Church in the First Century*, and it gave a whole different slant on the church and church life. The early church was into relationships and meeting together in homes. I'm not so sure about this whole megachurch approach."

They continued discussing what they had learned and sorting things out. What especially impressed Pastor Dorset was the audiovisual setup at Spring Harvest Church. It certainly outclassed Heartland's meager sound system and overhead projector!

Pastor Dorset and the others gave their report at the next meeting of the Vision and Planning Committee. They talked about what they had learned and shared the things that seemed especially relevant to Heartland.

Darrell Dorset talked about the video system. "I think it's time we do some upgrading," he said. "We need more microphones, better sound mixing, and new speakers. And if we upgrade the sound system, this would be a good time to add the video component." Pastor Dorset had already done some research on audiovisual systems and how much they might cost.

The committee considered this and other ideas the team had brought back from the Creative Church Leadership Conference. After a couple of months, the committee gave its report to the church board. It was professionally done, with charts and graphs. It showed how the church had grown and analyzed its financial picture. The report evaluated the church's different programs, making projections and recommendations. It also recommended a churchwide program of small groups—and a name change. "After researching our church's identity and our image in our target area, we believe our witness would be enhanced by a small change in name. We recommend that Heartland Evangelical Church be renamed Heartland Christian Fellowship."

The name change kicked up a lot of discussion, but since it was a fairly minor change and didn't involve any doctrinal shift, eventually it was approved. "After all, 'Christian' is a biblical word," Pastor Dorset pointed out, "and it says who we are. And we do want to emphasize the *fellowship* aspect of our church."

The proposal for a small-group program was referred to a special task force to figure out what would work best at Heartland Christian Fellowship and begin making plans.

Pastor Dorset, however, was especially interested in the new audiovisual system and pushed hard for it. The church board blinked a bit at the cost, but in the end approved the report and its recommendations, including the new system.

Six months later, the new audiovisual system was in place. Purchasing this system meant a sharp increase in the church budget. But with the church's projected growth, Pastor Dorset was sure there would be no problem.

The new system took some getting used to. The church hired a part-time audiovisual technician, a young man who had grown up in the church and had recently graduated from college. Pastor Dorset started illustrating his sermons with clips from movies and TV programs. He had to rearrange his schedule and the way he did his sermon preparation, but he felt the new system helped him communicate better.

As the year passed, Pastor Dorset became quite comfortable with the new system. But he had some new concerns. He wasn't sure why, but statistics showed the church wasn't growing. Financial giving had risen only slightly. Monthly income was running below projections, and a bit below expenses.

Early one April morning Pastor Dorset shared his concerns with the Thursday breakfast group. "I'm not sure what's happening," he said. "Overall I think we're doing things better than ever before. But finances aren't keeping up, and attendance is flat."

He hadn't said anything about this to the group before because he didn't want to sound negative or cause any concern. But frankly, he was worried. And the breakfast group had become a place of open sharing.

"What do you think is happening?" Pastor Dorset asked. "It seems to me we're losing momentum."

"Well, I guess I have to agree," Ray Schilling said. "It's strange, after all the planning and strategizing and new ideas we've had."

Angie said, "It does seem like our programming has improved. But I have a feeling we've lost something—I'm not sure what."

"I don't think we're really growing in community," Jim said. "Remember how we used to share and pray for one another in the small groups? I really don't see that happening now."

"Well," Pastor Dorset said, "Let's pray about this. What does God want to tell us? If we're headed in the wrong direction, we'd better locate the problem and get back on track." The group agreed to pray about this and to seek God's guidance over the next few weeks.

Back in his office, Darrell Dorset tried to figure out what had happened over the past year. He couldn't understand it all, but the more he thought about it, one thing did stand out. His people, especially his key leaders, had spent a lot of time in committee and board meetings over the past year. The focus had been on planning and especially on improving the church building and its audiovisual system. Maybe they had gotten their eyes off the essentials. The church was busy—maybe *too* busy? Maybe the church wasn't really nourishing its "first love."

# Questions
## for Group Discussion or Personal Reflection

1. How large was the group of believers that first influenced you to take the claims of Jesus Christ seriously?
2. Describe the group of believers that guided your growth in becoming a committed follower of Jesus Christ.
3. How large is the group of believers that provides you with the most significant Christian fellowship today?
4. Regardless of the size, what are the traits of this group that are most meaningful and significant to your life in Christ?
5. What did Pastor Dorset and his leaders learn at the Creative Church Leadership Conference that was helpful?
6. How would you evaluate the changes Heartland made? What do you see that was positive or negative about the changes they made?
7. Why do you suppose the Heartland church stopped growing?
8. What do you think Heartland Christian Fellowship should do now?
9. Do the marks of the church discussed in chapter one illuminate this discussion in any way?

# 5

## THE DNA OF CHURCH STRUCTURE

### *New Wineskins*

Where can we find material for church structure that fits the church's basic DNA? If megachurches, house churches, and business models are not the best sources for new wineskins, then where should we look?

To really be Christ's body in the world, the church needs structures that match its DNA and that work in the world. Wineskins must be both compatible with the wine of the gospel and appropriate within particular cultural contexts. Three sources are especially promising for helping churches recover the dynamism of the New Testament church.

### The Bible

The Bible is our primary source for effective church structure. While this should be obvious, sometimes Christians resist going to Scripture for the answer to the structure question. Some claim the New Testament teaches nothing about the *form* of the church. Others argue that biblical examples of church structure are not really relevant today. Strangely, the church seems to have an inbred aversion to building ecclesiastical practice on Scripture—call it a blind spot.

Evidence of this blind spot is everywhere. A seminary has high on one of its buildings the words:

## CENTER FOR BIBLICAL PREACHING AND CHURCH LEADERSHIP

Notice the adjectives. The *preaching* is to be *biblical,* but *leadership,* by implication, comes from church tradition. Why doesn't it read, "Center for Church Preaching and Biblical Leadership"? Such language is typical and represents a common mindset. Surely, however, leadership in the church should be based as much on Scripture as preaching should be.

Here are four basic reasons why Scripture must be our primary source for church structure.

1. *The Bible is God's unique revelation both of Jesus Christ and of his body, the church.* Evangelicals claim to believe in biblical authority and to make Scripture their primary rule for faith and practice. But we have a blind spot when it comes to ecclesiology. Seldom do North American Christians mine the depths and apply the authoritative teachings of Scripture regarding the nature and practical operation of the church, except in very limited areas. The Bible is God's unique revelation as to *what the church is*—its very DNA—and how it is to function. But much church practice, especially in North America, would suggest that we don't really believe this.

2. *Ecclesiology is a primary focus of Scripture.* Much of the Old Testament focuses on what it means to be the *people* of God. Most of the New Testament highlights the new community of the Spirit formed around Jesus. But evangelical theology often misses this biblical emphasis.

Clearly, ecclesiology is a key theme of Scripture. The New Testament is all about Jesus Christ, head and body. As Robert Coleman pointed out years ago, the Gospels show that Jesus spent more time in forming his community of disciples, the church in embryo, than in preaching to the crowds.[1] Acts is the story of the formation and extension of the Christian community and reveals many insights about church life. The letters of Paul and other New Testament writers give us a rich, profound, fully faceted Christology that invariably leads to ecclesiology: "Live [corporately] a life worthy of the calling you have received" (Eph. 4:1). "Walk as Jesus did" (1 John 2:6). Likewise, the essential teachings on *soteriology* (the plan of salvation), even in the Book of Romans, are all ecclesiologically grounded (note especially Rom. 12–14).

The amount of space given in the epistles to the nature of relationships within the Christian community is striking. Notice especially the dominant use of the pronoun "you" in the plural (meaning "you-all!") rather than the singular, the rich stratum of "one another" passages, the teachings on spiritual gifts, and the prominent use of "body of Christ" and other organic metaphors. The New Testament is about Christian community—what it is and how it is to function.

This rich biblical treasure leaves us with a disturbing question: Why do we *not* go to the Bible for our ecclesiology, when the church is a primary focus of Scripture? There are historical and cultural reasons for this. Historically, the churches of the Reformation (with the exception of the Radical Reformation) have focused so sharply on the plan of salvation—soteriology—that they have neglected God's plan for Christian community—ecclesiology. Culturally, the Protestant tradition has been so marked by individualism that it has largely neglected the corporate nature of Christian experience.

For these reasons, we often approach Scripture with blinders on. We misread much of the New Testament, individualizing what has corporate meaning and neglecting reconciliation on the human plane while rightly stressing reconciliation with God. It is not that the Bible has little of practical relevance to say about the church and its structures. It is rather that we have not taken seriously what is clearly there. As we will show later, this neglect of Scripture has impoverished our ecclesiology.

3. A third reason we should turn to Scripture for new wineskins is *the example of the early church* that we find there. The New Testament church, for all its imperfections, was the most dynamic embodiment of the gospel that history has yet seen. A powerful gospel movement grew out of the initial days after Pentecost and, within decades, shook the world.

So we need to delve into the *experience* of these early Christian communities (not just the explicit biblical teachings about the church) when we face the issue of wineskins. Most of the essential information about the early church is contained within the New Testament. As Paul said of the Old Testament, the New Testament record of the church was "written to teach us" (Rom. 15:4).

We can learn much from the experience of the earliest Christian communities. Michael Green's book *Evangelism in the Early Church* and Rodney Stark's *The Rise of Christianity* are helpful and prophetic at this point. In large measure, these books are really about ecclesiology. Stark, for instance, shows that the genius of the early church's growth and witness was not its strategy or organization but its embodiment of Christian virtue in countercultural yet culturally engaged community.[2]

4. Finally, we should go first to Scripture for guidance on church structure because *Scripture uniquely combines church and mission*. There is very little distinction between "church" and "mission" in the New Testament. "The church does not have a mission; the mission has a church," as someone has said. Biblically, this is true. But we must ask, *Why* was this the case in the New Testament? What can we learn to help us develop the kind of Christian communities in which it becomes unnecessary to put the word *missional* before the word *church*? The

Bible offers essential and highly relevant material for answering these questions.

The suggestion that we turn to the Bible for new wineskins is often met with skepticism. Historically, people say, that attempt has failed. It has led to arguments and divisions and to different and competing traditions—for example, episcopal, congregational, and presbyterian ecclesiologies. But there is a way around this problem. It comes in part through paying attention to a second source of material for new wineskins: the history of renewal movements.

## Learning from Renewal Movements

Much can be learned from the ways in which God's Spirit has repeatedly renewed the church throughout history.[3] Renewal movements offer helpful material for church structure. At least four insights from the history of church renewal can help us in the quest for new wineskins.

1. *Renewal movements set the issue of church structure within the broad sweep of history.* Renewal movements raise the question of history, including a theology of history. They remind us of the relativity and variety of cultural contexts and that the church has survived and thrived in radically diverse social, political, and economic settings. W. A. Visser 't Hooft reminded us in *The Renewal of the Church* that the church has an extraordinary capacity for renewal, even under the most difficult circumstances and at times when it appears totally dead.[4] Thus the church's experience of repeated renewal is a source of instruction for us today.

2. *The history of renewal teaches us about the renewing work of the Holy Spirit.* How does the Spirit renew the church? Key patterns can be found. The Book of Acts has often been called "the Acts of the Holy Spirit." The Holy Spirit is the real agent in the significant and startling growth and witness of the early church. But the Spirit did not work alone—or magically, like some impersonal force. The Spirit worked *through people*, through the flesh-and-blood church of Jesus Christ. Just as Jesus is "the same yesterday and today and forever" (Heb. 13:8), so the Holy Spirit is active in all times, making Jesus Christ real to people. The church will never outgrow the Holy Spirit, because God is always a step ahead of us. The Spirit draws us into the future that God has for us, for his church, and for the whole creation (see Rom. 8:1–23).

Since Pentecost, the church has continuously been in the age of the Spirit. But Spirit-guided renewal never points to the Spirit himself. Rather, it lifts up Jesus, always helping the church to be Christ-centered and to carry on Jesus' work.

We may sense the Spirit's presence daily in our prayer and Bible study times. But on occasion, the Spirit moves powerfully over the Christian community. Many years ago, at Spring Arbor High School and Junior College, the Spirit came upon a chapel service in remarkable power. Students began confessing sins and repenting at the altar. Some were saved. Others were filled with the Spirit. A "holy hush" lasting for days settled over the school. People said they sensed God's presence the moment they stepped onto campus. It would be hard for anyone who lived through those days to deny the reality of the Holy Spirit or his sweet, gentle, persuasive power in peoples' lives.

Some twenty years later, a group of urban ministers were gathered on the top floor of a tall building overlooking downtown Minneapolis, Minnesota. About seventy workers had gathered from a dozen cities for an urban ministry conference. The meeting was drawing to a close with communion. As the bread and wine were passed, each one sensed the flowing of the Spirit's presence and power. Some began weeping; others got up and went to their colleagues, either to mend relationships or simply to pray together. Through the windows we could see below us the hurting city. Within our spirits we heard Jesus saying, "Come, give your life for those who are hurting." We knew this was God's Spirit.

Glance back through history, and you'll see that God has repeatedly worked in similar ways. The Holy Spirit is the renewing Spirit who convicts, cleanses, gives gifts, and reshapes the church for faithful mission. The Spirit works to restore the church to biblical faithfulness, often by bringing biblical truth to the forefront of the church's focus—truth that has sometimes been eclipsed by tradition, institutionalism, or sin. The Holy Spirit brings people to faith in Jesus Christ, renews the church, and moves out ahead of the church to awaken people to their need of Christ. He is at work to "renew the face of the earth" (Ps. 104:30), and he will finally bring the kingdom of God to total fulfillment.

God says by his Spirit today, as in the past, "See, I am doing a new thing!" (Isa. 43:19). That "new thing" ultimately will be the fulfillment of the promise that every knee will bow before Jesus Christ (Rom. 14:11; Phil. 2:10) and that the kingdom of this world will become "the kingdom of our Lord and of his Christ" (Rev. 11:15).

We can discern what the Holy Spirit will do in the future by looking at what he has done in the past. Examining the history of renewal, we find helpful principles for the life and structure of the church today.

3. *Renewal movements show us that deep renewal often begins at the periphery, or the margins, of the church.* Seldom does it begin from the center or from established church leadership.

One compelling example comes from the history of Roman Catholicism, where renewal has often taken the form of new religious orders.

Typically these orders (of both men and women) have been founded by figures with no authority other than their own charisma, endowed by the Holy Spirit: Francis of Assisi, Benedict of Nursia, Scholastica, Clare, Angela Merici. In the occasional periods in Roman Catholic history when the church sought a reform pope, generally it turned to an uncorrupted monk from one of the orders. Thus God worked to renew the church.[5]

So today, in our quest for effective wineskins, we should look at what God is doing at the margins of the church. Here we may be able to *see* what the Spirit is saying to the churches.

4. Finally, *renewal movements help restore a Trinitarian balance in the church.* Renewal movements may not be uniquely Trinitarian and don't always have a coherent or balanced Trinitarian theology or practice. But they implicitly teach a Trinitarian ecclesiology. Renewal movements typically stress the "new work" of the Spirit. Renewal generally breaks forth at times when the church has forgotten the renewing work of the Spirit and no longer expects God to do a new thing. But suddenly a new movement appears, usually at the margins of the church and usually celebrating the presence and power of the Spirit. These movements generally have a fairly simple and direct argument: Just as God worked in the early church, so he now pours out his Spirit afresh, doing something new and restoring the church to vitality.

Renewal movements restore the accent on the Spirit to the life of the church. Such movements understand that God creates communities of personal interrelationship so energized by the Holy Spirit that they make Jesus Christ real and new and alive in new contexts. Thus these movements tend to reenergize *theology*. It then becomes the church's *theological* task to reflect on this dynamic and articulate a full-orbed Trinitarian ecclesiology.[6]

A key to vital church life is the recovery of a biblically based Trinitarian theology that takes its primary cues from God's action in Jesus Christ and from Jesus' continuing work in the church through the Spirit. In this sense, renewal movements point us in the right direction. In renewal movements we see how God works by the Spirit and through Scripture to vitalize churches.

## Lessons from Ecology

Granted the primacy of Scripture and the value of studying renewal movements, where in our contemporary, quickly globalizing culture do we find clues that may help us build effective wineskins? The most promising place to look is today's increasing sense of ecology. Ecological models operate at a deeper conceptual and metaphorical level than business models and are therefore more promising as a resource for new wineskins.

An ecosystem is the most complex level of organization in nature. It is made up of communities and their physical environments. In the same way, the church as the body of Christ is the most complex social organization. Its complexity includes both spiritual and physical dimensions and potentially incorporates everyone from the least to the greatest, from the poor to the rich. The church includes all people of every race and in every time and place who believe in Jesus Christ.

Here are some reasons why viewing the structure of the church ecologically can help us in the quest for better wineskins.

1. *Ecology is more in tune with the way God created the world than are commonly accepted organizational and institutional models.* As science shifts from mechanical to organic models, it is rediscovering the ancient concept of ecology. The key insight of ecology is that all creation (and particularly all life forms) is made up of complex, highly interdependent relationships. It is not possible to touch any one element in the system without affecting the whole. A key watchword of ecology is, "You can never do just one thing."

Ecology is much broader than environmentalism or biology. It has the potential to profoundly shape our understanding of how the universe operates. We are all part of a complex ecological web. Christians understand that this interrelatedness derives from God's activity as Trinity in creating and then sustaining the universe until the restoration of all things is accomplished (Acts 3:21). As we saw in chapter two, the church is likewise a complex organism with its own ecology, operating within the larger cultural and ecological environment. This has practical implications for church structure, as we will see.[7]

2. *The ecological model is more consistent with systems theory* than are other models. Systems theory studies patterns in complex interrelationships. We often learn more about the church from studying family dynamics and other social systems than from studying business models. Ecology takes systems theory a step further, revealing that every system operates within a larger system that constitutes all of culture and, in fact, the whole universe. We are part of a highly complex creation marked by interrelationship and interdependence.

As our awareness of this complex system grows, we find it necessary to replace older mechanistic, linear, and hierarchical models with ecological ones. Because ecology is much closer to biblical revelation and to the nature of God as Trinity, the church should seriously consider its implications in order to understand itself and to form faithful wineskins.[8]

3. *The ecological model is more in tune with where today's culture is headed than are other models.* Awareness of ecology is growing at every level of society. It will increasingly shape political, social, and economic discourse. Thomas Friedman argues in his highly acclaimed book, *The Lexus and the Olive Tree*, that an ecological perspective is necessary to understand the new global system. Globalization is a highly complex arrangement that must be understood multidimensionally. "It is the interaction of [multiple perspectives] that is really the defining feature" of the system, says Friedman. "There is increasingly a seamless web" uniting the diverse components of this new system, necessitating "an ecological perspective" in order to understand it.[9]

A second example of ecological thinking comes from John Chambers. As the visionary CEO of Cisco Systems, Chambers argues that "leading companies will . . . form an 'ecosystem' of partnerships in a horizontal, rather than a vertical, business model." He adds, "Companies participating in [such] an ecosystem . . . will emerge as the market and industry leaders of the future." Cisco's "ecosystem model," he says, allows the company "to remain agile, quickly enter new markets, and provide both breadth and depth of solutions through the ecosystem community."[10]

Rather than taking its cues from business, the church should note that business itself, at the cutting edge, is thinking ecologically. As the church starts to think ecologically—provided it keeps Scripture primary—it will discover a host of insights about the wineskins through which it may effectively serve as agent of God's mission in the world.

The church today thus has three key sources for developing functional wineskins: Scripture, renewal movements, and ecology. Using these sources, we can identify several key principles for church life and structure. These principles will be outlined in the next chapter. When based on these principles, churches *in any cultural context* can be faithful to God and effective in carrying out God's mission. These principles are sufficiently general to escape the limitations of the dead ends presented by megachurches, microchurches, and business models. Yet they are very fruitful for churches that are open to being creatively led by the Spirit.

———

## Heartland Digs Deeper

Darrell Dorset knew something was definitely wrong at Heartland Christian Fellowship. But he didn't know what. He began praying. He also began doing something he had seldom done before: fasting for most of Friday each week.

He wasn't really alarmed, because in many ways the church was doing well. People were still responding positively to his preaching and teaching. A couple he had thought were headed for divorce had a breakthrough spiritually and relationally. Their marriage was being renewed, thanks partly to the pastor's prayer and counseling. Occasionally there were conversions. And finances, though tight, weren't yet critical.

But Pastor Dorset sensed the church had lost momentum. The life of the church seemed increasingly routine. And the church certainly wasn't having much impact on the city.

Around this time, three things happened that dramatically changed the picture. They appeared to be random events, but Darrell was convinced God's Spirit was subtly working behind the scenes.

First, Darrell's wife, Beth, became seriously ill. She lost weight and had no energy. The doctors couldn't figure out what was wrong. Only after months of testing did they diagnose a chronic intestinal disorder. With rest and medication, Beth began slowly to recover.

Beth's illness was like a blow to the stomach for Darrell. Beth had always been his main support. Now that support was gone, and he had to uplift and encourage her. The kids, now young teens, were great sports and helped take up the slack. But Darrell was hit hard and had trouble concentrating on his church work. He did, however, spend more time in prayer and found his prayer life deepening. The Bible also came alive to him in new ways as his study was now sparked by an increased sense of his own need.

The second surprise came from Jim Richards. Jim worked as the manager at Johnson Center Tractors and Equipment Company, which was on the highway that led into town. The business was growing, and Jim had recently hired two new employees.

Jim wasn't especially outgoing, but he did have a deep love for people. Most of the men in his store were already Christians, but the two new workers were not. Jim began praying for them. When he got the chance, he gave gentle words of witness.

Several weeks later, at the Thursday breakfast meeting, Jim spoke up as prayer concerns were shared. Pastor Dorset had just updated the group on his wife's condition and requested prayer for her.

Jim said, "Something interesting is happening at work. Those two new guys I told you about—Gary and Willis—well, they're both beginning to ask interesting questions! The other day Gary wanted to know how I became a Christian. And Willis asked me to pray for him and his wife—they're having some problems. I'd like you all to pray for these guys."

Everyone promised to pray. Pastor Dorset asked Jim if he thought Willis and Gary would be open to meeting with Jim for some prayer and Bible study. Jim didn't think so, but he said he'd ask.

A week later, Jim could hardly wait to talk with the Thursday morning group. "Guess what!" he said. "I got to talking more with Gary and Willis, and they both said they'd like to meet and study the Bible together. Their wives are interested, too. In fact, Jan and I are having them over Saturday night and we're going to talk about it and get started."

This was a surprise to Pastor Dorset. First, he hadn't thought Jim would take that much initiative. And second, he had doubted that Gary and Willis would respond positively. "I should have had more faith!" he said to himself.

One Sunday morning several weeks later, as Pastor Dorset was getting ready to start the worship service, he noticed two families he'd never seen before walk in. He wondered who they were. One was a biracial couple. But then Darrell saw Jim Richards with them and figured these people must be Gary and Willis and their families. He offered a quick, silent prayer that God would in some way speak to them during the service today.

The third surprise came as a result of Bill and Angie Silver picking up a book on revival somewhere and reading it together. The book had put new questions in their minds and hearts. Soon they were talking about it in the Thursday morning group.

"The book's called *An Endless Line of Splendor: Revivals and Their Leaders from the Great Awakening to the Present,*" Bill said. "It's by Earle Cairns, who taught history for a long time at Wheaton College. It talks about the Great Awakening in America and England and Germany. I never knew there was a Great Awakening in Germany."

"It also tells the story of the nineteenth-century revivals," Angie added. "There was actually a revival among the Confederate troops in the Civil War!"

"I had heard of D. L. Moody," Bill said. "The book tells about him, too. And many other evangelists and revivals." Bill added, "You know, this book has got me thinking. Are there still revivals today? How important is revival in the life of the church?"

"I'm sure God's Spirit always wants to revive and renew us," Pastor Dorset replied. "And to renew the church. Whether it's through a dramatic revival or in quieter ways, God wants to make the church alive and vital—a living organism, the body of Christ."

In fact, Darrell Dorset had already been thinking along this line. He had decided to do a more in-depth Scripture study of the church and of the Holy Spirit—partly because of his own need and partly because of his concern about the church. Mostly he studied the New Testament, but he also went back and reviewed those times in the Old Testament when God had sent renewal or revival to Israel. He found he was gradually starting to think differently about the church. *What does it mean to go "back to the basics" in church life?* he asked himself. He was struck with the "one another" passages in the New Testament. *Is our church really living this way? Certainly not as much as it should be,* he decided.

But through all these things—Beth's illness, Jim's new Bible study group, and Bill and Angie's questions about renewal and revival—Darrell Dorset could sense his own experience and understanding of God deepening. He thought he sensed it in others, too—especially in the Thursday morning breakfast group.

One chilly morning in early November as the breakfast group was discussing these things, Ray Schilling spoke up. "You know I teach science at the high school," he said. "We've just been studying about ecosystems. Well, I had a new thought as I was having my devotions. You remember Paul says in Colossians 1 that all things were created by Christ and 'in him all things hold together.' I'm wondering how that relates to the environment and to ecosystems. Seems to me it connects. I mean, there's a wonderful intricacy to ecosystems, and I think it tells us something about God."

"Makes sense to me," Darrell Dorset said. "But what does that have to do with the church? Or revival?"

"Just this," Ray said. "Maybe the church is a kind of ecosystem. Everything ties in to everything else."

"I'm not sure I know what you mean," Jim said.

"Well, look," Ray said, patiently. "Look what's happened in our church family over the past year. Beth's sickness has touched us all. Jim's Bible study group has inspired us and given us some new ideas. And some new people! And then, Bill and Angie have been reading that revival book. That also ties in. Maybe the Holy Spirit is already renewing us, or reviving us, through all these things."

The next day Pastor Dorset was working in his study. He finished up his sermon and started thinking about the church. The task force on small groups was to meet next Tuesday night. Maybe he should go back over the ideas they had written up earlier and see how he felt about them now. He wasn't sure the original plan still fit and wondered if the church had dug deeply enough in its planning.

# Questions
## for Group Discussion or Personal Reflection

1. When you were ten years old and heard the word "church," what visual image immediately jumped into your mind?
2. Having read this chapter, what visual image will you now carry in your mind for the word "church"?
3. What image of the church do you feel will be most useful when you attempt to explain your faith to an unbeliever?
4. How would you describe Heartland Christian Fellowship at this point in its life?
5. What signs do you see that God is already at work, bringing renewal to Heartland?
6. How do unexpected personal crises and troubles (such as Beth's illness) affect the life of a church?
7. Do the marks of the church discussed in chapter one illuminate this discussion in any way?

# 6

---

# Genetic Material for Vital Churches

A church's genetic code is complex, but it is not a total mystery. The Bible is like a codebook. It provides the key to the church's DNA, through divine revelation.

From the biblical material on the church, illuminated by the history of church renewal and insights from ecology, we may distill some key principles. In this chapter we discuss five theological and four operational principles for vital churches.

These key principles draw together and underscore themes discussed in earlier chapters. Churches that embody these principles are more likely to find their true identity and really look like the body of Christ. Churches that ignore these principles may experience mutations in their development and degraded effectiveness in their ministries. They may grow, but the growth may be cancerous rather than a reflection of the DNA of Christ's body.

## Five Theological Principles

Here are five keys to help churches live consistently with their God-given DNA.

1. *The central focus of the church is worshiping God and serving his mission.* The primary passion of a vital church is God—worshiping him and serving him. This can so easily be accepted as a truism that we fail to see it as the central nervous system of ecclesiology—of the church

and its structure. The church is the community gathered around Jesus, willing to be his body, his mode of action in the world.

There is no conflict or tension between the worship of God and the mission of God. Authentic worship leads to mission. Worship that does not lead to mission is worship of a passionless, purposeless God. Such worship has lost a central truth of the Trinity—that the passionate shared love of the Father, Son, and Holy Spirit overflows to passionate concern for the care and restoration of his creation. Authentic worship leads to passion for God's kingdom and especially for reconciling persons to the love of God poured out in the life of Jesus Christ.

In saying that worship and mission are the central nervous system of the body, we mean that all the church's life and existence is to be ordered around this central passion. It is the primary task of leadership to be sure this happens.

2. *The church's life, both in concept and in action, should be based on organic and missional metaphors.* The church as body of Christ is a living social, spiritual, charismatic organism. It is alive. Thus the central biblical images of the church are all organic and ecological: body, bride, family, vine and branches. Even static "building" and "temple" images become organic ones: "living stones," a growing building, a temple animated by the Spirit (see 1 Peter 2:4–6; Eph. 2:19–22).

Metaphors and models are powerful. Think of the church as a building, and it becomes building centered and architecture dependent. Think of the church as an organization, and it becomes preoccupied with organizational forms and programs. Think of the church organically, and it focuses on what makes for healthy life.

The Bible presents the church as a unique kind of organism. It is charismatic because it is born in grace *(charis)* and functions by grace (the *charismata,* or gifts of the Spirit).[1] And it is missional, serving the mission of God. The church is unique because it is the only social organism in all creation that can be called the body of Christ. Yet due to the consistency of God's created order, it is an organism with its own ecology. Thus it can be understood ecologically and organically.

Organic images not closely tied to the mission of the church, however, can be static and self-serving. This is where the history of renewal movements helps us. The church is the social movement of the Spirit for the sake of God's kingdom.[2] Vital churches, therefore, should be based in images that are both organic and missional.

This need is a fundamental principle for church structure, as we will show. The wineskins that best serve the church are organic, ecological ones. They are missional models that help us understand the church as a social movement in service of the mission of God.

3. *Vital churches maintain a healthy balance of worship, community, and witness.* All three elements are key. They interact with and depend on each other. As mentioned in chapter three, this is important for mission as well as for the church's internal health.

This is a theological principle. That is, *worship* is central because of *who God is.* The purpose of worship is not primarily to give people a fulfilling worship experience, but to glorify God and extend his mission. *Community* is essential not just because people want to enjoy a social experience, but because the Holy Spirit has touched their lives, prompting a deep love for and a costly commitment to one another. *Witness* is essential not because the church needs volunteers for its programs, but because the love of God impels people into the world, full of love and a passion for justice. Here is an ecological balance grounded in who God is and in what he has done and is doing through Jesus Christ and through the power and inspiration of the Holy Spirit.

This principle is true theologically, and it is proven true in practice. Every church we have seen that is vital and strongly missional maintains this balance. Its worship life is animated and deeply authentic, its social infrastructure works to build and advance accountable discipleship, and its witness makes an impact on the world through a combination of evangelistic, servant, and justice ministries. Each element of the church's ecology reinforces the others. In fact, understanding this ecology of worship, community, and witness helps us diagnose pathologies in the church—reasons why a church is not vital.[3]

This threefold ecology corresponds nicely with Christian Schwarz's "eight quality characteristics," as outlined in his book, *Natural Church Development.* His model of the church is organic (or "biotic," as he puts it), and focuses more on church health than on church growth. In all these ways his model is similar to ours, though he puts less emphasis on justice and a theology of the kingdom.[4]

4. *The central task of leadership is to build an apostolic, ministering community.* God raises up leaders to equip God's people for the work of ministry (Eph. 4:11–12). While pastors do many things, the overriding task that gives pattern and focus to everything else is the equipping of the whole community for effective mission. Preaching, counseling, planning, and all else should be tested by this central principle: Does it help the whole church to be in ministry, an active agent for the kingdom of God?

This central focus for leadership rejects the clergy/laity dichotomy as heretical. To be a Christian is to be a minister. To be a disciple of Jesus is to engage in completing the work Jesus began. To be a member of the body is to have a function, a ministry, in the body. Professional pastoral leadership is endorsed only in the sense that pastors should carry on their work with excellence. They should become experts in multiplying ministry.

Underlying this principle is the charismatic nature of the church and the doctrine of the priesthood of all believers. Every Christian is charismatically gifted. Each is a priest before God for missions in the world. And each is a servant of Jesus Christ and collaborates or co-labors with him in the work of the kingdom. In New Testament perspective, all Christian leadership is charismatic (based on spiritual gifts; Eph. 4:7–16) and is rooted in character, as exhibited by the fruit of the Spirit and the "mind" of Jesus (Phil. 2:3–13 nrsv; Gal. 5:22–25). Leadership gifts vary but are based on one fundamental principle: building a diverse community of disciples who are all engaged in the church's apostolic mission (1 Cor. 12:1–28; Eph. 4:11–12).

This central leadership principle interacts smoothly with the ecological balance of worship, community, and witness. Leaders do not attempt to turn all church members into evangelists, or social activists, or disciplers. After all, church members don't all have exactly the same DNA or combination of gifts. Wise leaders, therefore, help each member find a vital place in the body so that the *whole body* may function in a healthy way (Eph. 4:11–16). Some members will minister primarily in worship, some in building accountable community, and others in direct witness in the world. What a beautiful blend! It is the whole body that is called into mission through the ecological interrelationship of all its members.

5. *Vital churches exist as a countercultural missional community.* As a "missionary minority," they constitute the counterculture of the kingdom. This principle interacts with and supports the other theological principles already mentioned.

The call to be a countercultural community is not a summons to disengage from culture or from social transformation. Rather, it affirms that the church's essential life is centered in Jesus Christ and in a shared social commitment to God's kingdom. This centered commitment impels the church into apostolic engagement with the world. Vital churches show that Jesus' words about being salt and light, about being in but not of the world, are fundamental principles of church life and structure. They are not teachings first of all about our individual lives, but about the nature of the Jesus community, the body of Christ. Healthy churches maintain a vital balance between being too much in or too much out of the world. They maintain a creative tension between distinct social identity and transformational social engagement.

These five theological principles give shape and direction for church life, especially for leadership strategy. In our experience, the most effective church leaders are those who, consciously or intuitively, practice these principles.

## Four Operational Principles

The five theological principles lead naturally to action. Consistent with the theological principles, the following four operational principles provide the genetic building blocks for churches that fulfill their kingdom mission. These keys can help leaders build vital churches. Effective, faithful leaders will:

1. *Evaluate all structures and programs by organic and missional principles.* If you are a church leader, use the above theological principles as means of ongoing assessment.

- Is the central focus of our church the worship and mission of God?
- Is our life based in organic and missional images and metaphors?
- Do we have a dynamic balance of worship, community, and witness?
- Are leaders equipping all the members for God's mission?
- Is our church authentically a countercultural community engaging the world through the power of the gospel?

Congregations can be evaluated by these tests. Leaders can take steps accordingly to build effective, faithful churches. But take care to avoid the twin dangers of "sacralizing" structures so they can't be touched or changed as necessary, or of "secularizing" them, forgetting that structures, though purely functional, do reinforce values and worldview assumptions.

2. *Build an effective infrastructure of accountable small groups.* There are many ways to do this; the specifics vary according to context. But all Christians need face-to-face accountable community. This has been a constant in all great, transformative renewal movements in history.

Apostolic churches find ways to network small groups so they truly help members find, and be effective in, their niche in ministry. This is a key leadership challenge. The genius of the church is the dynamic ecology of worship, community, and witness and the mutually reinforcing rhythm of small group and large group. An infrastructure of healthy small groups is essential in making this ecology come alive.

3. *Build a leadership team that collectively models the character of Jesus Christ.* Effective leaders know how to build teams. This principle is based theologically on the fact that no human person is head of the church; Jesus Christ is. And he exercises his headship through the *body*, not through one person. Effective leadership is Christ centered. Pastoral leaders should build leadership teams based on character, spiritual gifts, and a sense of call to ministry.

No congregation can be equipped for ministry by just one person. It requires a team (as Philip Jakob Spener argued two hundred years ago).[5] Team leadership may follow a variety of models and can operate within quite different church polities. But the principle is clear: The biblical model is not a solo pastor, but pastors who know how to extend their leadership through forming teams of mutual vision, vulnerability, interdependence, and equipping for ministry.

4. *Minister the gospel to and with the poor.* This is a biblical mandate reinforced by church history. Those gospel movements that have embodied Jesus' passion "to preach good news to the poor" have lasted longest, have most transformed society, and have been most effective in winning people to Christ. John Wesley's comment on Hebrews 8:11, "for they all shall know me, from the least even to the greatest," is relevant here. He observed that the saving knowledge of God has always proceeded and will always proceed "not first to the greatest, and then to the least," but from the least to the greatest.[6]

No matter what the social context, God invites his people to join with him in ministering to, with, and for the poor. Such a ministry is always prophetic, because it runs directly contrary to the assumptions and values of the world system—and counter to every worldly church system.[7]

## A Lesson from History

An illustration from history ties these nine theological and practical principles together. The attitude and actions of John Wesley in eighteenth-century England give a glimpse of these principles in actual practice.

"In religion I am for as few innovations as possible. I love the old wine best," wrote John Wesley at age eighty-six. Some people must have scratched their heads at this, since for fifty years Wesley had adopted innovation after innovation as he led the Methodist movement in its spread over the British Isles and across the ocean to North America. Many people thought Methodists were fanatics. Wesley was criticized for all kinds of upstart new ideas, from preaching in the streets to forming unauthorized cell groups. People were incensed that Wesley spent so much time among the poor, drawing national attention to the dreary plight of coal and tin miners. Why didn't he stay put as a parish priest or stick to teaching at Oxford?

John Wesley (1703–91) was a rare blend of conservative innovator and radical Christian. The secret of his genius is not hard to find. He said his favorite subject was Jesus Christ. His secret was unswerving loyalty to Jesus and deep roots in Scripture. Wesley could see how the church in his day, while professing to be Christian, was actually drowning in traditionalism and spiritual lethargy. So he pointed the church back to Jesus and to the early church.

Wesley's freedom to evaluate, conserve, and experiment grew out of his own spiritual journey. After his Aldersgate "heartwarming" on May 24, 1738, Wesley had a new sense of the freeing power of the Holy Spirit. He had a new passion to satisfy people's spiritual hunger and a new freedom to change forms and patterns that no longer worked.

Wesley started out rigidly "high church" in his theology, but God did not let him stay there. In some ways, he was still a high churchman at his death. He conserved the best of the Anglican and Catholic traditions. But he also learned to be remarkably flexible and unconventional. Looking back now, we can see that he applied three key tests with regard to the church and its structures.

### 1. Does It Work?

The first key to Wesley's success was the *test of functionality*. All we do in the church must contribute to mission—getting the job done. Structures and practices are valid only if they help the church fulfill the mission of Christ.

In many ways, eighteenth-century Anglicanism was dysfunctional. People were crowding into London and other cities, but the church went about its routine business, serving mostly the rich and socially well placed. The gospel was not being preached to the masses, yet the church was largely unconcerned. It had neither the passion nor the structures to reach the common people.

Wesley's response was to innovate. Partly this was by choice, partly by necessity. As he began to preach salvation by grace, through faith (not by church attendance or good works), he was soon banned from most Anglican pulpits. So he took the gospel to those who would hear.

Wesley's greatest innovations were outdoor preaching, nurture and discipleship groups (called "class meetings" and "bands"), and building a team of young, modestly educated men and women whom he sent out to preach the gospel. Most of these "lay" preachers proved quite effective, and Wesley poured his energies into training and guiding them. Training was mainly "on the job." They learned by doing, by reading Wesley's sermons, tracts, and letters, and by time together.

Wesley also focused on the church's broader role in society. He had a passion for social justice and national righteousness. This led him to a number of practical steps. He agitated to reform prisons, liquor laws, and labor conditions. He set up loan funds for the poor. He campaigned against the slave trade and smuggling. He opened a dispensary and gave medicines to the poor; worked to solve unemployment; sometimes set up small businesses. He personally raised and gave away considerable sums of money to people in need. For him, this was all part of Christian mission.

Wesley borrowed most of his innovations from others, but he borrowed wisely. He had a practical test when considering such innovations: Will this help people experience the love of God and carry out the mission of Christ? If so, let's try it—whatever the source or history, so long as it is consistent with Scripture.

Functionality was Wesley's answer to traditionalism. To those who said, "We've always done it this way," he asked, in effect, "Does it work?"

## 2. Is It Alive?

The second key to Wesley's effectiveness was the *test of vitality*. The church of Jesus Christ must be vital, alive. Renewed by the Spirit, the church visibly shows forth the life of Jesus. If it doesn't, something is wrong and must be changed. Wesley worked constantly to renew the Church of England and to keep Methodism vital as a renewing body within the church.

Wesley's impact began when he started carrying the gospel outside the four walls of the church building. His friend, the evangelist George Whitefield, had gathered a large congregation of coal miners at Kingswood, near Bristol, in early 1739. Here Whitefield preached regularly in the open fields. Wesley frowned on such outdoor preaching. He had been "so tenacious of every point relating to decency and order," he said, "that I should have thought the saving of souls *almost a sin* if it had not been done *in a church* [building]."[8]

Whitefield urged Wesley to take over this unique congregation so he could return to America. Wesley hesitated, but after seeing Whitefield at work, he knew God was in this ministry. So he began proclaiming "in the highways the glad tidings of salvation," offering Christ to some three thousand people.[9] The crowds grew, and soon Methodist congregations were formed all over England. Wesley discovered that when the people stop coming to the church, it is time for the church to go to the people.

Wesley and his associates did not win popular praise for their efforts. Leslie R. Marston notes, they "were called mad enthusiasts because they would free the gospel from the confining gothic arches of established religion and release it to the masses in street and field, to the sick and unclean in hovel and gutter, to the wretched and condemned in Bedlam and prison."[10]

Wesley was a devout churchman. He was also a realist. He saw that many people simply would not attend traditional services. It meant entering an alien world. And even those who did attend failed to receive the more personal spiritual help they needed.

Wesley knew that vitality meant more than numbers. In his journals he often noted Methodist growth or decline in various places, but he always saw numbers as symptomatic of something deeper. After "purging" from one Methodist group "all that did not walk according to the gospel," Wesley commented, "But number is an inconsiderable [i.e., insignificant] circumstance. May God increase them in faith and love!"[11]

Wesley believed as much in church discipline as in church growth. He knew that faithful churches don't always grow and that growing churches aren't always faithful. Yet when a congregation was declining, he generally suspected that some problem needed attention—perhaps false doctrine or incompetent leadership but more often little quarrels and disputes that had to be settled if the church was to be healthy. With the care and pain of a vinedresser who cuts back the grapevines, Wesley repeatedly pruned the Methodist societies of lifeless or unruly members so that the congregation could grow to become vital and strong. In America, Francis Asbury carefully followed Wesley's example in exercising such discipline, laying the groundwork for amazing Methodist growth in the early 1800s.

Wesley's antidote to institutionalism—the attitude that says, "We've got the right system; just go by the book"—was the test of vitality. He asked, "Is it alive?"

### 3. Does It Unite Us in Love?

The third key Wesley used was the *test of community*. Wesley had a keen sense of what it meant to be the *body* of Christ, the community of the Spirit in actual social reality, not just in theory. He said the church was called to "social holiness," meaning a community that lives out the holy love of God. Practically, social holiness called for structures and practices where close face-to-face community would grow and deepen.

Wesley created new and workable structures for *koinōnia*, or shared life. One of the first things he did was to form groups of about a dozen people, each group having its own leader. These were the famous Methodist "class meetings." Wesley soon discovered the spiritual dynamic of this small-group structure. He found that through such group participation the early Methodists "began to 'bear one another's burdens,' and naturally to 'care for each other,'" coming to a deep personal experience of Christian community.[12]

The Methodist system of groups, preachers, and various offices and functions opened a wide door for leadership and discipleship. By the time Methodism had reached 100,000 members, the movement must have had 10,000 class and band leaders with as many or more other leaders and workers, many of whom were women.

Remarkably, Wesley put one in ten, perhaps one in five, to work in significant ministry and leadership. Who were these people? Not the educated or the wealthy with time on their hands, but laboring men and women, husbands and wives and young folks with little or no training but with spiritual gifts and eagerness to serve. Community became the incubator and training camp for Christlike ministry.

Wesley's answer to individualism—the attitude that says, "What's in it for me?"—was the test of *community*. He asked, "Does it unite us in love?"

These illustrations from the ministry of John Wesley show it is indeed possible to be:

- Concerned about growing disciples, not just congregations
- Concerned about kingdom growth, not just church growth
- Concerned about turning multiplied thousands of unbelievers into disciples of Jesus, not just church members.[13]

History shows that the practical application of the principles outlined in this chapter can bring real vitality to the church. These principles are the genetic material that can help us grow churches that really are the body of Christ.

———

## What Does It Mean to Be "Body"?

In his personal Bible study, Darrell Dorset was digging deeper. He felt something was lacking *biblically* in his understanding of the church. He worked through Ephesians and Philippians, then the Book of Hebrews, as well as a number of Old Testament passages.

Darrell had been brought up to read the Bible devotionally. He dipped into it daily for his own spiritual nurture, and he studied it faithfully for sermon preparation. But as he examined the biblical teachings on the church, something dawned on him that he hadn't noticed before. You might say he found the body! Actually, he discovered something about himself. It hit him one day: *I've been reading the Bible to feed myself and for doctrine and sermon preparation. But I've been reading it pretty individualistically. I think I've been missing the "one-anotherness" of the New Testament teaching about the church.*

Later, looking back, Pastor Dorset described this time as a sort of "paradigm shift" in his own life and ministry. Only after a year or so had passed did he see how much his thinking changed during this time.

This shift had come about partly through more study of the Letter to the Ephesians. Darrell got interested in the idea of "edification," because he wanted to "edify" or build up the members of his church. He noticed that Paul speaks of "edifying the body of Christ" in Ephesians 4:12 and 16. Actually, that's what his old King James Bible said; *The New International Version* used the phrase "build up" rather than "edify." Pastor Dorset did a word study, checking other versions and reference resources.

"Edify," he said. "Edification. Edifice. This is building language. But what is being built? Paul is talking about Christ's body—building up the whole body of Christ."

All this was familiar, of course. What was new was that Darrell Dorset was seeing for the first time that Paul—and, in fact, all the New Testament writers—is talking about building up, strengthening, and maturing the church in its community life and interrelationships. Paul isn't talking so much about the "edification" of individual believers. It's not the individual Christian who gets "built up" as Christ's body, Darrell Dorset noted. It is the "whole body"—everyone together. That seemed to be what Ephesians 4:16 is saying.

This was a new insight for Pastor Dorset. Once he saw it, he was surprised he hadn't noticed it earlier. It seemed so obvious. *It's the* whole body *that needs to be built up,* he thought to himself. *It's about really becoming a community, the body of Christ. I suppose that in some sense if everyone is not growing, no one is growing. Or at least not growing as much as they might.*

Meanwhile, the church was nearing a decision about small groups. The task force had met a few times and was working on a plan. The basic idea was to set up a system so everyone in the congregation would have a small group he or she could go to.

But Pastor Dorset felt uneasy about the plan. He brought it up as a prayer concern on Thursday morning.

"We certainly need small groups," he said. "I'm convinced they're necessary to really 'build up the body of Christ.'" And he shared a bit of his own Bible-study discoveries.

"But I'm not sure this is the right approach. For one thing, a lot of our people don't really *want* to be in a small group. They feel they're too busy, or they don't see the need for it.

"Also, I'm not sure we're spiritually ready. Where will we find leaders who will turn this into a living reality, not just another program?"

The others in the Thursday breakfast group were a little surprised by this, but they tried to understand where their pastor was coming from. "We had good success with those groups we had a couple of years ago," Ray said. "Don't you think these groups would be at least as successful—maybe more?"

"I would hope so," Pastor Dorset said. "But I'm not sure we're clear enough yet just what we're getting into." In the back of his mind, too, was the fact that he had heard of churches that had tried small groups and their attempts hadn't worked out well. "Small groups are out of fashion," one pastor had told him.

As Darrell thought more about this, he decided to propose something different to the small-group task force. "I'm in favor of small groups, and I think we ought to move ahead with this," he said. "But there's something I want us to do first. I want us to ask, What kind of church do we want to be? What does it really mean to 'build up the body,' or to 'grow up into Christ'?"

Pastor Dorset proposed that the task force members—in fact, the whole church board and all his key leaders—take some weeks to work through these questions biblically. Some of his people scratched their heads; this seemed to be slowing progress. But they trusted his judgment and were happy to go along with it if he felt that was the right thing to do.

Over the next three months, Pastor Dorset led the church through a process of discovery. He drew up an outline of key Scriptures that he wanted everyone to study. But he also handed out a list of questions about how these Scriptures related to the life of Heartland Christian Fellowship. In some ways it was similar to the study the church had done a couple of years earlier, only this one went deeper.

"I want us to really dig into these Bible passages," he said. "But that's not all; I want us to ask ourselves some key questions.

"First, are we really functioning as the *body* of Christ, in the way the Bible describes it, here at Heartland? Second, does our worship really focus on God and on his mission for us? Third, are we as a church really doing the work of Christ? Fourth, are we training and equipping our people for *ministry*, not just to be good, loyal church members? And finally, are we, as a Christian community, 'in but not of' the world, as Jesus said we should be? These are tough questions."

It took time to work through this study. But the feedback Pastor Dorset got from the Thursday morning group, as well as from others, showed him that the process was worth the time.

By now it was early spring. Trees were budding and daffodils were nodding in the breeze. Darrell Dorset felt the promise of springtime as he drove to meet the breakfast group on Thursday morning.

Angie Silver led the Bible study this particular morning. She had made some discoveries of her own as a result of the process Pastor Dorset had started.

"This morning we're going to look at 1 Peter 2:9–10," Angie said. They read the passage: "But you are a chosen people, a royal priesthood, a holy nation, a people belonging to God, that you may declare the praises of him who called you out of darkness into his wonderful light. Once you were not a people, but now you are the people of God; once you had not received mercy, but now you have received mercy."

"Now, does this 'you' Peter talks about here mean us, today, at Heartland Christian Fellowship? Or is it speaking only of the church back in those days?"

As Pastor Dorset listened to the discussion, he thought to himself, *They're getting it! We're starting to see what it is to be Christ's body, a royal priesthood, a people in service to God.* And he reflected on how Ray, Jim, Bill, Angie, and Linda had grown over the past couple of years, both in their Christian walk and in the depth of their understanding of Christ's body.

The small-group task force finally brought in its report. It looked much different from the earlier draft. The committee proposed not a program of small groups for the church but a simple process for starting a few small groups and letting them multiply. They proposed that the pastor form a small-group leadership team of ten or so men and women who were interested in small groups and whom the pastor trusted for their maturity and commitment. This group would then draw up basic guidelines and begin to organize and oversee (really, "pastor") the new groups as they were formed. This leadership team would not only form groups but would also identify and train leaders for each group that was formed. And it would monitor each group's progress.

The proposal was approved by the church board. During the summer Pastor Dorset devoted a lot of thought and prayer to forming the small-group leadership team and to how the small groups would function, grow, and multiply.

# Questions
## for Group Discussion or Personal Reflection

1. Why was Pastor Dorset uneasy about the initial proposal for small groups at Heartland Christian Fellowship? Do you understand his concern?
2. What new insight did Pastor Dorset get about "edification"? Why was this important?
3. What did Pastor Dorset mean when he said to himself, "They're getting it"?
4. Do you see any signs that organic and missional models or metaphors are beginning to take hold in Heartland Christian Fellowship?
5. Which of the principles discussed in this chapter do you see illustrated in this part of the story of Heartland Christian Fellowship?
6. When you think of the church as the body of Christ, where do you see yourself within that body? Use your imagination. Are you a nose, a red blood cell, a toenail, a stomach, the conscience?
7. Explain your function and contribution to the body. Why is the body healthier because you are part of it?
8. What is one thing you have the ability and desire to do in the body but feel would not be well received or appreciated?
9. Are there organizational changes that could be made in your church that would make your ministry or personal contribution to the body more effective?
10. How can these three questions be applied to your own church?
    - Does it work?
    - Is it alive?
    - Does it unite in love?

# 7

## THE DNA OF MISSION

"Mission is the DNA of the church," says Baptist missiologist William O'Brien. Mission draws the church and all creation "toward a common future: fulfilling the purpose for which [they were] created."[1]

How can we understand the church's mission in a way that matches the church's essential DNA and is also consistent with God's design in creating the world?

Here we face tough issues, because we run into deeply rooted Western cultural ideas that have infected the church. To understand the church's DNA biblically, we have to understand the cultural soil in which most American and European churches have been nurtured. In particular, we have to address three key cultural concepts: *hierarchy, ecology,* and *psychology.*

Heartland Christian Fellowship, whose story we are following in this book, was facing these issues without knowing it. As a church, were they structured hierarchically or organically? Were their relationships centered in God or just in good psychology? Were they a living, breathing organism with a unique ecology or just a religious club? A careful reading of the Heartland story shows that these issues were always just below the surface. Only occasionally did they become visible. Yet they shaped the church's mission and ministry.

In this chapter and the next, we explore the DNA of the church and its mission in terms of these three key ideas: hierarchy, psychology, and ecology. We bring Scripture to bear in examining these concepts. The goal is to peel back layers of culture so that we can see the church's mission the way God intends.

103

Take, for example, the issue of ecology. Many Christians see ecology as having nothing to do with the church or its mission. Does the church have no redemptive word about things like air pollution, endangered species, or poisoned rivers and streams?

## God's Church and God's World

Christians have a unique angle for looking at ecology and the whole created order: Jesus Christ! Jesus is Lord of the church and its mission, and he is Lord of creation and of culture. We must keep this fact before us as we look at ecological and cultural issues.

The Bible says that "the whole creation [groans] in labor pains," awaiting the day when it will be "set free from its bondage to decay" and share in the full salvation Jesus is bringing (Rom. 8:21–22).[2] What then is the meaning of God's action in Christ for the created order? And what does this say about church life and the DNA of the church's mission?

The Bible teaches that "Christ came into the world to save sinners" (1 Tim. 1:15). Salvation in Christ is, first of all, new life in Christ through faith in him. But salvation also includes all of God's creation and looks forward to "the time of universal restoration" (Acts 3:21), to "new heavens and a new earth" (2 Peter 3:13). God in Christ through the Spirit is working to "renew the face of the earth" (Ps. 104:30).

Most Christians have not thought deeply about ecology or about God's purposes in creation. Too often the church has tried to address ecological concerns (if it hasn't in fact ignored them) without first asking what a *biblical* understanding of ecology might entail. Yet we live in an age where ecology has grown from a scientific concept to a broader cultural worldview. Ecology is emerging as a key worldview lens for many thinking people. It helps us understand not only the church (as noted in chapter 5) but also God's world and the church's mission within it.

We might think that the Bible doesn't say much about ecology. But in fact, the biblical revelation about creation and about Jesus Christ gives us a profound understanding of ecology. We will misunderstand today's ecological crisis unless we see it in terms of God's work in Jesus Christ. A Christocentric understanding of creation offers key insights for dealing with questions of ecological and economic justice and thus for presenting a holistic gospel of healing for all people and for the whole earth. This approach leads to a fuller understanding of the DNA of the church's mission.

It is possible to understand ecology *Christocentrically*.[3] This means, first of all, understanding that all creation finds its center in Jesus Christ,

Savior and Lord, the Word made flesh, whose richly textured yet remarkably consistent portrait fills the pages of the New Testament. We begin with Jesus, the one "who was handed over to death for our trespasses and was raised for our justification" (Rom. 4:25), who "appeared once for all at the end of the age to remove sin by the sacrifice of himself," and who "will appear a second time, not to deal with sin, but to save those who are eagerly waiting for him" (Heb. 9:26, 28).

Note especially how Jesus Christ is pictured in Ephesians 1:9–10, Colossians 1:15–17, and Hebrews 1:3. These passages give us key insights. They teach that Jesus Christ is the radiance or "reflection of God's glory," "the image of the invisible God, the firstborn of all creation," through whom all things were created, in whom "all things cohere,"[4] and through whom all things will be brought into ecological harmony. At the center of a comprehensive understanding of ecology stands Jesus Christ. This is the key to integrating the concerns of ecology, justice, evangelism, and our own lives. Thus it is a key to understanding the church's mission.

## Ecology: An Inside or an Outside Question?

The claims of ecology are pressed on us by scientists, by political activists, and by Christians concerned about responsible stewardship of the created order. For most Christians, however, ecology is a question that comes "from the outside," from society or the surrounding culture, not "from the inside," from the heart of the gospel itself. Biblically, however, ecology is really an "inside" question. Scripture teaches that God created, sustains, and redeems the world through Jesus Christ, by the power of the Holy Spirit. Whatever is true about the ecology of God's created order is a part of the Christian faith and worldview. Therefore ecology is not foreign to the Christian faith. It is *integral* to it. We should see ecology as a biblical and fundamentally Christian concern.

There is a reason why ecology seems to come to us as an outside question. Generally, theology has not paid enough attention to biblical teachings about creation and the relationship between Jesus Christ and the created order. Consequently, most Christians are unprepared to enter the "eco" debate.

We must dig down to the underlying issues. What is the question that ecology, as an emerging worldview or interpretive framework, attempts to answer? The underlying issue is the *principle of coherence*. Is there any such principle? Ecology (which is actually based on a metaphor) is the current scientific answer to that question. But historically other answers have been given. We will examine some possible answers to the profoundly ecological question, How does everything hold together?[5]

Every person, educated or uneducated, assumes some principle of coherence.[6] We all believe there is some force, some "glue," that holds everything together. Our understanding of ecology, then, depends on how we understand that force, or principle.

From Greek philosophy, on through the Roman tradition, medieval European culture, and British and American thought, one can trace what this principle of coherence has been. In fact, the Eurocentric tradition is built on the story of three ideas about what holds everything together—what the central principle is that unites the physical universe, human life, even politics and economics. These ideas are misleading, however, and can lead to a false understanding of the universe (physical and spiritual) and of ecology. They need to be critiqued biblically and theologically in order to properly understand the church and its mission.

As noted above, these three powerful culture-shaping ideas are *hierarchy, psychology,* and *ecology.*

## Hierarchy: The Great Chain of Being

Christianity has claimed that its central principle of coherence is God, or Jesus Christ, or the Christian Faith, or the Bible. Too often, however, this is a hollow claim. The central organizing principle of Eurocentric culture—never effectively challenged—is the principle of *hierarchy.* The universe, and therefore all social relationships, have been understood as a vertical ladder or hierarchy.[7]

For the most part, this view has been accepted uncritically by the church. While one can cite exceptions in individual lives and in various expressions of the church throughout history, hierarchy has been the generally accepted concept.

For Christians, this uncritical acceptance of hierarchy is a problem. Hierarchy has been *read into* Scripture, Christian theology, and ecclesiastical structures for fifteen hundred years. Many Christians believe that the universe is hierarchical, that the church and the family are hierarchical institutions, and even that the Trinity itself is a hierarchy![8] The unexamined, uncritical acceptance of hierarchy is a *primary cause* of our difficulty today with the whole issue of ecology (and church life, as well). It is hard to think hierarchically and ecologically at the same time.

For many years I (Howard) resisted the notion that hierarchy is incompatible with what the Bible teaches about the universe, society, and the church. Unknowingly, I had absorbed the assumption of hierarchy while growing up. It was a kind of cultural genetic endowment. Hierarchy runs in the genes of Western (and other) cultures. Only by a long process did I come to question this. It took years even to recognize the question: Where does the Bible actually *teach* hierarchy? Obviously Scripture gives many *examples* of hierarchy, but it never teaches that hierarchy is normative for society or the church.

What is hierarchy, essentially? It is *a vertical structure of at least three levels.* Primary authority resides at the top, and each descending level is under the authority of the higher levels. Position in the hierarchy corresponds to rank within the whole. Hierarchy can be applied to the social order (Who's on top?) and also to the cosmic order. The cosmic order is often seen as the basis for existing social arrangements, making them legitimate and not to be questioned.

Hierarchy can be defined narrowly or broadly. The French anthropologist Louis Dumont defined hierarchy as "the principle by which the elements of a whole are ranked in relation to the whole" and argued that "in the majority of societies it is religion which provides the view of the whole" so that "the ranking will thus be religious in nature."[9] In this broad sense, hierarchy is virtually inevitable, says Dumont. As soon as we make evaluations and distinctions, we create hierarchy. Seen in this light, any classification system is hierarchical.

We are using *hierarchy* in the narrower and more common sense of a vertical structure of a least three levels, however. For clarity, we call this *vertical hierarchy.* This is a principle of arrangement that implies levels of rank, status, or perfection. The visual image is that of a vertical line, ladder, or pyramid.[10]

In this understanding, an army, a 1950s-style corporation, and the authority structure of the Roman Catholic Church are all hierarchies. The very words *hierarch* and *hierarchy* are religious terms that trace back to the idea of what is sacred or consecrated and to those who lead or rule in sacred things. The idea of a graded hierarchy grows from this root.

In contrast, ecology is not hierarchy, because the principle of organization is not vertical gradation. The image is not a vertical line but a circle; not a pyramid but a network or living organism.

A family is not a hierarchy. The authority of parents over their children is not hierarchical authority. Many people do teach, of course, that the family should be a hierarchy: the father at the top, then the mother, then the children. The biblical view is more organic and ecological and sees the mother and father in mutual partnership, with a loving, relational authority over their children.[11] This biblical view is not hierarchy, properly speaking.

## Not So among You!

While hierarchical relationships are mentioned in the Bible, especially in the Old Testament, nowhere does the Bible teach hierarchy either as the nature of the cosmos or as the revealed pattern for society or for God's people. Jesus was clear about this, and his behavior was consistent with his teaching. He recognized hierarchy in society and in Jewish culture but prescribed something different. His sharpest words about this are in Matthew 20:25–28: "You know that the rulers of the Gentiles lord it over them, and their great ones are tyrants over them. It will not be so among you; but whoever wishes to be great among you must be your servant, and whoever wishes to be first among you must be your slave; just as the Son of Man came not to be served, but to serve, and to give his life a ransom for many." Jesus seems to be opposing both the abuse of power and the hierarchical structure on which power was based. (Matthew 23:1–12 teaches the same lesson in a different way.)

The New Testament does not teach hierarchy as the principle of either authority or organization in the church. Not long after the New Testament era, some church leaders began advocating a vertical hierarchy of bishop-priest-deacon. But the New Testament gives no hint that these terms were originally understood hierarchically—or even understood as "offices" in a technical sense. "Bishop" *(episkopos)* and "elder" *(presbyteros,* from which we get the words *presbyter* and *priest)* were flexible terms, at times used interchangeably (as in Acts 20:17–28 and 1 Peter 5:1–2). The "first apostles, second prophets, third teachers" of 1 Corinthians 12:28 is not a hierarchy. Paul's whole point in 1 Corinthians 12 is the organic relationships in the body, not the hierarchical relationships of the Roman legions. Paul is speaking of historical sequence (how God planted the church), not of a hierarchy.

What happened? How have we come to read hierarchy into these and other New Testament passages? The answer is simple: Hierarchy was already so firmly embedded in ancient Indo-European culture that it seeped into biblical interpretation and ecclesiastical practice and overwhelmed the more radical, subversive New Testament teaching. The culprit, writes Colin Gunton, was

> the neoplatonic doctrine of reality as a graded hierarchy. From where, if not from such an influence, did the notion of hierarchy derive? There is scarcely biblical evidence worthy of the name. But [Thomas] Aquinas implies, without ever spelling the matter out, that the hierarchy of the church—[consisting of] an ontological grading of persons—is modeled on that of heaven.[12]

Thomas Aquinas spoke of a "chain of being" beginning with God at the top and ranging down through angels, human beings, animals in the order of their intelligence, and then plants and nonliving things. Medieval cathedrals often depicted this chain of being in their intricate carvings.[13] The idea became firmly rooted in Christendom and has persisted ever since. One influential culprit is the King James Bible of 1611, translated under government auspices, which betrays the hierarchical assumptions of seventeenth-century England in the way it renders the Greek text.[14]

The roots of hierarchy lie in cultural history, not in the Bible. Finding these roots means going back at least to Greek philosophy four centuries before Jesus Christ.

## Loosing the Great Chain

The philosopher Arthur Lovejoy traced the persistence and influence of hierarchy throughout Western culture. He defined hierarchy as "the principle of unilinear gradation" and traced the idea to early Greek philosophers including Plato and especially Aristotle.[15] Lovejoy summarized the inheritance these origins have bequeathed to the West:

> The result was the conception of the plan and structure of the world which, through the Middle Ages and down to the late eighteenth century, many philosophers, most [scientists], and, indeed, most educated [people], were to accept without question—the conception of the universe as a "Great Chain of Being," composed of an immense . . . number of links ranging in hierarchical order from the meagerest kind of existents, which barely escape non-existence, through "every possible" grade up to the . . . highest possible kind of creature . . . every one of them differing from that immediately above and that immediately below by the "least possible" degree of difference.[16]

Another author notes the relationship between science, theology, and worldview in the Chain of Being idea during the Renaissance:

> . . . there was [thus] established, from the very beginning of natural history, a principle which was long to remain authoritative: that according to which living beings are linked to one another by regularly graduated affinities. . . . [Renaissance science thus inherited] the idea of a hierarchy of beings; a philosophical dogma which Christian theology, following Neo-Platonism, had often made the theme of an essentially speculative interpretation of the universe [in other words, a worldview].[17]

The late medieval jurist John Fortescue wrote similarly,

> In this order hot things are in harmony with cold, dry with moist, heavy
> with light, great with little, high with low. In this order angel is set over
> angel, rank upon rank in the kingdom of heaven; man is set over man,
> beast over beast, bird over bird, and fish over fish, on the Earth in the air
> and in the sea: so that there is no worm that crawls upon the ground, no
> bird that flies on high, no fish that swims in the depths, which the chain
> of this order does not bind in most harmonious concord.[18]

Here the universe is viewed as a vertical ladder or chain. Everything
that exists finds its proper place and purpose in terms of its position in
the hierarchy—its link in the Great Chain. For millennia this concept
has given cosmic justification to oppression and social inequality. In the
eighteenth century, the British philosopher-poet Alexander Pope voiced
the accepted doctrine:

> Vast chain of Being! which from God began,
> Natures ethereal, human, angel, man,
> Beast, bird, fish, insect, what no eye can see,
> No glass can reach; from Infinite to thee,
> From thee to Nothing.—On superior pow'rs
> Were we to press, inferior might on ours:
> Or in the full creation leave a void,
> Where, one step broken, the great scale's destroy'd:
> From Nature's chain whatever link you strike,
> Tenth or ten thousandth, breaks the chain alike . . .
> All are but parts of one stupendous whole,
> Whose body Nature is, and God the soul.

Pope didn't fail to draw out the social implications:

> Order is Heav'n's first law; and this confest,
> Some are, and must be, greater than the rest,
> More rich, more wise; but who infers from hence
> That such are happier, shocks all common sense.[19]

The Great Chain of Being, with its notion of hierarchical coherence,
has thus been a background assumption of Eurocentric culture. Whatever its positive contribution in maintaining order, it has also been an
instrument of oppression. It functioned to support social inequality and
privileged interest. It may be that the very concept of hierarchy is essentially a mechanism to give cosmic justification for social inequity.

The Great Chain idea does have some attractive features. It insists on the relatedness of all things, has a principle of coherence, provides a sense of meaning and purpose. It has a certain beauty and symmetry, even a kind of ecology. It persisted because it was functional.

But the Great Chain of Being is a flawed image and an inadequate principle of coherence. It is hierarchical rather than truly organic. It is nonhistorical, failing to explain the real processes of history. As a philosophical idea, it lacks a scientific foundation. The "chain" that holds all things together also serves as a chain of oppression, binding everything into a static structure. Its cultural implication is a social hierarchy where men dominate women, the rich rule the poor, clergy dominate "laity," and humans subdue and exploit all "inferior" things. Thus the idea actually undermines a Christian worldview. Historically, it has damaged the church's DNA.

The instinct of connectedness in the Great Chain idea is sound, but it must be seen more ecologically and historically. Nature apparently has no vertical hierarchies. Yet it has order and system and historical continuity. It is constantly shifting and changing through time, but in ways that (at least in hindsight) make good sense.

Through the concept of the Great Chain, hierarchy became a cosmic principle genetically embedded in the Indo-European tradition. In the church, the cosmic theology of Pseudo-Dionysius' *Celestial Hierarchies* gave classical Christian expression to the idea of hierarchy. He said that heaven itself is a hierarchy of angelic beings, and the church's hierarchy reflects this heavenly one.[20] In this view, the universe is hierarchical in every dimension. Thus hierarchy answers the question: By what principle does the universe hold together?[21]

Incidentally, we may legitimately wonder whether the modern idea of evolution could ever have developed, or if it would have taken the "scientific" form it did, had it not been for the hierarchical Great Chain idea. For the Great Chain included the concepts of intimately related gradation and a scale of development that are also basic to the ideas of evolution and progress. One way of interpreting the rise of the evolutionary model is this: The vertical hierarchy of the Great Chain of Being turned sideways becomes a horizontal timeline. The accent shifts from space to time. Now the connection is not between earth and heaven, but between past and future. Spiritual ascension is transformed into social and material progress.

The Western tradition, reaching back before Christ, has through many centuries preserved the underlying presupposition of hierarchy as the principle of coherence in the cosmos. Only within the last two hundred years has hierarchy been seriously challenged, and even then only in partial and often ineffective ways.

From the time of the French Revolution on, however, social and political hierarchy has increasingly been questioned in the West.[22] Democracy and such notions as "All men are created equal" seem contrary to hierarchy, at least in terms of political systems. But democracy has not effectively dislodged hierarchy as an underlying cosmic principle. It is only in the last one hundred and fifty years or so—with the rise of psychology and, more recently, ecology—that the notion of hierarchy as a deep cultural metaphor has been largely displaced. Psychology and ecology, therefore, are the second and third contenders for a universal principle of coherence. These will be explored in the next chapter.

## Conclusion

What does this excursion into philosophy and cultural history say about the DNA of the church's mission? As a ground-clearing exercise, we have intentionally belabored the point about hierarchy in order to avoid misunderstandings later.

Hierarchy is in our cultural DNA (even in the church like a genetic mutation), but it is *not* part of the DNA of the gospel. We need to cleanse the old leaven of hierarchy from our understanding of church and mission or it will continue to infect and subvert missional faithfulness.

The church's mission must be radically centered in the person of Jesus Christ. In the following two chapters we explore what this means. We will see that the concept of ecology helps us understand how the church functions, but that ultimately we must focus on Jesus himself, for he is head of the body.

―――――――

## Unsettling Questions at Heartland

Pastor Dorset was faithful in his times of daily prayer and Bible study. He often spent a few minutes reading also about the lives of great men and women of the past—people like Martin Luther, Amy Carmichael, and John Calvin. He had a favorite place for his early morning devotions, a little breakfast nook just off the kitchen. He would fix a cup of tea or coffee and spend an hour or so with the Lord before Beth and the kids were up.

Two years had passed, and Darrell was thankful that both his family and the church were doing well. Beth had regained her strength. Both their children, now teenagers, had made solid commitments to Jesus Christ. The church was growing again.

Darrell was in the middle of an in-depth study of the Gospels. Some months back he had found himself thinking, *All this study of the church has been rich and, in fact, life-changing. But I want to get closer to Jesus. In all our focus on the body of Christ, I don't want to lose sight of the head!*

On this particular Monday morning, predawn light was just beginning to reveal the shadows of the trees in his yard as Darrell sat down with his open Bible. The passage he was working on was Matthew 20, beginning with verse seventeen. Jesus was on his way to Jerusalem, but he paused to warn his disciples what lay ahead. He even foretold his death and resurrection, though his disciples didn't get it. In fact, they were jockeying for position in the new kingdom they thought Jesus was about to set up.

Darrell was especially struck by verses 25–28: "You know that the rulers of the Gentiles lord it over them, and their great ones are tyrants over them. It will not be so among you; but whoever wishes to be great among you must be your servant, and whoever wishes to be first among you must be your slave; just as the Son of Man came not to be served but to serve, and to give his life a ransom for many."

Darrell thought about that for a long time. He recalled other passages about Jesus' self-emptying, about how "though he was rich, yet he became poor." He remembered 1 Peter 2:23 and looked it up: "When they hurled their insults at him, he did not retaliate; when he suffered, he made no threats. Instead, he entrusted himself to him who judges justly."

*That's talking about Jesus, the head of the body,* Pastor Dorset thought. *If that was Jesus' way, what does it say about our church? And about me, as a pastor and leader?* His prayer time that morning was especially deep.

Later that day, Pastor Dorset was reflecting on how God had worked in the church over the past couple of years. Heartland Christian Fellowship was seeing steady and accelerating growth. With an expanding, diverse network of discipleship cells and other small groups, the church had developed a warm sense of community. Heartland was helping many people put their lives together by introducing them to Jesus Christ.

But what was the congregation going to do about space? As the church grew, Pastor Dorset and his key leaders began to consider building a larger facility. They were just about at their limits, not only in worship space but also in space for classes and other activities. Pastor Dorset's first inclination was to preach a strong sermon on the need for expansion and to "cast a vision" for a bigger building. He was pretty sure people would follow his lead. But the more he prayed and thought about it, the more he was convinced he should wait and let the church wrestle with the issue awhile.

Heartland's building was located on a ten-acre plot of ground along the main road into town. There was plenty of land for expansion, but the back of the property fell away into a swampy area unfit for building. What should the church do? This became a topic at church board meetings as well as at the Thursday breakfast group.

A committee was appointed to study the matter. Pastor Dorset met with the committee and outlined the church's needs, as he saw them. After several weeks of study, the committee proposed a solution. Their plan called for filling in the swamp in order to provide enough land for a larger building and expanded parking. This would give plenty of space for the congregation to grow. It would meet the church's needs, the committee felt, for at least five years.

Most of the church liked this plan. But Ray Schilling, the science teacher at the local high school, raised unexpected questions. What was the ecological significance of the marshland the church owned? How would filling it in disrupt the wildlife in the area? What kind of witness would the church be giving if it didn't face these issues?

Ray first raised these questions at the Thursday morning breakfast group. Pastor Dorset was surprised, though he was glad Ray was thinking about these matters. Just as long as he didn't keep the church from moving ahead!

"You aren't one of those tree huggers, are you, Ray?" Jim Richards teased.

Ray laughed. "No," he said, "though maybe we'd all be better off if we hugged a tree now and then."

Angie said, "Well, is this just a planning problem? I mean, is it just a matter of figuring out how not to disturb the wildlife too much?"

"Actually, I think it's deeper than that," Ray said. "You know I try to relate Christian faith to my work as a science teacher. The Bible talks about how nature shows God's wisdom and care. I know the swamp on our property doesn't look very pretty, but it's home for a lot of creatures. I've walked around some back there with the kids. It's a whole ecosystem."

"OK," Bill said. "I suppose we should do what we should do. Be good stewards, and all that. But that's not as important as our church and evangelism and people's eternal destiny. We need to keep things in perspective."

"I understand," Ray replied. "And I don't suppose most of the church sees this the way I do. Actually, our property is part of a wetland that's important not just for wildlife but for our county's whole environment."

Ten years earlier, Pastor Dorset probably would have seen this matter differently—more like Bill seemed to. But something had happened as he started to think organically about the church and the kingdom of God. He was ready now to hear what Ray was saying—and to see the deeper issues. And he was less bothered now that Ray didn't automatically accept his view as pastor. Earlier that would have irritated him.

"I suppose some folks might see this as a conflict between evangelism and ecology," Pastor Dorset said. "But maybe it isn't. We need to ask what is really at stake here, from a gospel standpoint. How do the different parts of the church's mission fit together? Maybe Ray is right that we as a church have some responsibility for this land—responsibility to God first, as Creator, but also to our community and even to the land itself."

Bill wasn't sure he agreed, but he was willing to think more about it. And Jim said, "Well, I'll have to admit Ray has raised an interesting question and put a wrinkle in things. I was just about ready to send in the bulldozers! I've got a couple of them over at Johnson Center Tractors and Equipment, you know, just waiting to bite into that good dirt!"

"Well, we're not quite ready for *that!*" Pastor Dorset smiled.

Before leaving that day, the group prayed for guidance in solving what looked like a tough dilemma.

Meanwhile, the building committee continued its work. Ray met with the committee and shared his concerns. He brought some maps and charts that explained the ecological importance of the church's land and how it related to the adjoining property.

Pastor Dorset also met with the committee and gave his views. He sensed that some people on the committee wanted him simply to tell them what the church should do. Ten years earlier he might have done that, but the more he understood the church (and himself), the more he realized that as a community—a living organism—the church had to make up its own mind. His role was to guide, not to dictate.

The committee chairperson said, "Okay, let's look at our options. We certainly don't have enough space to build unless we do something about that low area. Will we have to move somewhere else? Let's work on this and see what we can come up with. I think God will help us."

# Questions
## for Group Discussion or Personal Reflection

1. What does it mean to you personally to realize that all creation finds its center in Jesus Christ? How does this knowledge affect your thinking about the mission of the church?
2. This chapter identified *hierarchy* as a vertical structure of at least three levels. Do you think your church is structured hierarchically? What is convenient about a hierarchical structure? What is dangerous about it?
3. Suppose your own physical body were structured hierarchically, so that instead of a direct nerve link to the brain, messages from your fingers had to travel through the "authority" of the hand, wrist, arm, elbow, upper arm, shoulder, and neck before getting a decision. How long would it take you to accomplish the mission of putting just one bite of food into your mouth?
4. What do you appreciate most about the fact that the church is a body with Jesus Christ as the head, functioning smoothly and efficiently, much like your own body?
5. What is Pastor Dorset beginning to learn about the relationship between Jesus Christ and his body, the church?
6. Why do you think Heartland Christian Fellowship has begun to grow again?
7. As Heartland Christian Fellowship wrestles with the need for larger facilities, what factors does it need to take into consideration?
8. How do you think Pastor Dorset handled this situation? How would you describe his leadership style?
9. Should the Heartland church be concerned about the swampland at the back of its property? Why or why not?

8

_____

# Mission beyond Psychology and Ecology

In previous chapters we have seen the importance of ecology and ecological models. Ecology and genetics are closely related. Both have to do with *living things*—what they are like and how they behave. We are seeking to understand the church and its mission and structure organically, in terms of the life that comes from God and flows through the church into the world.

To better understand the DNA of the church's mission, we have been looking at Western cultural history. We now turn from *hierarchy* to *psychology*, then return to a deeper discussion of ecology and the ways it helps us decode the church's DNA.

Over the past century or so, our society has been saturated with psychology and, more recently, with ecology. Psychology and ecology, however, can be mere cultural fads. We want the church to be grounded in Jesus Christ, not in culture, so that the church can *serve* the culture in Christ's name. However, we need to examine these two ideas and forces—psychology and ecology—that have deeply shaped our culture. How do they relate to the church and its mission?

There are, of course, proper psychological and ecological dimensions of the church's mission. But psychology and ecology have their limits. In this chapter we examine the pluses and minuses of psychological and ecological models and show their relevance for understanding the church's DNA.

## Psychology: The Triumph of Personal Experience

The rise of psychology in the twentieth century and the growing emphasis on personal experience produced a competitor for hierarchy as the glue of society. Psychology since Freud and Jung offers an alternative worldview. In response to the question, What holds everything together? psychology answers: Our consciousness and feelings—that's the glue. Not some abstract hierarchical principle ("bricks in space" as someone has termed it) but *the realm of personal experience.* Here the motto is not "I think; therefore I am," but "I feel; therefore the universe is." Hierarchy collapses. The top and bottom of the vertical line shrink to one point: the thinking, feeling person—me. Subjectivity becomes the meaning of the universe—not transcendent reality but inner experience.

This is now our culture's reigning ideology. It is the dominant presupposition that colors everything else—our thoughts, values, and actions. And its influence continues to grow, even as ecology begins to challenge it. Experience, understood psychologically, is the dominant mode of postmodernity.

Psychology is very influential in the church as well. Whenever we think that worship is primarily about our feelings rather than about who God is or what our mission is in the world, we show our debt to this omnipresent psychological orientation.

The rise of psychological consciousness has many benefits, of course. In fact, we are not speaking of psychology *per se,* as a science. We are drawing attention to the fact that for most people today, personal experience serves as the principle of cosmic coherence, what really "holds things together." Psychological subjectivism has become the dominant mentality (and emotion) of our time—in effect, a worldview. Personal experience serves as the interpretive metaphor for cosmic significance. We feel that it is our own experience that holds the universe together (an awful burden, when you stop to think about it!). In fact, we now understand "holding it together" as a psychological state rather than as a reference to the actual structure of the universe. Phrases like "getting a grip," "falling apart," "breaking down," and "having it together" now more likely describe psychological or emotional experiences than physical objects.

As a principle of cosmic coherence or as a worldview metaphor, however, psychology fails. It is not up to the job. There are three reasons for this.

First, the psychological perspective is individualistic and self-focused rather than unifying and other-embracing. Although psychology speaks incessantly of "relationships," the focus is really on the *subjective expe-*

*rience* of relationships rather than on the interrelatedness of people. As a worldview principle, psychology is essentially self-centered and offers no adequate basis for self-transcendence.

This in turn creates other problems. In the Western world, with its rampant individualism, consumerism, and self-justifying technology, the psychological model opens the door to demeaning exploitation and manipulation. The primary example of this is modern media advertising, where every proffered product is really the merchandising of a new experience. "Experience the difference." "Have it your way." "Just do it!" This viewpoint gets in the way of effective, Christlike ministry.

The second problem with the psychological model is that it overvalues the human at the expense of the nonhuman creation. Man and woman in their self-conscious subjectivity become the measure of all things. The nonhuman world has value only to the extent that we experience it. Earth is nothing more than a planetary theme park, a sort of DisneyGaia put here to sustain our kaleidoscopic enjoyments. Without human life, earth would have no significance. Such thinking is the malady of modern and postmodern humanism.

Ecologists insist that we can't continue to live on earth as though the planet is mere stage, stimulus, and scenery. They remind us that humanistic psychology is profoundly unecological. Our very experience, and certainly our health and well-being, depends on the wider world. Of course, by itself, even ecology provides no adequate answer as to *why* it is important to maintain the earth's ecological well-being. In philosophical terms, it is not clear why the well-being of the whole biosphere (or the whole cosmos) should be more important than the well-being of human persons. To answer this question we need something else. In fact, we have to look to the person of Jesus Christ.

The third and most basic reason psychological subjectivity fails as a principle of cosmic coherence is that it is fundamentally untrue. It mistakes a part for the whole. It focuses on one or two dimensions to the exclusion of the full multidimensionality of the cosmos and of human experience. It is a false reductionism. In theological terms, it inverts the relationship between creature and Creator. The psychological worldview is a modern-day example of what Paul describes in Romans 1: "They exchanged the truth of God for a lie, and worshiped and served created things rather than the Creator, who is forever praised" (Rom. 1:25).

Postmodern society does not lack proposals for transcending these difficulties. Probably the most common, at least in religious circles, is to raise subjective human experience to the level of a cosmic phenomenon. The universe itself is conscious, or coming to consciousness. New Age thought is a popular example of such thinking. This is a form of cosmic humanism, the ultimate anthropomorphism (mindset that attributes human traits to nonhuman things).

Although the idea of "cosmic consciousness" is popular among some thinkers, it is not a biblical idea. It is an unworkable principle of coherence and inadequate for Christian mission. It owes more to ideologies of evolution, progress, and psychology than to Scripture.

## Ecology: Complex Organisms in Interrelationship

If hierarchy and psychology fail, what about ecology? With the rise of ecological science, do we finally have the key to a worldview that is comprehensive in scope, symbolically powerful, and confirmed by science? Does it give us an adequate basis for understanding the church's mission?

The idea of ecology has itself been evolving. Thirty years ago "ecology" was used narrowly. One studied the ecology of particular organisms, like plants or cells. But over the past generation, with the rise of environmental issues, ecology has become a cultural metaphor. We are thinking ecologically. More recently, ecology has begun to emerge as *the* metaphor for the cosmos. It is starting to challenge hierarchy and psychology as the assumed universal principle of coherence.[1]

In this worldview, the whole universe is an eco-web and can best be comprehended ecologically. Ecology is the new science, the new consciousness, and the new metaphor of our time. Increasingly we "eco-" our words, inventing terms like *ecoconsumerism, ecoterrorism, ecofeminism.* As Theodore Roszak wrote, "This tiny neologistic flag flies above our language like a storm-warning meant to signal our belated concern for the fate of the planet. . . . [It] reveals our growing realization of how many aspects of our life that concern will have to embrace." He adds, "If psychosis is the attempt to live a lie, the epidemic psychosis of our time is the lie of believing we have no ethical obligation to our planetary home."[2]

## The Rise of Eco-Thinking

Seeing things ecologically is not new. It was common two thousand years ago, especially in Greek thought. Our word *ecology* traces to the earlier Greek view. *Ecology* means the study of the "household" (*oikos* in Greek, source of our "eco-" words). Ancient Greek thinkers used the words *oikonomia* and *oikoumenē* (the source of our words "economy" and "ecumenical") to speak about how everything in the city-state and everything in the cosmos is connected. Thus economy is an ecological idea, though we haven't thought of it that way in the Western world for two hundred years.[3]

In 1968 the editor of *Natural History* magazine compared the rising notion of ecology with the ancient Chain of Being idea discussed in the last chapter. He wrote:

> That all things in the universe are intimately related is an ancient but still pervasive thought. . . . Not even today has it been banished as a popular notion of the moral order of the living world. . . . We are now . . . redefining and relinking the great chain. But instead of a system of rank based on a philosophical or theological scale of values, we are developing a system that recognizes the actual workings and consequences of relationships. . . . While many of us tend to endow the word that describes the science of the new chain—and that word is ecology—with mystical properties, the fact is that the science itself is concrete, precise, and empirical. Nevertheless, it is reordering our conception of the world, of the chain, as profoundly as a great religious idea might.[4]

In many respects, ecology *is* the great new discovery of our time. So it is important that we, as Christians and as world citizens, think clearly about it. Ecology is increasingly seen as *the* key concept. Ecology concerns everything on the earth—microbes, chemicals, insects, water, trees. Until recently ecology has been seen mainly as a matter of the body, not of the spirit—really a one-sided, unecological view. But a change is coming. It will not do to allow a gap between body and spirit when we think ecologically.

Society today is discovering an expanded notion of ecology. This is inevitable as science and imagination probe the interface of mind and matter, spirit and body. Here we find the deeper meaning of ecology. Once we understand that the lives of snails and sparrows are linked to those of human beings in a dozen ways, the meaning of ecology gradually expands to include every other aspect of human life and well-being. As Christians, we have rich resources in Scripture to help us explore this question. Jesus' parables, of course, are based on this close connection between the physical and the spiritual world. That's what makes them work.

Ecology helps us understand how the world works. How important is a previously unknown plant or insect discovered in the rain forests of Central America? We can't answer until we really know its ecology—how it affects and is affected by its environment and by other life forms. We may think the plant or insect is unimportant. But suppose we find that it produces a chemical that can cure a dreaded human disease. Suddenly something thought unimportant becomes hugely valued! And if the whole earth has value, the significance of a plant or animal is not found only in its relationship to humans. The nonuseful, nonmedicinal plant has its own special value, perhaps, from the perspective of God's creative purpose.

Ecological science encourages us to presume significance even where we have not yet found it. Ecology really leads to a philosophical intuition: *Everything is significant simply because it connects with everything else*—even if we don't yet understand the connection. If anything is important and everything is linked, then every part is important. Again, in this sense ecology is like genetics. It helps us perceive connectedness; it gives coherence. We marvel at God's creative work and how everything in his creation fits together.

Ecology underscores the twin truths of unity (or wholeness) and diversity (or distinction). For ecology to exist, there must be *parts*—things that can be numbered and counted—that make up the whole. Ecology requires number (whether people, insects, elements, particles, concepts, or whatever). And meaning arises from relationships between the parts. This is consistent with the pairing of the *unity* and *diversity* of the church that we noted in chapter one.

By definition, ecology must consider *every* dimension and influence that touches the life of an organism or ecosystem. Sometimes even ecologists forget this. A study of a city's ecology, for instance, would be faulty if it failed to consider the effects of air pollution or the economic and cultural loss as middle-class professionals flee to the suburbs. And it would have to consider much more remote influences, including those from the past as well as economic or climatic factors half a world away.

Ecology insists that every influence must be counted. If we apply this ecological insight to society and culture, we find we must consider not only physical, economic, social, and political factors but also mind and spirit. Ecology is not complete if it ignores these more elusive realities, even though they are harder to count, analyze, and measure. The Christian worldview has much to contribute here. Conversely, ecology can help the church perceive the breadth and interconnectedness of its mission.

Ecology teaches us that all things are interdependent and connected. The world is a complex phenomenon of many interwoven parts. God's creation is marked by interrelatedness: Man and woman in mutual relationship, love in relation to truth, the individual in relation to society, humanity in relation to the environment, the present in relation to past and future.

Yes, the universe is profoundly ecological. And yet ecology is not the whole story. We are still being simplistic if we make ecology the fundamental principle of the universe. The Christian view is that ecology fits into a larger story—the story of what God is doing in Jesus Christ. The Bible gives a deeper understanding of ecology, which we may call *coherence in Christ*.

To decode the DNA of the church's mission, we need more than ecology. We must grasp the implications of New Testament teachings on who Jesus Christ is—not only to the church, but to the world and the whole creation.

———

## Heartland's Growing Pains

Heartland Christian Fellowship really had to do *something* about its space problem. Pastor Dorset remembered reading somewhere that if the sanctuary is more than 80 percent full on Sunday mornings, newcomers won't come back, and growth will stagnate. Well, Heartland was already beyond that point. Most seats were filled during the Sunday worship service. People had to come early to get a good seat. Pastor Dorset trained his people to leave vacant seats at the back of the sanctuary and at the ends of the aisles for new people and latecomers.

Meanwhile, the building committee continued looking at their options. Could they knock out a wall and add another fifty or one hundred seats? What about a second Sunday morning service? Or if they built a new sanctuary, what would they do about the wetland at the back of their property?

The small-group coordinating team was now functioning. It worked well in starting and multiplying a whole network of various kinds of groups. Most of these small groups seemed healthy. People were growing spiritually and deepening in their love and care for one another. Working with the coordinating team, Darrell Dorset had developed a network of small-group shepherds. Each shepherd (or pair of shepherds, for most of them were couples) had oversight of four to eight small groups. And the groups were now scattered all over the city, most of them meeting in members' homes.

Pastor Dorset met weekly with the small-group shepherds. This group of leaders now totaled thirteen, not including himself. Finding a meeting time that worked for everyone had been a problem, and they had to shift the schedule a couple of times. Right now they were meeting Sunday evenings at eight-thirty. For Pastor Dorset, this gathering had become a very high priority because it was key to everything happening in the body.

At the shepherds' meetings, Pastor Dorset tried to accomplish three main things: get an update on how the groups were going, including any special needs; make any necessary decisions about the groups or about forming new ones; and further encourage and equip the group shepherds. During the year that had passed since the formation of the small-group leadership team, Pastor Dorset found that next to Sunday morning worship, these team meetings were the high point of his week. Yes, there were problems—always people problems of one sort or another. But it was exciting to see God changing lives through the groups as they undergirded the overall life and witness of the church.

Pastor Dorset discontinued the Thursday morning breakfast group now that all its members were involved in the small-group network. In fact, Jim Richards, Ray and his wife, and Bill and Angie Silver were now all small-group shepherds. Pastor Dorset realized that the Thursday morning breakfast group had actually served as an equipping structure to multiply leaders in the church—leaders whose ministry was grounded in their own maturing growth.

One Sunday night in mid-November, Pastor Dorset was late to the shepherds' meeting due to a phone call. When he walked in, he found Ray Schilling talking with another of the shepherds, Sherry Adkins.

"I've noticed the same thing in one of my groups," Ray was saying. "I think we should bring it up in the meeting tonight."

"What's that?" Pastor Dorset asked as he took his seat.

"Oh, Sherry was saying she thinks a couple of her groups are becoming too self-centered. They're having a good time, but people don't seem to be growing in ministry."

"Well, we can talk about that," Pastor Dorset said.

Later on, during the shepherds' reporting time, Darrell Dorset said, "Okay, Sherry, why don't you tell us about the problem you and Ray were discussing earlier."

Sherry summarized the situation of the two groups, as she saw it. "Actually, I think they've kind of stagnated," she said. "People seem to be pretty self-focused. I think they're measuring the group, and their own lives, too much by how they *feel* and are losing sight of ministry and mission."

Pastor Dorset was pleased that Sherry recognized this, because this was something he had stressed from the beginning. Groups exist for ministry, not just for mutual support, he had told them repeatedly. "As

Elizabeth O'Connor says in her book about the Church of the Savior, it's the journey inward *and* the journey outward," he often reminded the leaders.

Pastor Dorset used this occasion to help his leaders see how people today have been influenced by the pop psychology of personal experience. "Experience is very important," he said. "But we want people to *experience Jesus Christ* through the power of the Holy Spirit and to live for him. The more people really know God—the Trinity of Father, Son, and Holy Spirit—the more they will have a passion for God's work in the world, not just for themselves and their own needs."

Pastor Dorset stressed this, but through group discussion, he also helped the leaders find practical ways to keep the groups on track, not just for personal support and healing but, more importantly, for God's mission.

Pastor Dorset also helped the group of shepherds see how all these things—the network of groups, the leaders' meeting, Sunday worship, even the struggles over what to do about a larger building—were part of the organic life of the church. "Everything we do is tied to everything else," he said repeatedly. "In fact, I believe the spiritual deepening we're seeing in our church, our growth in discipleship as well as in numbers, will actually help us solve the space problem. I'm sure God is leading us, in his own way and time. We just have to be Jesus' body, and stay closely connected to him as our head."

# Questions
## for Group Discussion or Personal Reflection

1. What do you think were the keys to the success of Heartland's small groups?
2. How did Pastor Dorset track the groups and keep them connected to the overall life of the church?
3. Do you see signs that the church is growing in any of the marks of the church? Which ones?
4. In what ways can Heartland be described as a living organism or a growing body?
5. Can you understand how small groups can be too inward focused or self-centered? What can be done to correct that, or to prevent it?
6. What is your most meaningful relationship?
7. What is the source of the meaning you derive from this relationship?

8. Do you agree that our society often puts too much emphasis on psychology and experience? What is the right balance here for Christians?
9. Think back to the marks of the church discussed in chapter 1. Is there a natural balance or "ecology" to these marks?

# 9

## IN CHRIST

### *The Coherence of Mission*

The church's DNA is so powerful that it thrusts the church out into mission. This is what it means for the church to be *like Jesus,* the source of its genetic inheritance.

Viewing the church as a living organism, we have sought fresh insights into the church and its mission and structure. Now we can ask more pointedly: How can the mission of the church be understood in ways that are consistent with the church's complex DNA?

The previous two chapters have shown that we need to move beyond cultural understandings and metaphors (hierarchy, psychology, and ecology) to more specifically biblical ones. The church's mission is revealed in Scripture, not learned from culture. But mission must redemptively engage culture and must be incarnated in everyday life.

In this chapter we are seeking *genetic compatibility* between the church and its mission. The church and its mission must have the same DNA. They must be coherent with each other.

God's action in Jesus Christ by the power of the Holy Spirit is the key to understanding Christian mission. The good news of Jesus Christ offers the essential resources humanity needs to deal creatively and effectively with human sin as well as with issues of ecology, the environment, social justice, and moral righteousness. Here the bold biblical claim that in Jesus Christ all things cohere (Col. 1:17) takes on deep meaning.

The church's mission must be *coherent.* That is, in that every part of the church's life, ministry, and mission must find their focus and their power is Jesus Christ. Jesus is the one who holds all things together and gives unity to all that the church is called to do.

In considering the *coherence* of mission, then, we are speaking not of an abstract principle but of real history—what God has done in Jesus Christ.[1] The central story is summed up by the apostle Paul: In Christ "God was reconciling the world to himself, not counting [people's sins] against them." So anyone who is "in Christ" is a "new creation" (2 Cor. 5:17–19 NRSV). The biblical picture of Jesus Christ is at once personal, ecological, and cosmic: "The creation waits with eager longing for the revealing of the children of God; for the creation . . . itself will be set free from its bondage to decay and will obtain the freedom of the glory of the children of God" (Rom. 8:19–21 NRSV).

According to the gospel, the decisive act in history was the resurrection of Jesus Christ. This was the key triumph over death and despair—the reversal of discord and incoherence. The bodily resurrection of Jesus is the cohesive event that makes everything new. After discovering the personal and cosmic significance of Jesus Christ, G. K. Chesterton wrote:

> On the third day the friends of Christ coming at daybreak to the place found the grave empty and the stone rolled away. In varying ways they realised that the world had died in the night. What they were looking at was the first day of a new creation, with a new heaven and a new earth; and in the semblance of the gardener God walked again in the garden, in the cool not of the evening, but the dawn.[2]

He who won the decisive victory over evil in his resurrection at a particular point in history will bring the story to final, glorious fulfillment in history. The goal of history is final harmony and reconciliation, justice and moral symmetry—the ultimate triumph of truth, love, and justice. The apostle Peter called it "the time of universal restoration" (Acts 3:21 NRSV).

## The Biblical Framework for Mission

This story of Jesus Christ does not occur in a historical vacuum. Jesus came "in the fullness of time" (Gal. 4:4, Eph. 1:10). The Jesus story is part of the larger history of God's action as revealed in Scripture. For our purposes, five elements of the larger biblical framework are decisive for understanding the church's mission. Reviewing them will uncover the broad biblical foundation of the church's role in the world:

1. *God created the universe.* "By faith we understand that the worlds were prepared by the word of God, so that what is seen was made from

things that are not visible" (Heb. 11:3 NRSV). The world belongs to God, not to private individuals, global corporations, or national governments. We have no right individually or corporately to mistreat it or to claim it solely for our own interests. The church must visibly reflect this truth in its life and ministry. This is part of the church's mission in the world.

2. *The created order is in some deep sense diseased because of sin.* The fall introduced a moral genetic defect. Although earth's nonhuman biosystems cannot sin, the created order suffers the "enmity" that human rebellion brought into the world (Gen. 3:14–19). "The creation was subjected to frustration" and is in "bondage to decay" (Rom 8:20–21). This complex spiritual, physical, moral, and ecological disorder is pictured graphically in the Old Testament:

> Hear the word of the LORD, O people of Israel; for the LORD has an indictment against the inhabitants of the land. There is no faithfulness or loyalty, and no knowledge of God in the land. Swearing, lying, and murder, and stealing and adultery break out; bloodshed follows bloodshed. Therefore the land mourns, and all who live in it languish; together with the wild animals and the birds of the air, even the fish of the sea are perishing.
>
> Hosea 4:1–3 NRSV

One would think the writer had been watching CNN! Christian mission begins with a profound awareness of this moral disorder and disease.

3. *God has acted in Jesus Christ to reconcile the creation to himself.* God is bringing re-creation through the God-man. In the biblical picture, God's plan is not to redeem man and woman *out of* their environment, but *with* their environment. Salvation is ecological in this amazingly comprehensive sense.

The New Testament makes clear the tremendous cost of Jesus' reconciling work—his life of obedience and suffering, his death on the cross. Precisely because Jesus "humbled himself and became obedient to death," God "exalted him to the highest place and gave him the name that is above every name." All creation will bow before him (Phil. 2:8–11). As both Savior and model, Jesus calls all who believe in and follow him to a life of discipleship, marked by the cross. This is why the apostle John says that Jesus' disciples must "walk as Jesus did" (1 John 2:6). Jesus forms a community marked by the cross, a community that shares the birth pangs of the new creation. Mission begins with the church truly *being* this community. Jesus' body must reflect the same DNA that found expression in Jesus' own life and ministry.

4. *God has given the church a mission in this world and in the world to come.* The redemption God is bringing promises a new heaven and a new earth. What does this mean? Biblically, it *does not* mean two very

common but lopsided views: It does not mean only saving the earth from oppression or ecological collapse, nor does it mean exclusively eternal life in heaven, with the total destruction of the material universe. Rather, it means the reconciliation of heaven and earth, the reign of God that is in some way the reconstitution of the whole creation through God's work in Jesus Christ.[3] If mission is really based in Jesus Christ, the God-man, it holds these dimensions together coherently, the way Jesus did.

5. *Our lives, churches, communities, and economies must be in harmony with the biblical principles of truth, justice, love, and organic interrelationship.* We can learn to think organically and ecologically in all areas, including our understanding of the church as an organic community rather than as a hierarchical institution. Perhaps today's growing ecological consciousness will help the church discover the profoundly ecological nature of God's working in nature, in the church, and in radical social reconstruction. Christians lift ecology to a higher level of understanding.

## The Jesus Worldstory

The church's mission is grounded in what God has done and is doing in Jesus Christ. In all it does, the church should reflect and extend the story of Jesus. This might be called the Jesus *worldstory,* because it is much more than a world*view.* The Jesus worldstory tells us how the world is held together and where it is headed. We are talking about the actual history of the universe God created and in which he is still working.

The whole universe, says the Jesus worldstory, reflects God's glory and creative energy. The universe is made to radiate and revel in God's majestic beauty. Birds and flowers, even rocks and planets, exist to glorify God and display his creative beauty. They do that by being fully what they are, as God created them. Human beings find their purpose in praising God, mirroring his glory, enjoying the earth, and pursuing God's purposes in the world. This is not demeaning, not bondage or slavery, because God is love, care, and creative energy. Just look at Jesus!

When the world is seen in this way, the significance of human life and of nature comes together. The purpose of life personally begins with knowing Jesus Christ as a living person. God offers this gift to us through our repentance and faith. Jesus invites us to deepen that relationship as we become the hands and feet of God's healing love in the world through his community, the church. Our purpose is to know and show God's loving brilliance in every dimension of life, including our interdependence with all of nature. We become part of a new humanity, a new community bonded together in Jesus and committed to Jesus-style life in the world. Together we work for *shalom*, the full flourishing of all God has made. We look forward finally to a renewed heaven and earth where God dwells (2 Pet. 3:13).

The universe is made to be home for humanity—for man and woman, who are unique among all creatures, so far as we know, in their combining of material and conscious spiritual existence. All creation reflects God's glory—God's "image." All creation is gifted with a spiritual DNA that reflects who God is. Yet only man and woman are uniquely and specially created "in the image of God." Our planet is, however, home for all the other material creatures God has made. Human beings have responsibility both to God and to their co-inhabitants of the cosmos to live in harmony with the created environment and to care for and nurture it.

In Jesus Christ we see that the universe is more than the material world. God created all things and is still living and acting in dimensions of life that are more than physical. We don't know what other beings or consciousnesses live at higher dimensions than our space-time world. Human beings may be but a small part of the conscious universe. The Bible speaks of various kinds of angelic beings and "powers." Some of these are in rebellion against God's design and have perverse influence on earth (Eph. 6:12).

Jesus, as a person in constant multidimensional communion with God (in the Trinity), provides the key to the interrelationship (the ecology) of all God has made. In the remarkable prayer recorded in John 17, Jesus said he wanted all who believed in him to "be one as we are one: I in them and you in me. May they be brought to complete unity to let the world know that you sent me and have loved them just as you have loved me" (John 17:22–23, authors' paraphrase). As the Persons of God's being—Father, Son, and Holy Spirit—are one, so Jesus wants all people to be joined in reconciled community. This community, in turn, is to mirror and nourish the reconciliation that God wills for "all things"—the whole creation.

The basis for this reconciliation is the creating, restoring, and re-creating action of God the Trinity. Every healthy human relationship is a reflection of God's internal communion. Our harmony with nature reflects the harmony of God's being. Our war with nature shows the disease of sin. Here is an awesome basis for ecological peace and for just human community, whether in marriage and family, neighborhood and nation, or the whole world. When we are in harmony with God through Jesus Christ by the Spirit, we are potentially in harmony with every other person and with the cosmos. We become part of the healing work of redemption rather than carriers of the disease.

History is the story of creation, alienation, and restoration through Jesus Christ. We learn from Jesus' own words that this reconciliation has begun but is far from finished. A battle rages between good and evil, light and darkness, hope and despair, justice and oppression, reconciliation and alienation. Every person is caught up in the battle, this struggle for the world's soul, whether they know it or not. The battle line runs through every human heart. But the victory of love, justice, and *shalom* is assured through Jesus' decisive conquest in his cross and resurrection. This assurance is the grounding for the church's life and mission in the world.

## Hierarchy, Psychology, and Ecology Revisited

The Christian worldstory centers in Jesus Christ and gathers up whatever is valid in hierarchy, psychology, and ecology. It integrates them as important but partial dimensions of the more comprehensive Christian worldstory and shows how they fit within the church's mission.

Understanding Christian mission in terms of God's action in Jesus Christ, we can make several conclusions.

1. While *vertical hierarchy* is rejected as contrary to the gospel and as arising from human sin, hierarchy in the broad sense of ordered interrelatedness seems true both theologically and scientifically. There is in the universe a basis for valuation and distinction. But this is not a vertical hierarchy. It is not based on power, money, race, gender, intelligence, charisma, or religiosity. It has an ethical and spiritual basis, for we live in a moral universe. It is grounded in that awesome synergy of love and justice that the Bible names holiness, and which theologically is comprehended in the doctrine of the Trinity. The Trinity is not a hierarchy, but is holy community without confusion or conflict. God is fully one and fully three, and the resolution of that seeming contradiction is found in the mystery of divine Personhood.

2. Coherence in Christ also integrates the valid insights of *psychology*. Personal experience does indeed undergird the universe—not as mere human or transhuman subjectivity, but as the Tri-personal God who can create, incarnate, and recreate. In God incarnate in Jesus Christ we see the deepest meaning of personal experience.

A special strength of the history of Jesus Christ is, in fact, its profoundly personal character. We find personality in the universe because its source, God, is a person. Further, the meaning of life is inscribed not in philosophies or theories but in the life and history of Jesus Christ. In him we see what it means to be person and to be human.

3. Coherence in Christ also integrates the dimension of *ecology* while giving it a deeper, fuller meaning. It is true, as ecology teaches, that the meaning of the part is in the whole and the meaning of the whole is in the parts. The universe is like a hologram, each part reflecting the whole. Coherence in Christ teaches us that ecology is more than a metaphor; it is a witness to the profound interrelatedness of the Trinity, of the created order, and of our relationship to Jesus Christ.

The good news of Jesus is *ecological* in a deeper sense than any scientific ecology, for it includes the ecology of existence in all its dimensions. God's economy is inherently ecological. It sees all things as coming from the same source, as now interrelated, and as sharing a common history and goal.

Designed and formed by God, the universe exists not just for itself, nor exclusively for humankind, but for fulfilling its potential to show God's beauty and love. This is the lesson God taught Job. Colin Gunton suggests,

> As the creation of the love of God the world is not impersonal process, a machine or a self-developing organism . . . but . . . has a destiny along with the human: [Its] destiny is to be realised along with and by the agency of the human creation, so that that which is not personal may come to be itself in being offered back perfected to its creator through Christ and in the Spirit.[4]

The doctrine of the Trinity is more compatible with an ecological understanding than it is with a hierarchical one. Whatever or whoever God is, God is *not only* one; God is three-in-one. The unity of God is found in the indivisible, ever-intercommunicating relationship of the Trinity. In the Christian view, meaning is therefore Trinitarian and relational. God is Trinity—a personal unity of Father, Son, and Holy Spirit, bound freely together in loving intercommunion. The doctrine of the Trinity is itself an intriguing intimation of the essential twoness and threeness of the oneness of meaning. It is an ecological conception— not a mechanical or hierarchical one. Just as human persons exist because God exists, so ecology exists because the Trinity exists.

For Christians, everything comes together in Jesus Christ. Coherence in Christ points us beyond both our personal existence and the ecological interconnectedness of all things to a greater multidimensionality— a complex reality of many dimensions and facets. This shows the significance of ecology, but also that ecology by itself fails to provide ultimate answers. The most consistent and credible worldview is belief in a personal God who is the creative source of the universe and also its sustainer, guide, judge, and culmination. This understanding coheres nicely with all dimensions of human experience, such as thinking, willing, acting, and storytelling.

## Life in Christ

All things cohere in Christ. Therefore, Jesus is the key to the future and the answer to the vexing issues of life in the present, including ecological concerns. This coherence applies to our personal lives, community lives, and our need for global peace and justice. It is key to the church's self-understanding.

*Personal life.* Our world is increasingly in crisis. This global crisis is rooted in a loss of a sense of personal meaning because of sin. At the deepest level, government, politics, and material prosperity cannot provide that meaning. But relationship with Jesus Christ can.

People who come to know Jesus personally find new and deeper meaning in their lives. In Jesus, people find meaning that transcends them and yet transforms them. Faith in Jesus gives inner purpose, unity, calmness, and confidence that at some deep level, everything is all right. This faith also gives a sense of calling and mission and of connection with the world. People criticize pie-in-the-sky Christians for being "so heavenly minded they're no earthly good." But throughout history those people most closely connected with Jesus, and thus most heavenly minded and inwardly grounded, have often contributed the most to social justice and human welfare.

*Community life.* Cooperative, shared life is a gift from Jesus. By lifting people above themselves, above their fears and prejudices, Jesus brings people together. The greatest, strongest gift of faith in Jesus Christ, throughout history, has been new, redemptive forms of community.

Can the global human family live in community and ecological harmony? Jesus Christ shows how: through respect and openness to every person and all peoples and through attitudes of cooperation and shared concerns. Jesus gives us the example. For those who know Jesus personally and who form his body, the church, Jesus provides the power to model community in millions of local situations and to build community globally.

*Global shalom.* Jesus Christ is the key to global peace and justice. He is the hope of history, for in him all things hold together and in him all things will find their final reconciliation and goal (Eph. 1:10).

Jesus is our hope through his example and the selflessness he engenders, but also in a more ultimate sense. Shortly after Jesus' ascension, the apostle Peter said that Jesus would "remain in heaven until the time of universal restoration that God announced long ago" (Acts 3:21 NRSV). We look forward, he said, to "a new heaven and a new earth" (2 Pet. 3:13). The apostle Paul said that because of our faith in Christ, we know "the creation itself will be set free from its bondage to decay" and brought to glorious freedom (Rom. 8:21 NRSV).

In his life, death, and resurrection, Jesus showed the way to confront and resolve the world's illness and disorder. This resolution comes not through force and manipulation but through lives committed to truth, compassion, and redemptive action. Intimate relationship with him and community grounded in him provide the center and source for personal coherence and ecological healing—and thus for the church's mission.

## Conclusion

Mission grounded in Christ is more than a philosophy or a moral cause. It is a call to commitment and engagement. If the history of Jesus were *only* a worldview or belief system, our attitude toward it could be merely intellectual. But the call that comes to us is not just an intellectual challenge. It is the appeal of a person: Jesus, who calls us to follow him in faith and to learn from him how to live on earth for both time and eternity. He calls us to a life centered in him, not to a mere set of ideas.

The gospel is friendly to all that is positive and humanizing in the world but deathly hostile to all that is destructive, dehumanizing, or pathological. Life truly grounded in Jesus cherishes the earth as good and worth caring for. But it opposes misunderstanding humans as nothing but one more species in the ecosystem.

Jesus lifts no race or nation in domination over others. The gospel values all people, east and west, north and south. From the perspective of the gospel we learn why civilizations rise and fall. The gospel opposes any "new world order" that oppresses people or demeans human dignity and freedom. Yet it promises a new world order of global peace, health, and prosperity—an order whose power and endurance saturate space and time yet stretch beyond them.

The rise of ecological consciousness may be God's gift to the church to help it discover a broader sense of mission. It can help the church comprehend greater dimensions of the truth that in Jesus Christ all things cohere. But it is in Jesus Christ himself, and in living together as his body, that we find the real DNA of mission.

Ecology says, *You can never do just one thing.* Organic, ecological understandings of the church and its mission that center in Jesus Christ say, *Synergize the many things you do in the one direction of the kingdom of God.* "Whether you eat or drink or whatever you do, do it all for the glory of God" (1 Cor. 10:31).

---

## Heartland Finds Some Answers

Heartland Christian Fellowship was nearing a decision about its space problem. The committee and the church board had studied the options. They had tried to base their decisions on a solid foundation—not just "What would Jesus do?" but what the church should do if it really is the body of Jesus Christ, Savior and Lord of the universe, and an outpost of the kingdom of God.

The building committee had started with what looked like a dilemma: Should we fill in the swampy area of our property in order to expand the sanctuary, or not? But the church soon found itself facing a deeper question: Does our mission as Christ's body include stewardship of the property we own—our little piece of earth?

Heartland Christian Fellowship found that viewing the church and God's saving plan organically and ecologically actually helped. The church decided that it had a responsibility both for evangelism and for the earth. It must both nurture the body and care for the land. As Pastor Dorset expressed it in one of the committee meetings, "We are responsible both for evangelism and for the environment, for two reasons. First, because God cares about both. But also because the two can't really be separated; each touches the other."

When Ray Schilling had first raised the question about environmental stewardship months earlier, most of the committee members were baffled. It had taken weeks for them to understand Ray's point. But they prayed about it and studied the issue. The committee formed two working groups, one to investigate the wetlands issue, and the other to consider creative options for handling the church's growth.

The whole process took nearly a year. Sometimes Pastor Dorset and the other leaders felt impatient. But finally the committee, and in fact the whole church, came to consensus on some key points. The church adopted the committee's recommendations. The results were more than Pastor Dorset could have hoped for.

First, with Ray's help, the whole church came to understand that its "swamp" really was an ecologically important wetland that sustained a multitude of birds, animals, and plants. The congregation worked out a plan to preserve the area from further "development"—and in the process involved the children and created a wonderful teaching and learning site. Heartland Christian Fellowship got a lot of good publicity out of all this, but that wasn't the point. The press coverage, however, probably boosted the church's evangelistic witness.

Second, Heartland grew more ecologically and aesthetically aware. It modified its landscaping, using native plants and trees, and refashioned the church's trimmings so that it fit more naturally into the landscape. Outsiders noticed, but that wasn't the point. The church was doing it to the glory of God.

Third, the church did address the space problem. After considering several options, it decided it really didn't need a larger sanctuary. Heartland decentralized, moving more of its functions into members' homes. It created, in effect, a network of house churches. In the sanctuary, Heartland replaced the pews with comfortable chairs and discovered it could accommodate a third more people in the same space, with a better sense of community and more flexibility. As the church continued to grow, it began plans for birthing a second congregation in a poor neighborhood where it now had two growing house groups.

These steps seemed to unleash a shock wave of creativity in the church. Heartland began holding a great outdoor "Servant Celebration" each summer, spending a whole weekend praising God for what he had done through them over the past year and enjoying the world God had made. ("Something like the Old Testament Feast of Booths," Bill Silver said.) It celebrated the lives that had been transformed and the ministries carried out. And the church also looked ahead, visioning for the future. Pastor Dorset always spent a good deal of time preparing for his talk at the Servant Celebration. He wanted to show how God had been at work, and he wanted to enlarge the church's vision for the future.

Heartland Christian Fellowship continued to grow, not only in numbers but also in understanding and practicing the good news of God's kingdom.

One Sunday night after the third annual Servant Celebration, Darrell Dorset stretched out on the couch at home to relax after a long day. Beth walked in from the kitchen. "You done good, pastor!" she said. "That was an inspiring and helpful message, I think. And I loved the video that

Jeff and Barb put together of the past year's events. It was fun to watch the kids and adults together at last fall's retreat."

"Yes," Darrell said, "I thought the whole celebration was great. We had a bigger crowd than we did last year. But I think we also had a greater sense of God's presence."

Darrell was quiet a few minutes. Then he said, "You know, Beth, things really come together in a beautiful way when we focus on Jesus Christ and watch him work through his body."

# Questions
## for Group Discussion or Personal Reflection

1. Why did Heartland Christian Fellowship take so long to decide what to do about their space problem? Were they wise to spend so much time in making this decision?
2. Is Heartland demonstrating *diversity, charismatic giftedness, local groundedness,* and *prophetic witness* as well as *unity, holiness, catholicity,* and *apostolicity?* If so, how? If not, where does it still need to grow?
3. How do the annual Servant Celebrations reflect the nature of the church as the body of Christ?
4. Does Heartland Christian Fellowship seem to have a healthy balance of ministry both for this world and for the world to come? Why or why not?
5. What difference does it make to know that God created and sustains the universe?
6. What difference does it make to know that God created and sustains your church?
7. What changes could help your church have a greater impact on the ecosystem in which your church is located?
8. What impact might these changes make locally as well as globally?

# 10

***

## THE CHURCH CONFRONTS GLOBALIZATION

Like it or not, all churches today are getting caught in the web of globalization. Our world is increasingly globalized—instantly linked by satellite, the Internet, and all kinds of business and entertainment connections.

What does this mean for Christ's body? If anything, globalization simply intensifies the need for the church to understand itself organically and to be clear about its own DNA—its own uniqueness. Churches alive with the DNA of the Spirit learn to live and witness so that globalization becomes an opportunity, not a threat.

In this chapter we will examine the challenge of globalization. And in the following chapter, we will explore the opportunities globalization opens up for the church. Churches alive with the Spirit are not called to go into cultural hibernation and shrink from global currents; they are called to engage in gospel globalization.

Globalization is not totally new! The Bible tells us the earth is the Lord's. "Let all the earth fear the Lord; let all the people of the world revere him" (Ps. 33:8). "How awesome is the Lord Most High, the great King over all the earth!" (Ps. 47:2). "Shout with joy to God, all the earth!" (Ps. 66:1). "Declare his glory among the nations, his marvelous deeds among all peoples" (1 Chron. 16:24; Ps. 96:3).

## The Earth Is the Lord's

"The earth is the Lord's!" This is the place to start in examining globalization. We serve a "global" God who "has the whole world in his hands." He is not shocked or threatened by globalization. God's plan has always been global. It has always encompassed the whole of history—and reached beyond it. Rather than feeling threatened by globalization, the church should understand that God is Lord of history. In his own way, God's Spirit will use globalization to bring about his purposes. And maybe he wants his body to help.

Globalization, therefore, is a biblical concern—a *gospel concern*—before it is a social, economic, or political issue. Christians care about the whole earth and all that happens in it because this is God's concern. In this sense, Christians are way ahead of the rest of the world. We have always known that the gospel is global good news! The gospel itself is a globalizing force.

We should beware of a nonbiblical view of the earth and global society. Christians properly focus on ultimate spiritual reality. Because of this, we easily assume that since spiritual reality endures forever and this world is passing away, the earth has no value or future except as it contributes to evangelism or church growth. But as God reminded Job, the whole created order is a testimony to God's greatness, creativity, and care (Job 38–41). The universe is a tapestry reflecting God's greatness. We should love what God loves and faithfully exercise the stewardship God has given us—a stewardship not only of the gospel but also of the physical earth and all its life forms, and of human society and culture, as well.

## The Deep Roots of Globalization

Yes, the earth is the Lord's. But it is facing new challenges today. Many of these challenges get lumped under the term *globalization*. The roots of globalization are not found in this century, or in the last, however; they reach clear back to Genesis 11:1–9:

> Now the whole world had one language and a common speech. As men moved eastward, they found a plain in Shinar and settled there.
>
> They said to each other, "Come, let's make bricks and bake them thoroughly." They used brick instead of stone, and tar for mortar. Then they said, "Come, let us build ourselves a city, with a tower that reaches to the heavens, so that we may make a name for ourselves and not be scattered over the face of the whole earth."

But the LORD came down to see the city and the tower that the men were building. The LORD said, "If as one people speaking the same language they have begun to do this, then nothing they plan to do will be impossible for them. Come, let us go down and confuse their language so they will not understand each other."

So the LORD scattered them from there over all the earth, and they stopped building the city. That is why it was called Babel—because there the LORD confused the language of the whole world. From there the LORD scattered them over the face of the whole earth.

This passage shows that globalization is not new. "Come, let us build ourselves a city, with a tower that reaches to the heavens, so that we may make a name for ourselves and not be scattered over the face of the whole earth." There is a natural human drive to unify humanity. And there is also its opposite: an impulse to fragment, isolate, and insulate ourselves from each other; to form ethnic communities and live only with people like ourselves. Some have called these competing tendencies *globalism* and *tribalism*.[1]

Neither of these tendencies is bad or sinful. Both are God-given, part of the image of God in us—our spiritual genetic inheritance. We want to unite people together because we deeply know that we are all of one blood, that "From one ancestor [God] made all nations to inhabit the whole earth" (Acts 17:26 NRSV). But we also want to be especially close to those who are most like us—"our kind of people" who share the same language and culture. What turns globalism and tribalism into evils is the problem of sin and self-centeredness.

Genesis 11:1 says, "Now the whole world had one language and a common speech." This is not a judgment but simply a cultural description. The Bible doesn't say it is good or bad. The problem wasn't the cultural unity of the human race; it was something deeper.

Genesis 11 tells us the problem. This is a very up-to-date insight, because here we see the negative side of globalization. Note especially three statements:

"Let us build . . . a tower that reaches to the heavens."

"So that we may make a name for ourselves."

"Let us make bricks and bake them thoroughly."

We find in these statements three aspects of globalization that are still with us:

1. *Humanistic culture and religion.* "A tower that reaches to the heavens." By human effort alone ("Let us build . . ."), without reference to God, these people attempt to raise a new culture and religion. It is clear

from Mesopotamian history that this "tower that reaches to heaven" was partly a religious shrine. It was a theological statement. These people were going to climb to heaven by their own efforts.

All culture is religious at heart. In this case, the people intended to build a society based on humanistic faith. Building the tower was an act of rebellion against God. It was an attempt to create a substitute Eden, as Jacques Ellul makes plain in *The Meaning of the City*.[2]

Globalization today expresses this same urge. It seeks to create a *global culture* based on human cleverness. This tendency has within it the seeds of a commercialized, secular religion in which all earth's peoples are joined together by common economic ties. Its religious power is found precisely in the fact that it does not seem to be religious. Globalization is twenty-first-century humanity's "tower that reaches to heaven."

2. *Egotism and hubris.* This is the second striking thing in Genesis 11. We're going to "make a name for ourselves," the people say. *Hubris* means "insolent pride" or "arrogance"—precisely what we find here. Based on human-centered culture and religion, the people expect to be famous, "number one" in all the earth. Today this tendency translates as preoccupation with fame, celebrity, advertising and propaganda, and "winning" at all costs in business. What are these obsessions, if not today's forms of hubris? Nearly all advertising appeals to self-interest, and many advertisers reveal the same characteristics in themselves.

Global businesses speak of "branding," making a trademark so well known that it is recognized instantly throughout the earth. Examples include Coca-Cola, Marlboro cigarettes, Nike, and Levi jeans. "Let us make a name for ourselves" is a key slogan of contemporary globalization. Unfortunately, this mentality often seeps into the church as well.

3. *New technology.* "Let's make bricks and bake them thoroughly." And that's just what they did. "They used brick instead of stone, and tar for mortar." Building a tower of bricks and tar sounds rather primitive, but at the time it may have been something of a technological breakthrough. It shows the importance of technology. You can't build a tower without proper materials and the technical skill to use them.

Technology is a powerful tool. How it is used depends in large measure on a culture's values and virtues. In this case, technology was being used for the wrong purpose, and it brought God's judgment. It was technology in the service of rebellion against God.

One of the driving forces of globalization is ever more sophisticated technological development. But technology-driven globalization is not new. The history of globalization is the history of technological innovation, from ocean-going sailing ships, to the telegraph, to the Internet.[3]

The roots of technical globalization go back at least to Babel. Granted, the "globalization" of Genesis 11 was not really the whole globe. It touched but a part of the earth and a small population. The point is, the same *human cultural tendency* was there, exhibiting the same dynamics that give us full-blown globalization today.

All culture is cumulative, building on itself. Each generation builds on the previous one, adding new ideas, new techniques, and new stories. Yet the three cultural tendencies discussed here have continued all through history. They lie behind today's globalization. Globalization is a history-long human project. As time goes on, it becomes increasingly sophisticated, reaching into more and more areas of human life and culture.

One could get the impression from Genesis 11 that God opposes globalization. He confused the people's language and "scattered them over the face of the whole earth." God's action, however, was not aimed at their desire to be unified, or to "globalize." Rather, God acted because of their rebellion against his plans and purposes. *God has his own way of globalizing.* There is a proper gospel globalization. "Go, make disciples in all nations" is emphatic globalization. But healthy globalization honors God as sovereign, recognizes his history-long redemptive plan, and sees Jesus Christ as Lord of history.

We need to have a deeper understanding of globalization and its implications for the church. Let us consider four features of globalization that make it especially significant for the church's nature, structure, and mission.

## The Marks of a Global Society

Despite its long roots, globalization today is different from times past. We see the flowering of trends that have been long at work, particularly since the rise of capitalism, worldwide navigation (leading to colonialism), and industrialization. Four key features of emerging global society are qualitatively different from times past. These realities pose challenges the church has never before faced.

### Digitized, Wireless Technology

The roots of computerization, the Internet, and wireless technology go back two centuries to the harnessing of electricity and to related developments in mathematics and physics. Two more recent breakthroughs led to the development of modern computers: the transistor (leading to the microchip) and digitization. These developments are the basis for all software. In the last ten years, electronic digitization has brought us the Internet, cellular phones, compact discs, and high-definition television. But this is only the beginning.

Digitization is the technique of translating complex information into numbers by reducing everything to ones and zeroes. Almost everything can now be numbered, or quantified. In theory, everything, from emotional states to great works of art, can therefore be computerized. This has a profound cultural impact. Digitization reinforces the tendency of contemporary culture to value *quantity* over *quality* and to measure and evaluate everything numerically. This is a key mark of globalization, and especially of global economics.

Christians need to be aware of this deeply ingrained cultural tendency to value only what can be counted. Missions leader Jim Plueddeman says pointedly, "When we aim only at what can be measured, we ignore the more important goals of character, discipleship and holiness." Tom Sine has written, "Over the last fifty years society has changed dramatically in terms of its understanding of what's important and what's of value." Increasingly the message is that the only real values are those that are economic and quantifiable. "Western societies tend to see economic concerns as the ultimate concerns. . . . Many of us, including people of keen biblical faith, have been influenced by modern culture to define what is important and what is of value largely in economic terms."[4]

This tendency to quantify and to see economic values as primary leads to a second key aspect of globalization.

### All Life for Sale

Perhaps the most important feature of globalization is that it turns all of life and culture into things to be bought and sold. The word for this is *commodification*. Every human activity becomes a commodity, a product in the marketplace. *Commodification* is roughly synonymous with *commercialization*, but commodification is a better term for our discussion because it more accurately suggests the ever-increasing transformation of areas of life in the private household sphere into matters of the public economic sphere.[5]

A prophetic book on this topic is *The Age of Access: The New Culture of Hypercapitalism Where All of Life is a Paid-For Experience,* by Jeremy Rifkin. The global economy, Rifkin says, is "making a long-term shift from industrial production to cultural production."[6]

By "cultural production," Rifkin means that global business is now moving beyond goods and traditional commercial services to *every* area of life. Rifkin says we are entering a new era in which "people purchase their very existence in small commercial segments." Cultural production is "the final stage of the capitalist way of life, whose essential mission has always been to bring more and more human activity into the commercial arena." The progression from manufacturing and services to "commodifying human relationships and finally to selling access to cultural experiences" shows "the single-minded determination of the commercial sphere to make all relations economic ones."[7]

In areas of the world where globalization is in full swing, this process is already well advanced. More and more sectors of life are commercialized, rather than existing informally with no thought of using money. Rifkin writes, "The transformation from industrial to cultural capitalism already is challenging many of our most basic assumptions about what constitutes human society." In the new global economy, "culture becomes the most important commercial resource, time and attention become the most valuable possession, and each individual's own life becomes the ultimate market."[8]

Rifkin concludes, "Imagine a world where virtually every activity outside the confines of family relations is a paid-for experience, a world in which traditional reciprocal obligations and expectations—mediated by feelings of faith, empathy, and solidarity—are replaced by contractual relations in the form of paid memberships, subscriptions, admission charges, retainers, and fees."[9]

This is a challenge for the human race generally, but especially for Christians. Because of God's love for his world, Christians have a particular concern here—one that should engage the best Christian minds.[10]

What should be done? Rifkin says,

> Restoring a proper balance between the cultural realm and the commercial realm is likely to be one of the most important challenges. . . . Cultural resources risk overexploitation and depletion at the hands of commerce just as natural resources did during the Industrial Age. Finding a sustainable way to preserve and enhance the rich cultural diversity that is the lifeblood of civilization in a global network economy increasingly based on paid access to commodified cultural experiences is one of the primary political tasks of the new century.[11]

As the newest wave of globalization, commodification is taking over the culture in many places. It is like an infection, reaching more and more of life. Its tendency is to turn everything into monetary economics, undermining traditional community relationships built on trust, face-to-face intimacy, and experiences shared over time.

Commodification is powerful because it combines three social dynamics that already are vigorous in all Western societies: *technology, materialism*, and *individualism*. Society in places like Denmark, the United States, Japan, and South Korea has become highly technical and materialistic. In addition, much of Western culture, especially the United States, is very individualistic, which undermines community. This is vividly highlighted in Robert Putnam's book, *Bowling Alone: The Collapse and Revival of American Community*. Putnam notes that while increasing numbers of Americans go bowling, fewer are participating in bowling *teams*. Using a wide range of data, he shows that over the past quarter century Americans have become increasingly disconnected from friends, family, neighbors, and various social structures. This trend is drastically reducing the nation's "social capital."[12]

Through the processes of globalization, more and more nations are drawn into the global web of high technology, materialism, and individualism, leading to commodification. People increasingly live in a high-tech world and value the accumulation of material goods. Yet at the same time, people are increasingly isolated from one another. They find more and more areas of life passing into the marketplace. Much of their daily routine has become a matter of economic exchange—activities and experiences that are bought and paid for rather than exchanged informally and freely as in the days of their parents and grandparents.

Think about life fifty years ago in the United States. Most people prepared their own food and spent hours in family conversation and activities. They entertained themselves with games, reading, or storytelling. Today many Americans eat most of their meals in restaurants or fast-food outlets, spend little time together as families, and entertain themselves in passive, voyeuristic ways (watching TV or spending hours at the computer, for instance) that discourage community and physical activity. Or they go shopping, which further feeds both individualism and materialism. And they *pay money* for a growing number of things: restaurant meals, cable TV, Internet access, movies, music, designer clothing, and the many other products of the shopping mall, catalog, and website.[13]

Such things may not be bad in themselves, provided one's life is anchored in healthy, accountable community. But with the breakdown of marriage, family life, neighborhood interaction, and other community activities, the trend is worrisome. Life without community produces sadly unhealthy individuals who seek meaning and happiness in things that can't satisfy. The end result is alienation, depression, anger, and increasingly, violent acts against society.

Globalization in advanced societies brings *increased stress.* Surveys repeatedly show high, and increasing, levels of personal stress in the United States. This is a side effect of the globalizing process. Globalization feeds individualism and materialism while starving community and other social dynamics that give life deeper meaning.

The body of Christ is not exempt here. Two examples: Christian educational institutions and weddings. In the United States, Christian colleges and universities are increasingly signing marketing contracts with the makers of soft drinks, athletic equipment, and other items, giving these companies exclusive access to the students. The schools become marketing tools for global corporations. And even among Christians, weddings are becoming a commodity to be bought, with inflated prices for consultants, registered gifts, gowns, photography, and entertainment. The point is not simply the extravagance involved but also that the whole event has become a commercial production. The sacred, spiritual meaning takes second place. Weddings become commodities of the marketplace. Thankfully, some Christian couples refuse to go along with this and plan simpler, noncommercialized marriage celebrations.

How will Christian mission respond to this commodifying of every area of life? We need to reaffirm the basic Christian virtues of community, simplicity, and humanity. Christ's body should offer creative alternatives to commodification. The church will be countercultural at this point if it understands and lives in harmony with its own DNA.

## *Global Awareness and Interconnectedness*

Today we all know that we live in one connected world—even if we see the world mostly as a huge shopping mall! Globalization has produced a shift in human consciousness. No longer can business or religious leaders anywhere in the world think only locally or nationally. No longer do entrepreneurs or manufacturers operate in isolation from the global context. Even local businesses are plugging into global information networks to keep up with key developments.

Increasingly, sources of strategic information such as magazines, computer networks, and consulting firms are global or at least collect their information globally. A subtle shift in consciousness is occurring from local and national awareness to global awareness, not only in business but in society as well. If pastors aren't yet aware of this, a few minutes' conversation about these matters with a businessman or software engineer (or a farmer who has a global positioning system on his tractor) can be an eye-opening experience.

Anyone involved in economics, finance, or politics cannot help but be increasingly conscious of working in a global environment and being a world citizen. Consumers now buy products from all over the world. And what is true in people's business and commercial lives generally carries over to other areas, deepening global awareness. Children will be more globally conscious than their parents were. In the next forty years, two generations will come to maturity with a keen sense of global consciousness—people who know that their address is not Chicago or Nairobi or Seoul, but Planet Earth. Placeless email addresses already signal this new global culture.

Global and regional trade agreements promote this interconnection and awareness, as well. Broad international arrangements such as the World Trade Organization (WTO) and the North American Free Trade Agreement (NAFTA) have been controversial because they hurt certain businesses and, if not crafted fairly, lead to oppression and environmental degradation. But these trade agreements have a positive side also. In Mexico, NAFTA seems to be sparking greater democracy; the 2000 presidential election, in which the opposition party won for the first time in modern history, signals some positive effects of NAFTA. Whether China's entry into the WTO will feed greater democracy there remains to be seen, but it is a possibility.

Increased global awareness and linkages can be a very positive development for Christian mission, also. But the church must understand what's happening in our world and know how to respond. We have a global faith, and we belong to a global Christian community. Within the church, we should encourage the sense of being *world Christians*—citizens of God's reign throughout the world, profoundly committed to world mission and deeply aware that Christians everywhere, if really Christ's body, share the same DNA.

### Global Symbols and Images

In the new global economy, people become highly sensitive to symbols. Things-in-themselves mean less than what they symbolize. This does not necessarily mean less materialism. It can mean more, as things from jeans to jobs are bought, not for what they are in themselves, but for the brands, names, values, or other meanings tied to them.

This aspect of globalization shapes a mushrooming global youth culture. Earth is home to a "worldwide mass of [800 million] teenagers, who crave the latest trends [and] pay little attention to cultural boundaries," notes Erla Zwingle. The need and tendency of youth "to be linked is a principal force in the emergence of a global culture."[14]

Global culture focuses on symbols and images. On one level, this is just smart marketing. More basically, it is a shift from *things* to the *connections between things*—in other words, it constitutes a new focus on the patterns that hold things together rather than on hardware or goods or material products. Increasingly, the real product of businesses is services, not goods. Banks and insurance companies speak of the new services they provide as their "products." The most valuable assets of globally networked enterprises are not factories and warehouses and finished goods; they are now services, networks, brand names, and intangibles like reputation and influence.

Globalization accents the role of images and brings a new focus on linkages, connections, and patterns of relationship. Significantly, the global model is more organic than mechanical, more flowing and flexible than fixed and final. This suggests for the future a new sensitivity to networks and patterns that hold things together, perhaps countering the postmodern tendency toward diversity and disintegration.

This *could* be a positive development. It is very different from the view that has ruled the recent past, which was based on the science and philosophy of the Renaissance and the Enlightenment in Europe. In some ways this "new" mentality may actually be closer to that of societies less touched by modern culture and more aware of the patterns, textures, and connections of all of life.

This new sense of global connectedness could be helpful *if* Christians and others of goodwill learn to take advantage of it. But if it is used mainly to make a profit for businesses and investors, it will create emptiness and injustice, harming people and communities (especially those who are already poor) just so the profit margin of a global corporation can swell.

Consider an example: Wal-Mart is now the largest merchandiser in the world. Over a twenty-year period, Wal-Mart built hundreds of stores in or near small towns and cities across the United States. Because of discount prices due to their huge size, these superstores drove thousands of local shops out of business. Local stores simply couldn't compete. But now Wal-Mart is closing hundreds of its own stores and building even larger superstores near major cities. The reason is profit. Wal-Mart closes stores that don't make enough money, even though this brings further economic deterioration in the affected area and leaves ugly vacant buildings that Wal-Mart refuses to rent to competitors.

Globalization for profit alone inevitably leads to just such large-scale injustices and inequities. For example, AIDS medications are too expensive to be used in poor African nations because the patents and profit margins of American and European pharmaceutical companies must be protected. This is what happens when profit is the *only,* or overriding, force. Globalization must be humanized by other motives, including an enlightened sense of mutual responsibility for the welfare of the whole earth. The AIDS medications example is in fact very instructive. In recent years humanitarian groups have put enough pressure on the global pharmaceutical industry that some companies have started providing AIDS medications to Africa at greatly reduced cost. Globalization *can* be humanized if Christians and others of goodwill exercise firm but compassionate influence.[15]

Globalization is reaching everywhere. Consider an example from Kenya that shows how globalization touches Christians as well as non-Christians. An American missionary reports that the churches of Kenya have their own "Generation X." He notes,

> Exposure to the world's political, technological, economic, and social climate is contrasted with the frustrations of life lived in a third world country with its inherent limitations for meaningful opportunities for self-advancement. Kenya has computers, the Internet, MTV, America's sit-coms, cellular phones, Hollywood's movies, and exposure to cutting edge world trends. These all titillate the sense and minds of Kenya's youth. Sitting in a small crude church structure listening to a marginally educated pastor preaching a seemingly irrelevant sermon brings little satisfaction to many of [the church's] young people.[16]

Thousands of similar examples could be cited. Many such examples reveal the downside of globalization. Yet Christians can use this very force to hold up the image of a just, equitable, righteous society—the hope of the kingdom of God.

Let us ask, then: What opportunities does globalization offer to churches that understand what it means to be Christ's body? To this we turn in the next chapter.

––––––

## Heartland and the World

Heartland Christian Fellowship is located in a medium-size city called Johnson Center. Most of the people in the church grew up there. But Pastor Dorset noticed that over the years, more and more of the newer members came from "faraway places, with strange-sounding names." Partly these people were drawn to the area by good jobs, especially since the Honda plant opened some years earlier. The plant was built about halfway between Johnson Center and another town thirty miles north. And a lot of smaller factories and businesses had now started up, with names like Emkei Products and R and S Services. Johnson Center was becoming globally connected.

Pastor Dorset was talking about this one day with Jeff Dryer, a software designer and a faithful member at Heartland. He had his wife, Barb, had put together the video for the last Servant Celebration. There wasn't much about computers, software, and digital wizardry that Jeff didn't know. Jeff and the pastor talked about how their city was becoming increasingly connected globally.

Jeff worked for a small company that designed software for engineering firms. The business was growing, and every once in awhile Jeff would fly off to places like Hong Kong and New Delhi to work on projects.

Last summer Jeff's work had taken him to Brasília, the capital of Brazil. Jeff took the time to visit a mission that Heartland Christian Fellowship supported. The mission worked with poor *favelados*, people who live in the decrepit shantytowns that ring the city. Jeff brought back on his laptop a high-tech video report showing the mission's ministries to the poor and a new church that they had just planted.

Heartland Christian Fellowship was growing in its missionary concern. Pastor Dorset was pleased. He was glad now that the church had been spared the heavy expense of a new sanctuary. Sure, they could have found a way to raise the money, but it would have been just about the *only* thing they could have afforded to do. Instead, the church now had many thousands of dollars more for missions and other redemptive ministries.

Shortly after he and Jeff had discussed how Johnson Center was becoming a global city, Pastor Dorset read a fascinating cover story in *National Geographic* about globalization. *I've got to talk this over with Jeff*, Darrell thought. He also wanted to talk to Ray Schilling about it because the article highlighted links between globalization and ecological issues—how new Mexican factories along the U.S. border were polluting local streams and rivers, for instance.

The more he thought about these things, the more Darrell Dorset saw that some key discipleship issues were involved. If Johnson Center was really becoming globally linked, what did this mean for Heartland's mission and for Christian living in the world? *Somehow, I've got to address this in my preaching*, Darrell thought.

At a special Sunday evening service, Jeff Dryer talked about the mission work in Brasília. He put together an excellent report, including prayer requests and a five-minute video clip. Pastor Dorset had Jeff's report duplicated and distributed it through the shepherds' network to all the small groups.

A week or so later, in the small-group shepherds' meeting, Bill Silver said, "You know what? The folks in our groups have gotten really interested in that new church in Brasília. They're wondering if we could send a team down there to help out." Pastor Dorset soon discovered that several people in the church had the same idea.

"Well, let's channel the ideas to our World Mission Group and let them chew on it," Pastor Dorset said. "Sounds like a promising idea to me. But we need to think it through."

The World Mission Group liked the idea. In fact, Jeff, an active member of this group, had already been thinking along these lines.

The idea bore fruit. About six months later, a group of twenty people from Heartland Christian Fellowship—five couples and several single people, including some teenagers—was preparing to fly to Brasília to spend two weeks with their Brazilian brothers and sisters in Christ. Pastor Dorset was especially pleased that Ricardo and Leda could go along, because they had family roots in Brazil. Another of the couples was Chinese American, fairly recent converts, and quite new to the church. "At least we won't look like a typical group of American tourists!" Jeff said.

As the time for the mission trip got nearer, however, Pastor Dorset began to have second thoughts. He really *didn't* want this to be merely a Christian tourist trip. He was thinking about what it meant for the church to be the body of Christ globally. *These Brazilian Christians really are our brothers and sisters,* he kept thinking to himself. He began to wonder if the trip was such a good idea. But he also thought about the image of the body in 1 Corinthians 12. *No part of the body can say it doesn't need the other parts,* he thought.

As he prayed about this, Pastor Dorset had an idea. *Let's make this a 1 Corinthians 12 kind of experience,* he thought. *If we're going to give, we're also going to receive. I wonder what our Brazilian brothers and sisters can teach us about being Christ's body.*

As it turned out, the Brazilian church had a lot to teach! The mission team planned its schedule so that half the time in Brasília was spent just getting acquainted with the Brazilian Christians and learning from them. They visited in the people's homes, some of which were just cardboard and tin shanties. They ate tasty beans and rice with them. They went to the church's home meetings and began to learn the joyful Portuguese songs. And each morning one of the church's pastors met with them for an hour and led them deeply into the Bible.

The Heartland team discovered that although this Brazilian church was very poor, some of its young people attended night school and had day jobs in the city. Jeff got acquainted with one young man who spoke nearly flawless English. Jeff was surprised to learn that this young man, Darivaldo, worked for the very company in Brasília that Jeff's company did business with. Jeff and Darivaldo talked together about computers and about ministry with the poor. "My dream is to start a new business that will create jobs for poor folks," Darivaldo said. And he told Jeff how he had been able to share his faith at work and at school.

When the mission team returned to Heartland, it had a lot to share. The team members felt they now understood more deeply what it means to be the church, and to be world Christians.

# Questions
## for Group Discussion or Personal Reflection

1. Does globalization touch your personal life? If so, how?
2. Share an experience that made you want to quote the old cliché, "It's a small world."
3. What worries you most about globalization? What gives you hope?
4. In what ways is globalization beginning to touch Heartland Christian Fellowship?
5. Do you think the mission trip to Brazil was a good idea? Why or why not?
6. Why did Pastor Dorset have some concerns or reservations about the trip? Do you think he was right?
7. Do you think Heartland is learning what it means to be global Christians? In what ways?
8. What new things is the Heartland church learning about the church's DNA?

# 11

## GOSPEL GLOBALIZATION

Like electricity, globalization has positive and negative poles. It can either do good or produce nasty shocks, depending on how you handle it.

Growing connectedness among earth's people is good. It can lead to greater peace, health, and prosperity. But due to human sinfulness, globalization also has its dark side.[1] In this chapter we look more closely at the challenges globalization poses and then explore the strategic opportunities it provides for Christian mission.

### The Challenges of Globalization

In the last chapter we saw what globalization is and some of the problems it brings. How does this relate specifically to the mission and DNA of the church? The globalizing process presents three major challenges that Christian mission must address.

1. *The challenge of commodification.* For the church, the danger here is falling prey to the world's marketing mentality and making the gospel itself a commodity. We need to see clearly that "though we live in the world, we do not wage war as the world does. The weapons we fight with are not the weapons of the world. On the contrary, they have divine power to demolish strongholds" (2 Cor. 10:3–4).

In his letters, the apostle Paul warned against commodifying the gospel. He was very concerned that he present the gospel "free of charge" (1 Cor. 9:18; 2 Cor. 11:7). He didn't mean his hearers shouldn't take personal responsibility for their own church and mission. Rather, he meant he would not "merchandise" the gospel; he would not turn it into a commodity, a matter of monetary exchange or gain. The church today must likewise be very careful about this. (Note 1 Corinthians 9:12–18.)

As mentioned earlier, a key aspect of globalization is *quantification*. This mind-set can easily infect the church. The quantification mind-set tends to value

Numbers over discipleship

Church growth over growth in Christlikeness

Large churches over small churches

Big events over small, informal processes

The quantification mind-set tends to measure "success" the same way the world does: Bigger is better. By contrast, the New Testament church was essentially a dynamic network of small units, mainly house churches. How did the New Testament writers view these churches? They urged them to "grow up into Christ," to "have the mind of Christ," and to "walk worthy of their calling." This is genetic, organic, relational language. The assumption of the New Testament seems to be that if the church is a genuine Christian community, living by kingdom values, it will of course grow numerically. Is this our assumption today?

Faithful churches measure their fidelity by the values of Christ's kingdom, not by those of the world. The church's being and calling come from Jesus Christ.

2. *The challenge of deteriorating community.* Commodification and other aspects of globalization tend to erode face-to-face community as a social reality and a basic cultural value. Healthy societies are based on trust and personal acquaintance, first at the family and neighborhood levels and then more broadly. Americans tend to think of Asian and African societies as much more communal than Western societies. But look at the long traffic jams in Seoul and other megacities. In most cars, you will see just one person! Or consider the massive migration in China of young women and men from small towns to the big cities, disrupting traditional family patterns. In many places around the globe, community is eroding and is being replaced by alliances and associations based solely on economics or entertainment. Christian mission must learn how to confront this.

3. *The challenge of the poor.* Globalization has dramatically increased the prosperity and well-being of millions of people in some places, but it has widened the gap between the rich and the poor globally. Data from reputable sources agree that overall the gap between the rich and the poor is worsening. A World Bank study suggests that globally, the gap

between rich and poor nations will widen still further over the next decade. United Nations research shows that whereas in 1965 the poorest 20 percent of the world's population earned 2.3 percent of global income, that percentage has now dropped to about 1.4 percent. Thus economic globalization is "dramatically expanding the wealth of the richest 20 percent while at the same time shrinking the resource base of the poorest 20 percent."[2]

Part of the global cry of the poor is the problem of migrants, new immigrants ("legal" or "illegal"), refugees, and displaced persons. The number of people living in refugee camps or on the margins of society has reached staggering levels—almost 22 million people. About 41 percent of them are in Asia, 28 percent in Africa, 23 percent in Europe, and 8 percent in the Americas. Of these displaced persons living in extreme poverty, the United Nations High Commission for Refugees classifies 13 million of them as "refugees"[3]—more than the population of Singapore, New Zealand, Norway, and Panama combined. Globalization is not helping this situation and in some ways makes it worse.

Globalization needs to be *humanized* by values that come from the Christian faith and from the best virtues of the world's religious traditions.[4] As Tom Sine notes, "the very greed that makes the free-market economy work so brilliantly in efficiently producing goods and services . . . undermines its capacity to work justly on behalf of the poor and the marginalized. . . . The free market and free trade will never improve the lot of the marginalized unless people of faith and compassion make it happen."[5]

People of faith and compassion *can* make it happen. The church of Jesus Christ has a key role to play. And globalization provides the church with key opportunities.

## The Opportunities of Globalization

Globalization opens up many opportunities for incarnational mission. Three of these opportunities are especially crucial.

1. *The opportunity to provide worldview answers.* Globalization raises a host of worldview issues. This is a major opening for Christian mission! As globalization puts more and more people in touch with each other, it undermines the exclusive claims of every worldview. People begin to ask worldview questions in new ways. Why do some people I know see things totally differently? What is the real meaning of life? Where is the world really headed? What is the value of human life? Only the Christian faith can provide *true* and satisfying answers to these questions. This is an open door for Christian mission.

2. *The opportunity to build life-affirming Christian community.* Community building has always been the church's peculiar strength. Community is a fundamental value of the gospel, as the New Testament teachings on *koinōnia* and being "members of one another" in the body of Christ make plain.

Globalization erodes community life. As globalization spreads, therefore, community-building opportunities for Christians will grow. This plays to the church's basic strength. Community, like mission, is in the church's DNA. The challenge is to build churches that actually model the life-affirming community pictured in the Bible.[6]

Similarly, Christians have strategic opportunities to help build a more just global economic community. Christ's body has much to offer here. "One of the positive aspects of globalization," Tom Sine notes, "is that the United Nations and a number of Christian organizations are beginning to build new partnerships with corporations to enable poorer communities to participate" in significant economic growth.[7]

3. *The opportunity to evangelize and plant kingdom communities among the world's poor.* Jesus said, quoting from Isaiah, "The Spirit of the Lord is on me, because he has anointed me to preach good news to the poor. He has sent me to proclaim freedom for the prisoners and recovery of sight for the blind, to release the oppressed, to proclaim the year of the Lord's favor" (Luke 4:18–19). When at its best, the church has often taken this Jubilee announcement as its great commission. It was John Wesley's text the day he first preached to the coal miners at Bristol, England, in 1739—one of the turning points in Christian history.[8]

This is a day of unprecedented opportunity and responsibility for evangelizing globally among the poor, the oppressed, the marginalized, and the displaced of the world. Such witness means both bringing people to faith in Christ and introducing them to the virtues of justice, mercy, and truth—in other words, the realities of the kingdom of God.

## The Marks of Gospel Globalization

The church today—the *global* church that truly acknowledges Jesus Christ as Savior and Sovereign—is called to the work of gospel globalization. Gospel globalization means faithful Christian mission that confronts head-on the challenges of globalization, and does so in the spirit of Jesus and the power of the Holy Spirit. We are to be heralds and *examples* of the good news of God's kingdom. As we have seen, to evangelize in the biblical sense means to spread the good news of God's reign, God's new order for people, nations, and the entire creation. This can be done effectively only by churches that understand and live out the DNA of Christ's body.

Gospel globalization requires certain basic qualities. To fulfill this call, the church needs to exhibit the following six marks of mission.

1. *Deep grounding in God's Word.* We look at Scripture with the "new eyes" that globalization provides us. Wearing globalization glasses, we see that God has always been concerned about the whole earth. The gospel has always been for everyone everywhere. It is designed to build a new global humanity, the worldwide people of God. As noted earlier, God has always had a global plan. In Scripture, that plan is often called the kingdom of God. Paul also calls it the "economy" of God, as in Ephesians 1:10, where we read that God has a plan (*oikonomia,* economy) for the fullness of time to bring everything into proper relationship under the headship of Jesus Christ.

Perhaps we need a new "global hermeneutic"—a new way of looking at Scripture. We don't mean interpreting Scripture through the lens of economic globalization or of new ideologies. Rather, we mean immersing ourselves so deeply in Scripture that its life becomes our life, its worldview our worldview—until God's priorities and passions become our priorities and passions.

Practicing such a global hermeneutic—living daily in Scripture and in Christian community—we find that globalization was God's concern long before it was today's news. God has a plan for the nations and for his whole creation.[9] We need to see this, to immerse ourselves in it, so that we can avoid past errors, such as seeing our own nation or race or church as God's central concern. We need to hear again, over and over, God's prophetic word to Peter: "Do not call anything impure that God has made clean" (Acts 10:15). We must not let anything keep us from carrying the gospel, in all its biblical dimensions, to all who need to hear and accept it.

2. *Global awareness.* Gospel globalization also requires an expanding global consciousness. Christians need always to see the life of the church in terms of worldwide Christian witness. This means we should know what is going on in the world. Leaders in Christian mission, especially, must keep themselves informed as to the dimensions of globalization and the resulting challenges and opportunities raised for Christian mission. This has special importance for missions training programs. New missionaries should know what is going on in the world and how to interpret it from the perspective of a biblical Christian worldview. Likewise, every local church needs a sense of global mission.

We also need to cultivate a conscious sense of the worldwide church. Suffering Christians in central Africa and Christians in refugee camps in Thailand are our brothers and sisters in Christ. They are our own family; we share the same ecclesial DNA. Impoverished Christians in Haiti as well as affluent believers in Japan are our kin in Christ. We need to cultivate a vivid sense of mutual interdependence in Christ's body worldwide—a sense of what it means to be God's global family, the community of the kingdom of God.

3. *A Christian view of culture, nations, and creation.* Gospel globalization requires a Christian view of culture, nations and peoples, and the created order. Globalization forces us to think globally, and that is good. Christians *ought* to think globally. But they also need to be grounded in local Christian community, for Christ's body is both universal and local.

Here the global church has a major agenda: to develop a biblically Christian understanding of the nature of culture, to comprehend the essence of *peoplehood*, and to envision what God intends for the world he has made. This challenge includes concern for the environment—the physical earth, which is God's handiwork. God has given humanity stewardship of the earth. Christians should lead the way in caring for the environment as part of our spiritual responsibility.

The Bible provides rich resources for developing a Christian view of culture and creation. Most mission theology has paid little attention to these strands of biblical revelation. In a globalized world, this opportunity cannot be ignored. If Christians do not provide answers, the answers will come from non-Christian sources or will be understood simply in economic terms. A Christian worldview that encompasses these areas is real missionary work.[10]

4. *Reconciliation as the dominant note in mission.* Gospel globalization requires a new emphasis on *reconciliation* as the central theme in Christian missions. One of the most profound summaries of the gospel is found in 2 Corinthians 5:14–19 NRSV:

For the love of Christ urges us on, because we are convinced that one has died for all; therefore all have died. And he died for all, so that that those who live might live no longer for themselves, but for him who died and was raised for them. From now on, therefore, we regard no one from a human point of view; even though we once knew Christ from a human point of view, we know him no longer in that way. So if anyone is in Christ, there is a new creation: everything old has passed away; see, everything has become new! All this is from God, who reconciled us to himself through Christ, and has given us the ministry of reconciliation; that is, in Christ God was reconciling the world to himself, not counting their trespasses against them, and entrusting the message of reconciliation to us.

The New Testament similarly stresses reconciliation in Ephesians, Colossians, and Galatians. God has broken down the barriers between Jew and Gentile, rich and poor, slave and free, man and woman. In Christ, God broke through the barriers of race, class, and ethnicity that divide earth's people into warring camps.

The apostle Paul and his coworkers consistently gave *visible witness* to this reconciliation through cross-cultural church-planting teams and in the churches they established. Look at the multiethnic partners Paul brought together in his team—Silas, Timothy, Luke, Tychicus, Phoebe, Junia, Persis, Trophimus, Erastus, Aristarchus, not to mention Priscilla and Aquila.[11] These folks and others made up Paul's missionary network. They both *taught* the gospel of reconciliation and *lived it* in their team relationships with one another. People could *see* the body of Christ.

In a globalized world, reconciliation through Jesus Christ must be a primary—perhaps *the* primary—focus and mode of mission. Yet often this is not the case. Missiologist Wilbert Shenk notes, "The theological theme of reconciliation has never played a central role in missionary motivation and the theological rationale for missionary witness." The focus has been "on the individual's need to find peace with God and to develop a personal ethic that would support personal faith commitment." Christian missions have generally operated in a one-way *sending mode* based more on the Great Commission than on reconciliation. From the standpoint of a biblical ecclesiology, this is one-sided and misses the need for transcending and healing racial and ethnic divisions. In the Western church, mission is often also overly individualistic. Shenk observes, "Theology of mission [today] needs to be recast so as to embrace the human situation comprehensively."[12]

In other words, Christian mission focuses not only on the reconciliation of the sinner to God, but on all the biblical dimensions of reconciliation—all the ways in which God is "reconciling the world to himself." Francis Schaeffer helpfully pointed out years ago that Christian mission works to heal the four alienations or divisions resulting from the fall: alienation between humans and God, alienation from (or within) oneself, alienation between humans, and alienation from nature.[13] These are the spiritual, psychological, sociocultural, and ecological alienations that afflict the whole human family. They are all kingdom concerns. They clarify our mission agenda for the age of globalization.

5. *Kingdom evangelism.* Gospel globalization calls the church to kingdom evangelism. It requires the kind of apostolic ministry, worldwide, that genuinely seeks first God's kingdom—and extends the good news of his righteousness and justice to all the peoples of earth. Kingdom evangelism understands that in the gospel of the kingdom, there is no split between personal evangelism and social justice. Both are part of

the good news of God's reign. The gospel is global good news—good news to the whole creation and all people who inhabit it.[14]

Churches that understand the DNA of Christ's body will preach and incarnate salvation in all its biblical dimensions: healing, justice, and redemption. In the power of the Holy Spirit, sustained by prevailing prayer, the church can be God's healing force throughout the earth. People first of all need healing of their alienation from God and one another. They also need healing within families and communities as well as between ethnic groups. And the land itself needs healing (2 Chron. 7:14). The church is God's instrument for all such health. Through the church, God's Spirit can unleash a global "epidemic of healing."

Gospel globalization understands that *church planting is the front line in kingdom evangelism.* By the power of the Holy Spirit, God brings healing to his creation through the church and its obedience to the gospel of reconciliation. The logic of gospel globalization is very simple. If kingdom Christians can make a redemptive difference in the world, "letting their lights shine" and showing forth signs of the kingdom in all areas of life, then the world needs millions more of them! The world needs millions more Christians—not merely "believers" but genuine disciples of Jesus Christ, faithful citizens of God's kingdom who avoid being seduced by the dark side of globalization. And they must come from all earth's peoples, "from every tribe and language and people and nation" (Rev. 5:9).

There is only one way to avoid being seduced by the dark side of globalization, and that is through the life of genuine Christian discipleship in communities of God's reign. The church is called, through the power of the Holy Spirit, to create and nurture communities of the King.

The mandate of the gospel and of Old Testament prophecy, as well as the church's own DNA, makes it clear that the church must plant faithful Christian communities especially among the poor, the marginalized, the displaced, the oppressed, the suffering, refugees, those forgotten by the world—and especially among youth. Of all earth's population, it is the global youth culture that is most touched and shaped by globalization.

For these reasons, church planting is the number one priority of gospel globalization. But it is not enough merely to plant churches. It makes all the difference in the world—all the difference for the kingdom—what *kind* of church is planted. Genuine kingdom communities are called for, churches founded on Jesus Christ, empowered by the Holy Spirit, and filled with the gifts and fruit of the Spirit. They must be kingdom communities that are learning how to avoid the acids of quantification, materialism, and commodification by being solidly grounded in Scripture. And they need to learn from the best examples in the history of Christian mission to avoid the mistakes of the past.

Here is a significant ecclesiological agenda. We must examine the church's DNA from both a global and a local perspective, using the resources of Scripture and Christian history. Effective Christian mission requires a biblical understanding of the church. Rather than importing from the United States or Korea or elsewhere the models of the church that get the most media attention, the church should learn from places where local bodies of believers are quietly rebuilding society through genuine kingdom communities. Doug McConnell, International Director of Pioneers, says that one of the most pressing challenges facing frontier mission church planting today is "the critical need . . . to develop an ecclesiology. We are church planters but in some cases do not understand what a church is, either theologically" or in practice.[15]

We can learn much from the New Testament church. Look at the apostle Paul's church-planting methods. Normally he did not evangelize alone. He formed intercultural, interethnic teams. The church today can follow his example. Perhaps we have overlooked one of the most important and amazing aspects of New Testament missionary endeavor— the formation of interethnic teams to plant churches that visibly embody the gospel of reconciliation.

Wilbert Shenk argues that in a globalized world, we can no longer rely solely on "*monocultural* missionary teams as the primary model. In a world of manifold inter-civilizational conflicts, missionary teams ought to be intentional embodiments of the gospel that reconciles, heals, and restores across racial, denominational, and national lines." Shenk suggests that the dominant model of mission today "must be replaced with one based on strategic alliances and partnerships in mission, the heart of which is inter-civilizational teams commissioned to live and to proclaim that reconciling gospel that transforms enemies into friends."[16]

Fortunately, this is happening! Some missions organizations now employ intercultural and interethnic teams, even though this is difficult. Youth With A Mission (YWAM) has pioneered in such international, intercultural teams. Cooperation and partnership in global missions is increasing, especially in frontier church planting. Phil Butler, International Director of Interdev, cites the emergence today of "a completely new missions/evangelism infrastructure" in frontier missions. The key is partnership that demonstrates "God's people *can* work together over extended periods of time and with extraordinary results."[17]

Church planting based on the gospel of reconciliation that builds reconciled and reconciling communities of genuine disciples committed to the kingdom of God—here is good news! And here is an exciting agenda for Christian missions in the twenty-first century.

Billions of people the world over are being drawn into the web of globalization. They are being persuaded that their needs and deepest longings can be met by electronics, entertainment, or designer clothing—or by high-paying jobs in the high-tech industry. But this is a lie. Only Jesus Christ can satisfy the deepest longings of the human heart and the highest aspirations of culture. Only Christ's body offers community that transforms society and brings cultural and environmental healing. If we commit ourselves unreservedly to Jesus Christ, the Lord of history, and give ourselves fully to his mission in the world, we can make our own timely, unique contribution to that day when every knee will bow and every tongue confess Jesus Christ as Lord, to the glory of the Father.

6. *Tempering zeal with meekness.* Finally, gospel globalization means tempering zeal with meekness. Historically, the Christian mission has been carried out with admirable zeal. But zeal has sometimes hurt, raising barriers as non-Christians saw this zeal as arrogance or impatience. Zeal, often mixed with a failure to listen, sometimes overweighs wisdom.

For this reason, zeal must be tempered by another primary biblical virtue: meekness. Moses, one of the greatest leaders and missionaries for God, showed above all the virtue of meekness (Num. 12:3). Daniel, throughout his career as advisor to some of history's most powerful kings, had a flawless reputation marked by humility and meekness. Meekness is winsome almost everywhere in the world and is especially needed in the many cross-cultural places where the church is called into mission.

An effective tentmaker missionary in Malaysia, an American who has adapted deeply to Asian culture, cites an example of the importance of meekness. His ministry is primarily among Muslims. At one point a zealous Korean missionary joined his team, a young woman devoted to mission work and keenly focused on Muslim evangelism. The young woman befriended a Muslim lady and began to build a friendship. But after only a few weeks, the missionary aggressively urged her Muslim friend to accept Jesus Christ as Savior. The woman was offended and stopped coming for visits.

When the same thing happened a second time, the senior missionary helped this young zealot understand that while her zeal was admirable, she would never win Muslim women to Christ unless she had more patience and demonstrated meekness.[18]

Partly, the issue here is one of culture. Whatever other virtues they have, Americans and some other nationalities are not famous for meekness! Aggressiveness, zeal, making one's own way, and a "can-do" attitude are celebrated. Meekness is seen as weakness. Yet other cultures celebrate meekness as proof of strength and maturity.

A good example is the Thai culture. Some years ago, a Christian couple from Thailand, Ubolwan and Nantachai Mejudhon, entered Asbury Theological Seminary as doctoral students. Both had been Buddhists, and their courtship, marriage, and conversion to Christ make a fascinating story. Ubolwan and Nantachai embody the Thai value of meekness, deepening and expanding its meaning by their Christian commitment and the deep work of the Holy Spirit in their lives. Today they are effective Christian leaders in Thailand.

While at Asbury Seminary, Ubolwan and Nantachai decided to focus their doctoral research on the virtue of meekness. Supplementing their own experience by in-depth study, they showed the vital role of meekness in evangelism. For Westerners, reading their dissertations is a wake-up call. They show how most of us really do not value, or even understand, the profound biblical teaching on meekness.[19]

If the church wishes to engage effectively in gospel globalization, it will have to learn to temper its zeal for the gospel with the meekness of Jesus Christ. Meekness is part of the church's genetic inheritance from Christ (Matt. 5:5; 2 Cor. 10:1).

The body of Christ faces an unprecedented challenge as global society becomes increasingly linked. Yet, as we have seen, the church has unusual and powerful resources for meeting this challenge.

The church's greatest resource, however, is not its cleverness or strategy or history or even its numerical strength. The church's greatest resource is its genetic endowment from Jesus Christ—what it is in fact, and what it can be through the power of the Holy Spirit.

In our final chapter, we will turn from the challenges of globalization and cultural change to the day-to-day life of the church that is Christ's body. The point in decoding the church is not theory; it is life. Because the church has a certain kind of DNA, it lives a certain kind of life. We turn, then, to the life of the church, not only in its internal dynamics but also in its public discipleship.

---

## Heartland Discovers Gospel Globalization

Pastor Dorset liked to keep track of the church's statistics; they gave him a quick reading on how the church was doing. He watched not only the Sunday worship stats but also reports on the number and kinds of small groups and group attendance. He was interested even in the amount of food distributed through the church's food pantry. And of course he watched the financial picture carefully. These data were vital signs, he felt, of how Heartland Christian Fellowship was doing.

Darrell Dorset had long since learned, however, that such numbers are only *signs* of deeper realities. If he went to the doctor with a high temperature, for example, reducing the fever wasn't the doctor's only concern; he needed to examine the patient's overall health and find the deeper cause.

One thing Pastor Dorset and his key leaders especially watched was how much of the church's income stayed within the church and how much went to ministry in the neighborhood, the city, and the world. He was convinced that the growing proportion of the church's finances being spent in ministry and mission was a sign of health. Three years ago Heartland passed a key milestone, he felt, when for the first time more than half of its budget went to ministry beyond itself. And that large slice continued to grow. "It's a little like a person who is overweight shedding excess pounds," he had been heard to say.

Pastor Dorset focused especially on the vitality and genuineness of Heartland's worship, its internal community life, and its witness in the world. He always tried to understand what was happening in these three basic areas and how each impacted the others. Most of all, he worked and hoped and prayed that Heartland was "in all things grow[ing] up into" Jesus Christ, the head of the church, and "attaining to the whole measure of the fullness of Christ" (Eph. 4:15, 13). He now understood that this is what "edification" meant.

Darrell Dorset had a much clearer sense of priorities now than when he first came to Heartland eleven years ago. He had a better feel for what was primary and what was secondary. This sense of priorities brought him safely through three incidents that could have derailed Heartland Christian Fellowship.

First was the television program. Heartland Christian Fellowship had become well known in Johnson Center not only because of its growth but also through its broad range of ministries in the community. One day a representative of a local TV station called the church and asked for an appointment. Pastor Dorset met with the man and heard him out.

"We think you ought to put your church on TV," the man said. "We have a good slot open. You could broadcast your Sunday service, or maybe do some other kind of program. Think about it."

Pastor Dorset did think about it. In fact, he and his team of leaders studied the matter carefully. They looked at the cost, the equipment that would be necessary, the people it would take—everything they could think of.

In the end, Heartland decided against the TV program. "Maybe this is the right thing for some churches," he told the station representative, "but not for us, at least not now."

Heartland could have afforded the program financially. It had the resources. But Pastor Dorset gave the TV rep several reasons for the church's "No" decision. First, the church felt the money could be better spent elsewhere, especially in ministries to the poor—who probably wouldn't be much served by the TV program anyhow. Pastor Dorset was also concerned that the lion's share of the funds spent for TV would simply help sustain the station's business. It would boost their bottom line more than it would be a witness.

Also, Pastor Dorset was afraid the TV production would be an intrusion that would subtly affect the quality of the church's worship celebration. He was thinking not just of the cameras and staffing but also of the informal, sometimes unpredictable nature of Heartland's worship time. He didn't want to be under time pressure in his preaching or to cut short the moving of the Spirit during sharing and prayer times just to fit a program time frame. Darrell knew some of these problems could be solved by editing and broadcasting at a later time, but he didn't want to get into that.

Pastor Dorset had a more basic reason for declining the station's offer, however. "Our church is not a product we're trying to sell," he told the TV representative. "I don't think there's much of Jesus' call to discipleship that we could communicate over TV. Besides, you're already broadcasting three church programs. You don't need another one."

"But the program can help build your church," the TV rep said. "It's a great form of advertising."

Pastor Dorset responded, "We're really not much interested in advertising. We're doing fine by word of mouth. TV would give a false image of who we are." Ironically, this story got out, and a competing station ran a story about the church that "didn't need a TV program"!

The second incident that could have tripped up Heartland Christian Fellowship was a chance to buy a thirty-acre piece of property north of town, close to the bypass. It was prime property near a major interchange, with easy access. The price was right. But the church turned down the opportunity. There were several reasons, but the basic one, again, was mission related. "We have so many ministries going right here in our neighborhood," Pastor Dorset said. "We don't want to give them up, and we don't want to be a drive-in ministry. I've seen too many churches leave their neighborhoods behind and turn into religious shopping malls for middle-class professionals. I don't want that to happen to us." Pastor Dorset was thinking especially of a large going-and-growing church in another city. It once had a lively interracial, economically mixed congregation near the center of town. But then it had moved twelve miles away. The poorer folks from the old neighborhood, of course, couldn't or wouldn't commute that far. The congregation was no longer interracial or as mixed as it used to be.

So Heartland Christian Fellowship decided to stay put. Thinking about the decision later, Pastor Dorset said to himself, *I can't believe I'm reacting this way. Five years ago I would have jumped at the chance to buy this piece of land!*

This was not a decision against growth, but a decision for the kingdom of God. Heartland continued to grow, but in different ways. It was able to start three new congregations in the Johnson Center area, including one right downtown at a large apartment complex.

The third incident began with a letter Pastor Dorset received one day from an international missions organization that Heartland Christian Fellowship worked with. The mission wanted him to come and work with them full-time as a pastor to pastors and missionaries.

Pastor Dorset was shocked. He never expected such an offer. He and Beth thought and prayed about it, and he asked his key leaders for their prayer and advice. Was this God's call? If so, he was ready. He could see himself in this role; it would be a great opportunity.

But once again, Pastor Dorset said no. As he thought and prayed about it, God spoke very clearly to him. He had what amounted to a vision of churches being planted all over the world, among all the world's people groups, and of Heartland Christian Fellowship helping with that. He thought about all he had learned through Heartland's partnership with five or six different missions organizations and with groups like Habitat for Humanity.

*My heart is at Heartland,* he found himself saying, to himself and to God. Heartland Christian Fellowship had only begun to fulfill its global mission. Perhaps the time would come for him to go elsewhere, but not yet.

Pastor Dorset thought about the approaching World Mission Celebration, when the congregation would hear reports from around the globe and would commission seven of its own people to serve with several missions organizations in different countries.

A couple of days later, Pastor Dorset got confirmation that he had made the right decision. Bill Silver called. "I just had to talk to you," Bill said. "You know how God has been talking to us recently? Well, I've decided to take a leave from the high school. Angie and I are going to give a year or two to Youth With A Mission! What do you think of that?"

"Great!" Darrell Dorset replied. "You go. I'm going to stay right here!"

# Questions
## for Group Discussion or Personal Reflection

1. During your lifetime, have any parts of your life become a "commodity"?
2. Do you see commercialization or commodification shaping your church, job, or community in any way?
3. How wide is the reach of your church? Does it extend ten miles? Five hundred miles? Ten thousand miles?
4. How deep is the reach of your church? Does it touch the very poor? Does it cross ethnic divisions?
5. When is the last time your church planted a daughter church? What would it take to do so now?
6. Do you think Pastor Dorset and the Heartland church made the right decisions in the three incidents related? Why?
7. What aspects of "gospel globalization" did Heartland Christian Fellowship encounter? How did it deal with them?
8. What aspects or dynamics of globalization discussed in this chapter are *not* illustrated here in the experience of Heartland Christian Fellowship? How might the church respond to these?
9. In what ways is Heartland Christian Fellowship now demonstrating more fully the marks of the church, or more faithfully embodying the church's true DNA?

# 12

---

# THE DNA OF PUBLIC DISCIPLESHIP

Called on the carpet before King Agrippa, the apostle Paul said: "The king is familiar with these things, . . . none of this has escaped his notice, because it was not done in a corner" (Acts 26:26).

The DNA of the church thrusts Christians into the public square. The gospel calls us to public discipleship—beyond either/or Christianity.

In this final chapter, we will explore some dimensions of the church's public discipleship. Since we are using genetic and ecological models, we know that Christian living is both private and public, both internal and external, both material and spiritual. We know that Christ's body is very much in the world and yet not of the world.

We will examine several dimensions of the church's life that bridge the either/or divides that often infect the church and shape public perception of what the church is, what it does, and what it should be. The treatment here is illustrative, not comprehensive. Public discipleship is broader than the specific examples presented in this chapter. But these examples suggest a direction for, and the nature of, public discipleship that is consistent with the church's DNA.

## Grace and Love

Grace and love are two of the most common words in the Bible. "May the grace of the Lord Jesus Christ, and the love of God, and the fellowship of the Holy Spirit be with you all" Paul prayed in 2 Corinthians 13:14. He testified, "The grace of our Lord was poured out on me abundantly, along with the faith and love that are in Christ Jesus" (1 Tim. 1:14). Paul commended the Corinthian church because, he said, you "excel . . . in your love for us," and he urged it to excel also "in [the] grace of giving" (2 Cor. 8:7).

Clearly, grace and love are central ecclesial virtues. By God's love and grace the church is born. By the Holy Spirit, the church grows in love and grace—both in its internal life and in its public discipleship.

### Speaking Words of Grace

Why do New Testament instructions to the church constantly stress speech—how Christians should talk to each other? Much of the book of James is devoted to this, and the apostle Paul mentions it repeatedly. His words in Ephesians 4:29 are typical: "Do not let any unwholesome talk come out of your mouths, but only what is helpful for building others up according to their needs, that it may benefit those who listen." The church in its speech is to mirror God's grace. Why? First, because to do so reflects the character of God himself. But also because Christian relationships are the laboratory for Christian life in society—public discipleship.

One of the greatest privileges God has given us is speaking words of grace to one another. Words that become channels of God's love and mercy; that help rather than hurt; that bring healing and soothe upset spirits and troubled relationships.

Christians often wound one another because they speak out of frustration, confusion, or their own hurt. But as Christ's body, we can also speak words of grace. Our words can show that we understand others' pain—or if we don't understand, at least we want God's best for the other and want somehow to be an instrument of God's love.

One of the wonderful things about speech is that if we *do not* speak words of grace—if we speak words that wound or confuse—we can *then* speak words of amazing grace by asking forgiveness. In doing so, we show that, at a level deeper than our own hurt and frustration, we really do love and *want* to love the other—whether the other be spouse, child, parent, friend, supervisor, employee, or some brother or sister in Christ. Sometimes the most powerful words of grace come after words of ungrace. The one who receives words of grace can see that it is God at work in the speech, not (this time!) our own self-centeredness and self-preoccupation.

The power of speaking gracious words is that it doesn't require special times or occasions. Quite the opposite! Often the most gracious, attitude-changing words are those spoken in the daily push and pull of life, in those chance conversations or routine interactions that form the quick-setting mortar of our lives and relationships. This is what makes Jesus' life so attractive. Amazingly, he knew how to speak words of grace in day-to-day, seemingly chance interactions with people. Oh, that we might be more like Jesus!

A profound teaching of Scripture is that we *can*, by God's grace, speak words of grace. God can help us; he can grace us. We do not *have* to speak words of ungrace or *continue* speaking graceless words. Jesus can speak through us. He will and does speak through us—in proportion to our frequency of speaking with him and listening to him through the Spirit and the Word.

Speaking words of grace creates communities of love, openness, and creativity. It clears the way for the Spirit to do even greater things among us, bringing forth the full range of the fruit of the Spirit.

Graciousness in the Christian community does not mean there is no place for confrontation or for prophetic denunciation in society. Public discipleship can be tough, even as it is gracious. But grace clarifies the vision of the church. It helps the church distinguish between what are central kingdom concerns and what are merely minor peeves or frustrations, or perhaps even masked self-interest. The kingdom of God is a kingdom of grace as well as of justice.

## Living Lives of Love

In the body of Christ, speaking words of grace helps us live lives of love. It helps us create communities of love so that the church, as a contrast society, holds up before the world the true character of God's reign that is coming and is to come.

We are speaking here of genuine, godly love—not sentimental or self-serving love, the kind of "love" so common in today's world. We are to love as Jesus loved. "We love because he first loved us" (1 John 4:19). People talk easily about "unconditional love," as if this were the greatest, highest, noblest form of love. But is real love ever unconditional? Or is this a phrase that sounds good but really deceives? Does God love unconditionally? Is unconditional love, in fact, psychologically possible? At a fundamental level, these questions may be one, since our capacity to love is part of God's image in us.

This question of what love really is actually touches the heart of society's moral and ethical confusion. The world is adrift because it has forgotten who God is and the deep nature of his love. Modern ideas of love focus on emotion rather than character and on shifting feelings rather than considered commitment. We go astray ethically when we measure love by fallen, self-centered human notions and emotions instead of by God's character as revealed in Jesus Christ. Humanity will continue to drift unless it again grasps what God's love is—what it requires and costs.

Everyone likes the idea of unconditional love, no doubt. It must be the loftiest kind of love, something like the romantic cliché "endless love." But does unconditional love even make sense? Not without some clarification. Consider the following three cases.

A mother is having a test of wills with her two-year-old son. The young boy wants to continue playing with his toys, but it's time for bath and bed. Mom has already given him a five-minute grace period after his first howling protests. Now she insists he do as she says. She is not being unloving; her firmness is an expression of her concern for his well-being. Of course, the child doesn't see it that way. Or he doesn't care. He simply wants his own way. If he could speak his feelings, he would probably say, "If you really loved me, you'd let me do what I want!"

As adults, we have little problem identifying with Mom here. We understand a child's immaturity. Mom really is expressing love. But is it *unconditional* love? Perhaps, in the sense that she will continue loving her son even if he disobeys (at least if she is a psychologically healthy mother). But no, it is not unconditional love in a deeper sense, because love requires conditions in order to be fully expressed.

A more difficult case is that of Dick and Jane, who have been married for almost twenty years. (Forgive their names; their parents were reared in the forties.) Overall, their marriage has been a good one, and they have three healthy children. But problems have sprouted in the past couple of years. And now Jane has discovered that her husband has committed adultery.

Dick wants to continue the adulterous affair. He also wants his wife to accept it, like an up-to-date, sensible person, and let the marriage continue. What does real love mean for Jane in this situation? If she really loves him—*unconditionally*—won't she accept her husband on his terms, as an expression of her love? Or does genuine love require Jane to say, in effect, "Either I go or she goes." Sometimes (maybe always), genuine love requires conditions and choices. Otherwise, it is either cheap love or thwarted love.

Now we come to the third and ultimate case. The love of God, "greater far than tongue or pen can ever tell." Human love may fail, but surely God's love is unconditional, right?

But let's consider this. God created man and woman and put them in the Garden. He placed conditions there from the start: "You are free to . . . , but you must not . . ." (Gen. 2:16–17). Conditions run throughout Scripture, in fact. And the logic of this kind of responsible love under-girds the whole meaning of Jesus' coming, death, and resurrection.

If God's love were unconditional, the cross would be unnecessary. In this sense, God does not love unconditionally. He loved so much that he sent his Son. And he loves so much that he will not, *cannot*, forgive and accept us as his redeemed children except on the basis of Jesus' sacrifice. To do otherwise would betray the integrity of God's own character. Precisely for this reason, acceptance without cost or sacrifice would betray the essential nature of love itself. The cross is the ultimate proof that true love is never unconditional, because love always seeks to reconcile and to build a relationship.

Conditional love also underlies the interrelationships of the three Persons of the Trinity. Here we are talking of the most fundamental reality and mystery, and the deepest foundation of the church. Father, Son, and Holy Spirit love each other unreservedly and without limit, but not unconditionally. The condition of their mutual love is their mutual submission and self-giving. This is the most profound, most glorious, and most hopeful reality in the universe. In fact, it defines love.

True love is impossible without the potential for freely given response. Therefore, truly unconditional love, in its fullest sense, is impossible. This is because love is all about personal relationship and reciprocity. Genuine love is a relationship of mutuality between or among "sovereign" persons—"sovereign" in the sense that if love is compelled, it ceases to be love. Churches experience this when they move from evangelism to discipleship.

If God loved unconditionally, he would forgive and accept every person unconditionally (as many assume he does). No cross, either for Jesus or for us. But then the Christian message would be logically incoherent and psychologically unsound. It would be as shallow as the love of a person who always accepts another's behavior, no matter how offensive or destructive, without ever calling him or her to account. Ultimately, such "love" undermines genuine community, whether in the home or in the church.

Why doesn't God simply accept people (sinners) on the basis of Jesus' sacrifice, regardless of their response? Again, the answer lies in the nature of love itself. Without repentance, faith, and discipleship, a woman or man is not morally and psychologically capable of experiencing God's love in its redemptive and transforming power. Without such a response, what a person feels in relation to God is something less than God's love. It may be relief, psychological peace, or even a (false) sense of security. But it is not God's transforming love and, therefore, not salvation. If this is believed to be salvation, it is a deception.

God's love is conditional, not because God is a tyrant but because God is love. If God loved unconditionally, he would be less than God. Given the nature of personhood, conditional love is in this sense a moral and psychological necessity. It is grounded, however, not in psychology but in God's character as demonstrated in his acts in history. This provides the foundation for the church's love and grace.

Many people, probably even many Christians, think God's love is unconditional. Many have bought the sentiment of the popular song of the fifties, "He": "Though it makes him sad to see the way we live, he'll always say, 'I forgive.'" This is fuzzy romanticism and cheap grace, not the good news of Jesus Christ.

If Jesus' cross was necessary, then so is ours. To rely on God's "unconditional love" apart from Jesus Christ and apart from personal faith and discipleship is to trust in myth or mushy sentiment. The Good News is that God's love in Jesus Christ forgives, transforms, and empowers for righteous, compassionate living. The essential conditions of God's love are two: Jesus' death on the cross (costly grace) and our exercise of self-committing trust (genuine faith).

Apart from God's grace, we can do nothing to save ourselves. Our works can never save us (Titus 3:5). But this does not mean salvation is unconditional. Jesus shows us the true nature of love—and its breathtaking cost.

God *extends* his love unconditionally, no doubt. But the reception and fulfillment of that love has a condition: a response of repentance and faith that issues in a relationship of love.[1]

So it is also with the church. Christ's body is to be a community of loving discipleship. While it speaks words of grace, it also builds interrelationships of tough love—so that the character of Jesus Christ, the fruit of the Spirit, can grow in the community. This also is the DNA of Christ's body.

The effectiveness of the church's public discipleship is a reflection of its internal life—its graciousness, its costly love, and its commitment to God's reign in the world. Love and grace are the root; public discipleship is the fruit.

## Economic Justice

Since the church is called to inward and outward holiness—private and public discipleship—it is concerned with what goes on in economic life. Throughout church history, all the great reformers have addressed economic issues, from John Chrysostom and Francis of Assisi, John

Calvin and John Wesley, to Martin Luther King Jr., Tony Campolo, and Mother Teresa. In the matter of economic justice, we have the key precedents of Jesus Christ and the Old Testament prophets, who continually spoke about economic justice.

This is a really a matter of both private and public discipleship. How we value things, how we spend our money, and how we fit into the commercial-economic system touches every area of our lives. Economics is a spiritual issue because it is all about relative value.

But what about economic *systems?* Are they a gospel concern, or part of Christian mission? Throughout the centuries, the question has been hotly debated. Some have pointed out that Jesus spoke much about economics and that justice—including economic justice—is a basic concern of the biblical teachings about God's reign. Others have said that the Bible does not detail an economic system, but that free enterprise capitalism is the system most compatible with the Christian faith because of its emphasis on freedom and individual initiative. Some have even said that the Bible *teaches* capitalism or socialism!

Today capitalism seems to be triumphing globally. But that does not mean it should be exempt from Christian critique. Just the opposite. This is precisely the time to raise issues of economic justice as part of Christian public discipleship.

Capitalism arose with the decline of the Middle Ages, the growth of cities in Europe, and the Industrial Revolution. It was given classic expression in Adam Smith's influential book, *The Wealth of Nations*, first published in England in 1776.[2]

For two centuries, much of the debate in the West regarding economic systems has been between capitalism (in its various forms) and socialism (in its various forms). This was a debate within Western culture but also globally. It has also been a debate within the church. With the collapse of the Soviet Union, some have argued that this long debate has ended. Democratic capitalism has won.

While that judgment may be premature, it is clear that capitalism does have a powerful inherent dynamic. It shapes the lives of people and societies, increasingly so today through the process of globalization. That is precisely why it is an issue of public discipleship.

Capitalism as a system may be either humane or inhumane. Consider the situation today in Eastern Europe and Russia especially. The conflict between democratic capitalism and state-controlled socialism, at least in its Communist forms, is stark. Communism has collapsed and viable capitalism is struggling to be born. What are the alternatives? Some argue for democratic socialism, or for Confucian government-regulated capitalism (Singapore), or for an Islamic economic system.

Christians should ask, however, how and whether the energies of democratic capitalism can be harnessed for greater economic justice for all, since economic justice is a clear priority of the kingdom of God.[3] Capitalism is not *automatically* good or a blessing. This is abundantly clear from history. The actual effects of capitalism depend on other factors. Capitalism can be very inhumane, as eighteenth-century England and nineteenth-century America show.

A key question of public discipleship is, What *humanizes* capitalism? What makes it beneficial *to all*, not just to some? What makes it just and equitable, and thus consistent with the gospel?

This is a large issue that can't be dealt with in depth here. However, as a discipleship issue, it has practical meaning for local churches. Three things are needed to humanize the economic system locally and globally, and these are all issues of public discipleship:

1. *A sense of corporate responsibility and solidarity.* This is a matter of culture and community—how a society understands itself. For capitalism to be humane, society must have a sense of community; of mutual responsibility and care that serves as a check on individualism and greed. This must saturate the business world, the economic zone. Businesses are not exempt from social and ecological responsibility or from community solidarity. In fact, some cutting-edge businesses are aware of this and have taken the lead in economic fairness. They know that what is good for society and for the environment can also be good business practice.

These issues are matters of public discipleship for Christians who work in business or government. They are the church's concern as it disciples its members to know how to participate in society in a Christlike manner.

2. *Some regulation by government* generally is necessary to provide appropriate checks and balances. Greed and the profit motive (often the same thing, though not necessarily), can make capitalism very mean and exploitive.

The history of the United States in the 1880s and 1890s is a fascinating case in point. American industry was growing rapidly but was exploiting workers and, indirectly, farmers. A growing national conscience, the Populist movement, state and federal legislation, and the rise of the labor movement worked powerfully to humanize capitalism and its effects.[4]

Government has an *inescapable* role if capitalism is to be humane. The role of government to secure the general welfare requires significant limitations on capitalism. This is necessary in order to safeguard and ensure a just, equitable society and maintain balance between competing interests. From a biblical standpoint, this means a particular concern for the poor, the oppressed, and the marginalized—which is part of the very DNA of the church. Christians therefore should support government policies tht hold businesses accountable.

3. *A search for and commitment to more cooperative forms of capitalism.* There is still a "great economic debate."[5] Capitalism has various forms and can take various shapes. We do not yet know the full range of economic possibilities or, perhaps, of how the advantages and energies of capitalism might be combined with other economic forms.

Emerging global society urgently needs to further explore and study alternative forms of capitalism that involve more cooperative or shared ownership, joint state-private ventures, profit-sharing, and so forth. There are already many examples of such alternative forms in the world that should be studied. The church, as part of its public discipleship, can play a key role in this great economic debate because it brings to the table a unique perspective. It is concerned not with its own self-interest, but with the well-being of people everywhere—especially the poor, the oppressed, and the displaced.

Global society, and each nation individually, needs forms of economic organization that

- harness the power of capitalism, especially entrepreneurship and investment,
- have a lively sense of corporate social responsibility, and
- take into consideration environmental costs, working with rather than against the environment.[6]

The church has a key public discipleship role to play here. In the first place, some inevitable positive consequences seem to flow, normally, from the very existence of the church because of the moral and ethical values that Christianity introduces. But we need intentional action by Christians, especially with regard to the three items above: building a sense of mutually responsible, humane community; working for just legislation; and contributing to the economic debate about just and workable economic alternatives.

Capitalism is not "Christian economics." No one economic system is taught or endorsed in Scripture, though Scripture does reveal the fundamental moral, ethical, and ecological realities that must undergird any economic system.

Probably no one economic system is "right" for all times and places. Like genetics, economics depends on a complex range of factors, including the nature of the physical environment (climate, food supply, and available natural resources), the particular culture and its history, and relationships between cultures. Yet emerging global society may eventually arrive at some hybrid form of economics that becomes the dominant world system. The problem is that this could take either a just, humane, and democratic form or be unjust, exploitive, and totalitarian.

Capitalism has great power for both good and evil. As a system (not just the individual persons who manage and work within it), free-market capitalism must be Christianized. It must be humanized so that everyone's life is livable, with adequate economic opportunity. What Paul says about economics in the church is not a prescription for society, yet it does say something about the economics of the kingdom of God: "Our desire is . . . that there might be equality. At the present time your plenty will supply what they need, so that in turn their plenty will supply what you need. Then there will be equality, as it is written: 'He who gathered much did not have too much, and he who gathered little did not have too little'" (2 Cor. 8:13–15).

Humanizing capitalism is an issue of public discipleship. Churches that understand their DNA will readily see that this is true. Here is a role for the church as it sees itself existing not just for itself, but for God's reign.

## Responsible Earthkeeping

Economics and ecology really can't be divorced. Global warming and other environmental concerns are gradually driving this truth into the consciousness of societies, governments, and businesses worldwide.

In the United States, opinion polls show that the public generally favors taking care of the environment, even at a cost. A *USA Today* poll found most Americans agree with the statement, "Because God created the world, it's wrong to abuse it."

Happily, a growing number of Christians are putting feet to that sentiment. Their reasoning: God made the world, pronounced it good, and told us to care for it. God doesn't make junk, so we shouldn't junk the earth.

Evangelical Christians, among others, are becoming involved. Within the church, examples of environmental concern are not hard to find. The work of the Evangelical Environmental Network (EEN) and its magazine *Creation Care* is a case in point.[7] Ecological issues are often addressed also in the magazines *Sojourners* and *Prism,* the latter published by Evangelicals for Social Action.

For years World Vision International has built environment stewardship into its development ministry. In the Ansokia Valley in Ethiopia, a place ravaged by famine in the mid-1980s, World Vision has made a difference. Working with local residents, World Vision planted millions of trees for food and fuel and to stabilize the soil. The organization also pioneered drought-resistant crops and increased basic literacy. Now the Ansokia Valley is green and exports food to other regions. World Vision is demonstrating that the best humanitarian aid is ecologically sensitive.

Michigan's Au Sable Institute, begun by a small group of Christian biologists, is another example. Through its publications, seminars, and conferences, the institute has done cutting-edge work in Christian environmental concern for two decades.

Some Christian colleges have hired environmentally conscious administrators to help with energy conservation. Christian publishers are increasingly using recycled and environmentally safe paper and are recycling their wastes. For years Christians in inner-city churches have worked together in community gardens, neighborhood clean-up and recycling projects, and similar ministries that show practical concern for the environment. One might wonder how many of today's ecologists and environmentalists are quietly working out of a deep sense of Christian conviction.

These projects are all examples of public discipleship. They are consistent with the church's essential DNA. Today many Christians are practicing biblical stewardship of creation, showing that love for God and others extends to the care of what God has made.

Granted, environmental concern is hardly universal among Christians. Many politically conservative believers are put off by any mention of ecology or environmental issues. Some Christians still think that ecology is a purely secular concern. Some even see environmentalists as secular humanists or New Age conspirators. They deeply distrust the environmental movement. This fear need not block constructive action, however. From a Christian standpoint, the question is not the motives or politics of others who are concerned about the environment, but where a biblically informed and Jesus-motivated compassion leads us. As in other areas (family values, pro-life activism), Christians can make common cause with others on specific issues even while approaching these issues from very different assumptions or even worldviews.

Unfortunately, many North American Christians feel that ecology is of no deep concern to God. The physical world is of little value compared to the human soul. If the whole universe is to burn in a cosmic holocaust, why should we waste time trying to clean it up? In reply, Christian environmentalists cite a range of reasons for creation care, from the aesthetic to the economic and purely pragmatic. The deepest reason, however, is this: "The earth is the LORD's, and everything in it, the world, and all who live in it" (Ps. 24:1).

Nothing in the New Testament suggests that God's concern for creation was canceled by the coming of Christ. The opposite is true. In the risen Jesus Christ we see the firstfruits of a renewed creation, the promise of creation restored. So we seek God's help in being earthkeepers today as part of eyes-wide-open public discipleship.

Discipleship in this area can be expressed in specific practices. Here are some things Christians can do to show that we know the earth is more than a garbage dump:

1. We can teach our children a *biblical* perspective of the environment. This means avoiding both extremes: purely secular environmentalism, or nonbiblical overspiritualizing that undercuts responsible earth stewardship.

2. We can read up on the environment. A number of books and other publications by Christian writers and scientists are now available on this topic.[8]

3. As the body of Christ, we can demonstrate concern for God's creation. Christian churches are major holders of real estate, most of which is untaxed. These pieces of the environment should be demonstration plots for concern about God's world. Churches and Christian organizations should understand the ecology of the land they control. Their properties—from church lawns to college campuses—can bear public witness to the reconciling gospel of Jesus Christ.

4. We can recycle. Here good economics and good ecology meet. A few of us still remember our parents recycling tin cans and tires for the war effort during World War II. If patriotic wartime Christians could do that, certainly Jesus' disciples today can recycle our abundance of consumer trash, demonstrating a global patriotism that is really allegiance to the kingdom of God.

The goodness of God's creation, growing public support for earthcare, and Christians who are showing the way in the stewardship of the garden God has given us are things to celebrate. But the task has only begun. Public discipleship can have a yet much greater impact in leading the way in responsible earthkeeping.

## Praying for Kings and Presidents

The DNA of the church is comprehensive. That is, it involves all the church is and all it is called to be—whether in the home, the neighborhood, the Christian community or in economics, politics, and the environment. One theme of this book is that we must allow no either/or split between the inward and outward life of the church, between public and private discipleship.

This is true especially when it comes to the most fundamental and most important behavior of Christ's body around the world: prayer.

Training his young helper Timothy for pastoral ministry, the apostle Paul gave him specific instructions about prayer—instructions that nicely wed the private and public spheres. Churches, Paul taught, should offer up "requests, prayers, intercession and thanksgiving . . . for every-one—for kings and all those in authority, that we may live peaceful and quiet lives in all godliness and holiness" (1 Tim. 2:1–2). Presumably Paul meant Caesar and all other rulers. Writing today we would mention people like presidents Bush, Putin, and Fox, among others. We are to pray for all those in authority, whether they acknowledge that they serve under God's sovereignty or not.

Does the church obey God's Word here? A few years ago, while a different U.S. president was in office, when this verse was mentioned to a godly sister in the church she said, "Around here we don't pray *for* the President. We pray *against* him!" She meant this as a mild reproof to the church.

We should take Scriptures such as 1 Timothy 2:1–2 seriously as a part of our public discipleship—not only because this is God's Word but because prayer is a crucial way of entering into the work of God's kingdom. Such prayer keeps the church *constantly* bridging the public-private gap that often undercuts the church's public discipleship.

Whether the church is aware of it or not, it has a rich heritage of concern for the great moral, social, and political issues of the day. Abolition of slavery and the slave trade, widespread availability of health care, child labor laws, and many other reforms were the fruit of Christian public discipleship. Today, as in the past, Christians may differ greatly in their views on particular social issues, but they should all agree on one thing: our responsibility to pray for God to act in the affairs of nations and peoples and to move the world in the direction of the justice, mercy, and truth of God's reign.

## Priorities in Prayer

What should Christians pray for? What are proper prayer priorities? In a word, everything. But biblical injunctions highlight three special priorities: *the evangelization of the world, the renewal of the church*, and *God's will to be done on earth* in every area of life and culture.

The church should pray for the evangelization of the world because Jesus Christ came into the world to save all who will turn to him. Christians enter into that work through prayer. Paul reminded Timothy that God "wants everyone to be saved and to come to a knowledge of the truth" (1 Tim. 2:4). We should pray for the renewal of the church because God has placed the church on earth to continue and extend the work Jesus began. It can do this faithfully only as the Holy Spirit continuously or repeatedly renews the church. We should pray for God's will to be done on earth because Jesus specifically told us to and because this is part of "seeking first the kingdom of God" and its righteousness and justice. All our legitimate prayer concerns fall within these three priorities.

Many Christians do better with the first two priorities than with the third. We often neglect to pray for kings and presidents, or "for rulers and their governments," as Eugene Peterson translates it in *The Message*. Are we shortchanging God's kingdom in this area?

Most Christian prayer focuses on the church and on its own (especially physical) needs. That is probably to be expected. But it shouldn't be the extent of our prayers. God tells us to pray for all those in authority. We should pray for God's will to be done in the affairs of governments, businesses, and nations, for these realms all fall within the sovereign scope and intention of God.

Christians should be praying for leaders of city and state, for presidents and other leaders, for parliaments and courts. The church should pray for the United Nations, for leaders of other nations, and for the resolution of major issues and conflicts between nations and peoples. Such prayer would include, of course, leaders of business and other sectors, because God's concern is with *all* the "principalities and powers" that touch human life and either cooperate with or fight against his reign.

### God of the Nations

When we pray for these global concerns we bear witness to the fact that God is Lord of the nations. We become like the Christians in Acts 4 who prayed, "Sovereign Lord, you made the heaven and the earth and the sea, and everything in them" (Acts 4:24). Those first believers acknowledged that God was Lord of kings and governments, and they prayed for boldness to carry out their mission.

Since God is Lord of the nations, our prayers should circle the whole world. Psalm 22:28 reminds us that "dominion belongs to the LORD and he rules over the nations." In fact, God "foils the plans of the nations; he thwarts the purposes of the peoples" (Ps. 33:10). Does he not do this partly through our prayers? In Psalm 67:4, the worshiping choir prays, "May the nations be glad and sing for joy, for you rule the peoples justly and guide the nations of the earth." This is God's role, and we mysteriously enter into it through prayer. For we know that "All the nations you have made will come and worship before you, O Lord; they will bring glory to your name" (Ps. 86:9). This is the destiny of the nations. Perhaps we speed its coming through our faithful and persistent prayers.

Like the Jewish exiles in Babylon, we hear God saying to us: "Seek the peace and prosperity of the city to which I have carried you into exile. Pray to the LORD for it, because if it prospers, you too will prosper" (Jer. 29:7). Several times in Scripture we find God's people praying for nations and their rulers. Abraham prayed for God to preserve Sodom, Lot's home. Similarly today, our "political" prayers often grow out of some personal or family connection. Still, this prompts us to pray. We are naturally more sensitive to the needs of places we have visited and where we have friends and acquaintances. They become our prayer priorities.

God is Lord of the nations. We know the time is coming when "every knee [will] bow" and "every tongue confess that Jesus Christ is Lord" (Phil. 2:10–11); when "the kingdom of the world has become the kingdom of our Lord and of his Christ" (Rev. 11:15). So we pray with confidence, boldness, tenacity—and with anticipation. This is part of the mission of the church and part of public discipleship.

Recent history gives remarkable examples of the power of prayer in world affairs. Not many years ago Israel and Egypt were nearly at war, civil war looked inevitable in South Africa, and the Soviet Union loomed as a major threat. How things have changed! In each of these cases we can see the hand of God—and many godly men and women working behind the scenes. Because of the complexity of the church and of God's world, we can never trace an exact cause-and-effect influence of prayer. Yet few Christians can doubt that the remarkable peaceful outcomes to these crises owe something to prayer—probably much more than we imagine. Tennyson surely had it right: "More things are wrought by prayer / Than this world dreams of."

Such remarkable changes in world affairs spark hope that God's will really *can* be done on earth as in heaven, even in the affairs of nations, races, politics, and economics. Even when Christians can't fully agree on these issues, they can pray that God's will may be done; that the priorities of God's kingdom will be visibly realized. We pray in the certainty that the Messiah "will not falter or be discouraged till he establishes justice on earth" (Isa. 42:4). And as we pray, we often find that God works subtle transformations in our own attitudes and opinions. Perhaps increased prayer will bring the church to greater consensus on controversial social and global issues.

## *Prayer as Public Discipleship*

With the hope and certainty of God's ultimate hand in history, Christ's body can bring today's global issues to the throne of grace. Even as we pray for world evangelization and church renewal, we can pray for God's work among the "principalities and powers" of this age. Many issues today demand our concerted prayer.

Different parts of the church will recognize different priorities. We might easily list scores of pressing concerns. Events in our rapidly globalizing world cry for our prayerful intervention, however, especially in these tough crises:

- Central Africa
- Israel, the Palestinians, and their neighbors
- North and South Korea
- Bosnia, Croatia, and Serbia
- India and Pakistan
- Northern Ireland
- the global ecological crisis
- the AIDS epidemic
- the millions of refugees and displaced persons

These issues have an important common denominator. In each case, multinational efforts are underway to bring a just and peaceful solution. These efforts have much in common with the processes that led to key breakthroughs in South Africa and the Israeli-Egyptian crisis. People of goodwill but of different viewpoints are seeking real solutions. So these issues ought to be prime targets for prayer.

Many Christians and non-Christians have been sickened and saddened by the bloodshed and slaughter in Central Africa over past decades, particularly in Rwanda and the Congo. Instability and near chaos still reign through much of the region. Leaders from several African nations are trying to bring about long-range stability that will be just and economically viable. We can assist their efforts by our prayers.

Something similar is true in the other areas listed above. Four-party talks involving North and South Korea, China, and the United States are seeking finally to end the long Korean stalemate. The United Nations, NATO, the European Union, and even Russia are trying to bring peace and economic reconstruction to the Balkans. Fragile efforts continue to be made to heal the centuries-long wounds of Northern Ireland. Global environmental conferences such as those in Kyoto, Japan, and Buenos Aires, Argentina, seek consensus to limit the pollutants that scientists say are upsetting the world's ecosystem. Certainly all of these issues are fundamental prayer priorities where Christians can make a historic difference. Here are strategic, history-shaping opportunities for public discipleship.

The church may be tempted to view these issues more as threats than as opportunities. But Christians who understand the power of God and the direction of his work among the nations rejoice in the opportunity of being co-laborers for the sake of God's reign.

Christians in the past wrestled with the issues of slavery, temperance, child labor, and women's rights. Most of the early abolitionists were evangelical Christians who said that the work of revival and social reform went together. The church has a rich heritage, especially in the examples of those leaders and common people who agitated to end slavery in the United States and, somewhat earlier, the slave trade in England. Some were organizers and political activists. But thousands more were quiet prayer warriors who built the spiritual basis for social and political breakthroughs.

Such history can repeat itself. We face similar challenges today. International disputes, ethnic and tribal conflicts, abortion, and ecological crises are our public-policy prayer challenges. They can be controversial, because Christians don't always agree. Many Christians in the 1830s saw evangelical abolitionists as dangerous radicals who were moving beyond spiritual priorities. But God used these activists to build a consensus that said *everyone* deserves human dignity and opportunity, regardless of race.

Today's ecological crisis is somewhat parallel. Many Christians view environmental issues as irrelevant at best and demonic subversion at worst. Yet biblical Christians—even those who may disagree politically—recognize this crisis as a key prayer priority with serious consequences for coming generations. In the United States, conservative Christians are often more attuned to the abortion debate than to the ecological crisis, for understandable reasons. Yet we may wonder if our children will look back on our lukewarm response to today's ecological crisis the way we look at those in the 1840s and 1850s who refused to take a stand on slavery. Many people in that age said it wasn't a spiritual issue, or that they needed more information, or that they should concentrate only on evangelism. But kingdom Christians saw slavery as a moral issue and a call to public discipleship. They demanded Christian concern and prayerful intervention. And many thousands prayed. These Christians and their public discipleship were shining expressions of the church's true DNA.

Today the church should make such issues part of its public discipleship, first of all through prayer. All of the issues we have discussed fall within the orbit of Christian concern, of God's concern. They all involve God's reign.

### How Prayer Works

As the church prays for renewal, it can ask also that God give Christians everywhere a praying passion for "the nations" as they pray for world evangelization and the faithful extension of the church. Here is an agenda for pastoral prayers, Sunday school classes, prayer cells, house churches, and personal prayer lists. On their knees, Christians can push the world in the direction of God's reign. Only God can change hearts, and our puny efforts accomplish little if not supported by prayer. But God tells us that prayer is key.

How does prayer work? We don't fully know. Much mystery surrounds how God, in response to our prayers (themselves prompted by his Spirit), turns the hearts of kings, presidents, congresses, and international negotiators. Much of this remains a mystery.[9] But we do know this: As we pray about those things that are God's great concerns, we ourselves are changed. We become part of the solution instead of part of the problem.

For these reasons, we heed Paul's exhortation to Timothy: "I urge, then, first of all, that requests, prayers, intercession and thanksgiving be made for everyone — for kings and all those in authority, that we may live peaceful and quiet lives in all godliness and holiness. This is good, and pleases God our Savior, who wants everyone to be saved and to come to a knowledge of the truth" (1 Tim. 2:1–4).

## Conclusion

Of the many dimensions of public discipleship, these four can help the church achieve a fuller, richer expression of the church's DNA: living love and grace, teaching economic justice, practicing godly earth-keeping, and changing the world through prayer.

How can we make these areas of public discipleship practical in our lives together? We offer four suggestions:

- Live and walk in the Spirit. The best way to do this is through a life of daily prayer, Bible study, and close fellowship with other believers. Some form of small group is very useful here.

- Remember that the work of the Spirit is to form the character of Jesus in us. Therefore, seek to live the kind of holiness that we see in Jesus and open yourself daily to the Spirit's work.
- Look for signs of God's renewing work in the church and in the world. Praise God when you see him changing lives, healing families and churches, planting new churches around the world, and bringing peace among nations.
- Discover (or continue to grow in) the gifts and ministries God has given you. Assisted by the fellowship of the church, be a good steward of the gift for ministry that God has given you (1 Peter 4:10–11).

It is still true today that the Church of Jesus Christ is one, holy, catholic, and apostolic. It is equally true that the church, when faithful to the gospel, is many, charismatic, diverse, and prophetic. The more Christ's body demonstrates the fullness of its genetic inheritance, the more effective it will be in continuing Jesus' work upon the earth.

This book has explored some key dimensions of the church's inheritance. Viewing the church genetically, we have seen not only the complexity of the church but also ways to reach through that complexity to biblical faithfulness in structure, mission, and public discipleship.

Our prayer may be that the church increasingly live up to its inheritance. Meanwhile, God has given us his Holy Spirit "who is a deposit guaranteeing our inheritance until the redemption of those who are God's possession—to the praise of his glory" (Eph. 1:14). Animated by his Spirit, the church continues "giving thanks to the Father, who has qualified [his people] to share in the inheritance of the saints in the kingdom of light" (Col. 1:12).

----

## Public Discipleship in the Heartland

Pastor Dorset was flabbergasted. He had no warning that the attack was coming. It came, of all places, from Reverend Lucius Redstone of the Foundational Bible Church.

Everyone in Johnson Center knew about Reverend Redstone. His weekly radio broadcasts had become famous for their blistering attacks on various enemies of the True Faith. His church met on the east side of town in a medium-size building with white siding and a short, square steeple painted red, white, and blue.

In this week's radio blast, Reverend Redstone said Heartland Christian Fellowship was "becoming New Age." He mentioned Heartland's growing environmental concern. He accused the church of offering classes in transcendental meditation—which of course wasn't true, though Pastor Dorset *had* preached a sermon on the importance of meditating on God's Word, and some of the small groups used periods of silent meditation as a spiritual discipline.

Reverend Redstone also attacked Heartland for changing its name. "Remember, it used to be Heartland Evangelical Church. But several years ago it dropped 'Evangelical' from its name! It doesn't even call itself a *church* anymore! Just a fellowship! Here is a church—I mean a *fellowship*—that doesn't even want to be called 'evangelical'!

"We've been watching Heartland for a long time," he said, "and we've seen it slowly drifting away from the truth."

Darrell Dorset hadn't heard Reverend Redstone's blast, but one of his members gave him a tape of it. The part about the name change stung. For a long time Darrell had suspected the change had been a mistake. At least it hadn't done Heartland any good, as far as he could see. *But what is Reverend Redstone thinking?* he wondered to himself. *After all, 'Christian Fellowship' is just as biblical as 'Evangelical Church'—maybe more so!* There was no point, however, in changing the name back to Heartland Evangelical Church; that would only create more hassle and controversy. It would make it look like fiery Reverend Redstone was right.

Darrell Dorset listened to Reverend Redstone's attack and made a list of the charges. Should the church respond in some way? Heartland was becoming "New Age," Redstone said, not only because it talked about "ecology" and "meditation" (meditation, of all things!), but because some of the church's leaders had gone to a conference on global poverty that had been sponsored by an organization receiving funds from the United Nations. "Everybody knows the UN is pro-abortion," Reverend Redstone said. "And it's trying to take away our sovereignty as a nation! We should be denouncing the UN, not falling into its net!" Redstone also accused Heartland of changing the words of familiar hymns.

Pastor Dorset thought about Reverend Redstone's attack. *I guess our church does supply a lot of targets!* he thought—*at least for people looking for them.* Heartland had become well known in Johnson Center for its diverse ministries and its peculiar penchant to *not* do what other churches expected. Heartland now had home groups meeting throughout the city, and that upset some pastors who felt Heartland was invading their turf.

Two or three of Heartland's missions groups had also raised some eyebrows. One group had started rehabbing several old homes just east of downtown. Some members had even showed up at a city council meeting to help block plans to tear down two dozen old houses, which would have displaced a lot of families. Another missions group had adopted the motto "Peace with Justice" and was tracking places in the world where oppression and injustice were especially horrible. It printed up a small monthly newsletter intended just for members of the church. Apparently a copy had fallen into the hands of Reverend Redstone, and he had gone ballistic.

After listening to the tape of Reverend Redstone, Darrell Dorset wondered what to do. In some ways he was more amused than upset. But should the church respond? He prayed about it and talked it over with Beth and his key leaders.

A few days later Pastor Dorset had his regular meeting with his group leaders. Most of them had heard about Redstone's attack. "I've been praying about this," Pastor Dorset said. "So far, the Lord has told me just two things: One, don't retaliate or try to get even in any way. Two, pray for Reverend Redstone and his church. In fact, I may try to get together with him for lunch sometime—if he'll let me."

Pastor Dorset asked his leaders what they thought. Most had heard of the broadcast second- or thirdhand. "I actually caught the program," Roberto Ramirez said. "I heard it on my car radio. Pretty strong stuff!"

"What was the thing about changing hymns?" Jim Richards wanted to know.

Ray Schilling started to laugh. "I can explain that," he said. "In our home group, Greg Jeffords wanted to sing, 'In the Garden.' We did, but I suggested we change one word. One verse says, 'He speaks, and the sound of his voice is so sweet the birds hush their singing.' Well, I said, 'I think God likes the birds singing. Let's change "hush" to "start."' So we sang the song, 'He speaks, and the sound of his voice is so sweet the birds start their singing.'"

"How in the world did Redstone hear about that?" Bill Silver asked.

Ray said, "A couple of kids from Reverend Redstone's church are in one of my classes at the high school. We were talking after class about science and the Bible, and I said I think God takes delight in nature. I mentioned that song, 'In the Garden,' and how we had changed a word when we sang it in our group."

"Small world," someone muttered.

Pastor Dorset said, "Well, God is blessing us in what we're doing. I don't think we need to respond in any way. If we're walking with God, he'll take care of us."

The other leaders agreed.

"But I think we should pray for Reverend Redstone and his church," Roberto said.

The closing prayer time seemed to last longer than usual. Pastor Dorset "peeked" at one point. He glanced around the room and saw the earnestness on the faces of these committed men and women, his key leaders.

"Yes, Lord," Angie was praying. "We pray for the Foundational Bible Church. We pray for all your body throughout the world. Bring peace and healing, we pray."

Darrell Dorset closed his eyes. They were a little moist. The only words he could think of were "May your kingdom come. May your will be done on earth, as it is in heaven."

# Questions
## for Group Discussion or Personal Reflection

1. What are the key elements of your daily prayer life?
2. To exercise public discipleship as discussed in this chapter, what changes do you feel would be appropriate in your prayer life?
3. Is prayer in community a vital part of your church experience? What changes might be made for this to take on greater significance?
4. What is the economic impact of your church as an organization, and as individual members?
5. In what ways did Heartland Christian Fellowship "supply a lot of targets" for its critics?
6. How well do you think Heartland church handled the attack from Reverend Redstone?
7. In what ways is Heartland demonstrating public discipleship?
8. What challenges do you think lie ahead for Heartland Christian Fellowship?

# NOTES

## Chapter 1: Do Churches Have DNA?

1. Our approach here is considerably different from that of Richard Southern and Robert Norton in their book, *Cracking Your Congregation's Code: Mapping Your Spiritual DNA to Create Your Future* (San Francisco: Jossey-Bass, 2001). Southern and Norton view a congregation's DNA as spiraling strands of "mission" and "vision" bonded together by "values" but do not deal in depth with the church biblically and theologically, as we attempt to do here. Their book is mainly a manual about effective congregational organization. It could be useful for a church that already understands *what it really is* biblically and spiritually. Otherwise, it could mislead a church to think that its DNA is simply a matter of organizational effectiveness. As we will show, it is much more than that.

2. See Jaroslav Pelikan, *The Emergence of the Catholic Tradition (100–600)*, vol. 1 of *The Christian Tradition: A History of the Development of Doctrine* (Chicago: University of Chicago Press, 1971), 156.

3. G. C. Berkouwer, *The Church*, trans. James E. Davison (Grand Rapids: Eerdmans, 1976), 14–15. Berkouwer is speaking here specifically of the Belgic Confession, but the point applies more generally. Craig Van Gelder points out that the Apostles' Creed speaks of the church also as "the communion of saints." This describes "the social reality of the church" and may be seen as a fifth classic mark. Thus these "five attributes came to be the common way of describing the church over the next centuries." See Van Gelder's *The Essence of the Church: A Community Created by the Spirit* (Grand Rapids: Baker, 2000), 50.

4. Benjamin T. Roberts, "Free Churches," *The Earnest Christian* 1:1 (January 1860): 7–8. Emphasis in the original.

5. Ibid., 8.

6. Stephen Olin, "The Adaptation of the Gospel to the Poor," *The Works of Stephen Olin, D.D., LL.D., Late President of the Wesleyan University* (New York: Harper and Brothers, 1852), 1:346. Italics in the original. Roberts quotes this passage (and more) from Olin in his "Free Churches" article. This had been a common emphasis since the days of early British and American Methodism, but by the 1850s it was fading or even under attack within Methodism. Bishop Thomas Morris (1794–1874), who ordained Roberts, argued similarly in the 1840s in a sermon entitled, "The Privileges of the Poor," based on Matthew 11:5. This sermon noted that the answer Jesus sent to John the Baptist "afforded the most conclusive evidence of Messiahship, by showing himself to be the author of the very works which the ancient prophets had foretold Messiah should perform." Thomas A. Morris, *Sermons on Various Occasions* (Cincinnati: L. Swormstedt and J. T. Mitchell, 1845), 172–87.

7. Benjamin T. Roberts, "Gospel to the Poor," *The Earnest Christian and Golden Rule* 7:3 (March 1864): 70. Emphasis in the original.

8. Ibid.

9. Ibid., 72.

10. Ibid., 73. Emphasis in the original.

11. Some may ask: What does the Bible mean by the poor? Roberts and Olin assumed that was self-evident. In the Bible "the poor" generally means both the spiritually and economically poor and oppressed (and/or socially marginalized), often with no distinction between spiritual and material poverty except perhaps as nuanced by the context. Roberts meant primarily the economically poor and socially marginalized, who he said most feel their spiritual poverty.

12. See Howard A. Snyder, *The Radical Wesley and Patterns of Church Renewal* (Downers Grove, Ill.: InterVarsity, 1980; Eugene, Ore.: Wipf and Stock, 1996), 76.

13. Charles Van Engen, *God's Missionary People* (Grand Rapids: Baker, 1991). Though Van Engen's treatment is creative, he simply accepts the four classic marks as given. Not coincidentally, Van Engen hardly mentions the Radical Protestant tradition (which says much about the church) in a book devoted primarily to ecclesiology.

14. Typically, much of the dynamic of a new social movement springs from its immersion in the immediate social context, though it also maintains tension with that context.

15. This formulation admittedly is biased toward a more institutional interpretation of the classic marks. Obviously, the church in its movement stage should be (and often aims to be) one, holy, catholic, and apostolic in a dynamic, functional sense.

16. See Howard A. Snyder, "The First Charismatic Movement," chapter 1 in *Signs of the Spirit: How God Reshapes the Church* (Grand Rapids: Zondervan, 1989; Eugene, Ore.: Wipf and Stock, 1997), 15–28.

17. See Vinson Synan, *The Holiness-Pentecostal Tradition: Charismatic Movements in the Twentieth Century* (Grand Rapids: Eerdmans, 1997), rev. ed. of *The Holiness-Pentecostal Movement in the United States* (Grand Rapids: Eerdmans, 1971).

18. Theologically, there is a certain priority of apostles over prophets, as suggested in 1 Corinthians 12:28 and Ephesians 4:11. Apostles establish the church on the basis of and under the authority of Jesus Christ and have initial supervisory or oversight responsibility. Apostles are followed by prophets who stir up, inspire, invigorate, and pronounce judgment on the church. Both the New Testament and church history provide many examples of this. The so-called New Apostolic Reformation emphasizes this pairing of apostles and prophets to some degree, though its stress on the *office* and authority of apostles is misleading and potentially dangerous. See C. Peter Wagner, ed., *The New Apostolic Churches* (Ventura, Calif.: Regal, 1998), 13–25.

19. See Howard A. Snyder with Daniel V. Runyon, *The Divided Flame: Wesleyans and the Charismatic Movement* (Grand Rapids: Francis Asbury, 1986); Howard A. Snyder, "The Church as Holy and Charismatic," *Wesleyan Theological Journal* (fall 1980): 7–32.

20. See E. Stanley Jones, *Christ's Alternative to Communism* (New York: Abingdon, 1935).

21. We feel it is important to make a distinction between ministry "to the poor" and ministry "to and among the poor." Preaching *at* the poor and doling out blessings from a position of superiority is not authentic ministry. Authentic ministry means incarnating the Good News among the poor as Jesus did, through healing, teaching, preaching, and forming kingdom communities.

22. John Wesley, *Explanatory Notes upon the New Testament* (London: Epworth, 1958), 227 (commenting on Luke 7:22).

23. Karl Barth said: "The Church is witness of the fact that the Son of man came to seek and to save the lost. And this implies that—casting all false impartiality aside—the Church must concentrate first on the lower and lowest levels of human society. The poor, the socially and economically weak and threatened, will always be the object of its primary and particular concern, and it will always insist [as well] on the State's special respon-

sibility for these weaker members of society." Barth, "The Christian Community and the Civil Community," *Against the Stream: Shorter Post-War Writings 1946–52* (New York: Philosophical Library, 1954), 36.

24. The essence of God's holiness is love that disinterestedly does good to all, especially to the poor. Further, the biblical teaching on the *charismata* (spiritual gifts) is particularly good news for the poor because it teaches (and demonstrates!) that divine empowerment doesn't depend on status, wealth, education, or credentials but on the direct operation of the Holy Spirit. This is why "charismatic" movements (sociologically speaking) generally have been initially movements of the poor.

## Chapter 2: The Church: A Complex Organism

1. See also Rev. 1:20; 10:7; and related passages. In a development of great significance for later ecclesiology and sacramental theology, *mystērion* in the Greek New Testament came to be translated *sacramentum* in the Latin Vulgate.

2. See Avery Dulles, *Models of the Church* (Garden City, N.Y.: Doubleday, 1974), and the general discussion of models in chapter 1 of Howard A. Snyder, *Models of the Kingdom* (Nashville: Abingdon, 1991).

3. M. Mitchell Waldrop, *Complexity: The Emerging Science at the Edge of Order and Chaos* (New York: Simon and Schuster, 1992), 11.

4. See Jack Cohen and Ian Stewart, *The Collapse of Chaos: Discovering Simplicity in a Complex World* (New York: Viking, 1994); Murray Gell-Mann, *The Quark and the Jaguar: Adventures in the Simple and the Complex* (New York: W. H. Freeman, 1994); James Gleick, *Chaos: Making a New Science* (New York: Penguin, 1987); Ian Stewart and Martin Golubitsky, *Fearful Symmetry: Is God a Geometer?* (London: Penguin, 1993); Stuart Kaufman, *At Home in the Universe: The Search for the Laws of Self-Organization and Complexity* (New York: Oxford University Press, 1995).

5. Postmodernity, the society that is now replacing modernity in the West and in many respects globally, rejects the Enlightenment ideas of rationality, progress, order, and "metanarrative" (overarching coherent story) and is marked by irrationality, "nowism," the mixing of styles, and focus on the particular (the part rather than the whole). Though it is largely "deconstructive" (a favorite word of postmodernism), it has positive aspects for Christians in raising questions about our cultural history. See Howard A. Snyder, "Postmodernism: The Death of Worldviews?" chapter 15 in *EarthCurrents: The Struggle for the World's Soul* (Nashville: Abingdon, 1995), 213–30.

6. Bart Kosko, *Fuzzy Thinking: The New Science of Fuzzy Logic* (New York: Hyperion, 1993).

7. Military imagery is largely absent from the New Testament depiction of the church. The few places where it occurs (2 Tim. 2:3–4, for example) refer to self-discipline or to spiritual warfare "against the spiritual forces of evil in the heavenly realms" (Eph. 6:12), not to the church's corporate mission. Though there is military imagery in the Book of Revelation, the saints overcome "by the blood of the Lamb and by the word of their testimony" (Rev. 12:11), not by military organization or prowess. Throughout history, however, the church has picked up the military metaphor and used it in a destructive way to define the church's mission—as conquest, crusade, victory, and so on.

8. In keeping with complexity theory, no either/or distinction is intended here. Character is formed by behavior, and behavior expresses character. But as Jesus taught, character is more fundamental ("For out of the overflow of the heart the mouth speaks" [Matt. 12:34]).

9. Kaufman, *At Home in the Universe*, 26.

10. We have been told there is, in fact, a movie entitled *The Attack of the Fifty-Foot Woman!*

11. Literally, Acts 6:2–4 says, "It would not be right for us [Apostles] to neglect the Word of God in order to serve [*diakonein*, from *diakoneō*, "to be an attendant, wait upon"] tables. Brothers, choose seven men from among you who are known to be full of the Spirit and wisdom, whom we will appoint to this task [*chreias*, "necessity, task, or responsibility," not "office"] while we devote ourselves to the ministry [*diakonia*] of the word." Thus the apostles identify two forms of ministry, or *diakonia*: the ministry of distributing food to the needy and the ministry of the Word. Later church tradition turned the functional arrangement of Acts 6 into "the institution of the office of deacon."

## Chapter 3: Church, Trinity, and Mission

1. The fundamental missional nature of the church is cogently argued in Darrell L. Guder, ed., *Missional Church: A Theological Vision for the Sending Church in North America* (Grand Rapids: Eerdmans, 1998). Some of the thinking in this chapter is adapted from our responses to Guder's book.

2. *Trinitarian* is capitalized to make it clear that the reference here is to the Holy Trinity, not simply to a tripartite mode of analysis.

3. Guder, *Missional Church*, 81–82.

4. Colin E. Gunton, *The Promise of Trinitarian Theology*, 2d ed. (Edinburgh: T. and T. Clark, 1997), 79.

5. There is a doxological dimension to all the marks of the church. The church in its unity and diversity, its apostolicity and "propheticality," for instance, is to do everything to "the praise of [God's] glorious grace" (Eph. 1:6; 1 Cor. 10:31). All the essential marks of the church, if lived out faithfully, reflect dimensions of God's own character as Holy Trinity, and thus of the *missio Dei* (the mission of God). In other words, the church derives the missional bent of its DNA from its Trinitarian source.

6. See Howard A. Snyder, *Liberating the Church* (Downers Grove, Ill.: InterVarsity Press, 1983), 70–93, and *Radical Renewal: The Problem of Wineskins Today* (Houston: Touch, 1996), chapter 10. Relating to the eight marks discussed in chapter 1, *worship*, *community*, and *witness* may be thought of not as essential marks but as primary functions through which the church expresses the marks.

7. In the New Testament, "preaching the good news" or "proclaiming" or "telling" good news (the root of our word *evangelism*) often means specifically proclaiming the kingdom of God (see, for example, Matt. 4:23; 9:35; Luke 4:43; 8:1; Acts 8:12). The gospel is "good news to all creation" (Mark 16:15) and "for all the people" (Luke 2:10) and is particularly "good news to the poor" (Matt. 11:5; Luke 4:18, 7:22). It is clear from Scripture that the *content* of that good news is the kingdom of God in all its dimensions, the kingdom that is now available to us through faith in Jesus Christ (cf. Acts 5:42; 8:35; 10:36; 17:18). Therefore to "evangelize" (announce good news) involves more than personal evangelism or the saving of souls. Evangelism involves the full scope of "[God's] kingdom and his righteousness" and justice (Matt. 6:33), though the ministry of what is generally called "personal evangelism"—giving people the opportunity to consider the claims of Jesus Christ on their lives and respond in faith—has a certain priority because Jesus wants willing, trusting "fellow citizens" and "fellow workers" (Eph. 2:19; 1 Cor. 3:9; Col. 4:11) in his kingdom.

8. Sermon, "Salvation by Faith," in Frank Baker, ed., *The Works of John Wesley*, vol. 1, *Sermons I*, ed. Albert Outler (Nashville: Abingdon, 1982), 128.

9. See Gordon Cosby, *Handbook for Mission Groups* (Waco: Word, 1975); Elizabeth O'Connor, *Journey Inward, Journey Outward* (New York: Harper and Row, 1968); Steve Barker, et al, *Good Things Come in Small Groups: The Dynamics of Good Group Life* (Downers Grove, Ill.: InterVarsity Press, 1985); Richard C. Meyer, *One-Anothering: Biblical Building Blocks for Small Groups* (San Diego: LuraMedia, 1990); Ralph W. Neighbour, *Where*

*Do We Go from Here? A Guidebook for the Cell Group Church* (Houston: Touch, 1990); William A. Beckham, *The Second Reformation: Reshaping the Church for the Twenty-first Century* (Houston: Touch, 1995); Joel T. Comiskey, *Home Cell Group Explosion* (Houston: Touch, 1998); Gareth W. Icenogle, *Biblical Foundations for Small Group Ministry* (Downers Grove, Ill.: InterVarsity, 1994); and Joel T. Comiskey, *How to Lead a Great Cell Group Meeting* (Houston: Touch, 2001).

10. Note for example the way "members" and "body" are used in Romans 12:4–5, Ephesians 3:6 and 5:30, and Colossians 3:15.

11. As should be clear from the earlier discussion, we are not downplaying the need for a conscious decision to follow Christ, the exercise of faith, or commitment to the Christian community. But becoming a Christian is not "joining" an organization; it is being born and woven into a community, the body of Christ, by the action of the Holy Spirit.

12. Greg Ogden, *The New Reformation: Returning the Ministry to the People of God* (Grand Rapids: Zondervan, 1990). The church may be in the first stages of such a reformation, but the picture is very uneven, both in the U.S. and globally.

13. See Snyder, "Church and Culture," chapter 13 in *Radical Renewal*.

14. The divine *perichōrēsis* of the Trinity is thus reflected in, and carried over into, the life of the church. An especially helpful discussion is Colin E. Gunton, "The Community: The Trinity and the Being of the Church," chapter four in *The Promise of Trinitarian Theology*, rev. ed. (Edinburgh: T & T Clark, 1997).

15. Some theologians have tried to reconcile the Trinity and hierarchy, especially in the Western tradition. In fact, the two have been conceptually wed, with the result that hierarchy (grounded in pre-Christian Greek philosophical categories) has often won out over the Trinity! This is one of the underlying, often unconscious factors that make it difficult to conceive of ministry, leadership, and gender issues in biblical terms.

## Chapter 4: The DNA of Church Structure: Dead Ends

1. See Ezekiel 16:10; Exodus 26:14; Acts 18:2–3.

2. Over the years, the number of pastors and other church leaders we've talked with who have attended church growth, renewal, and leadership seminars and have come back discouraged and disillusioned has grown into quite a crowd. Mostly these leaders are from small and medium-size churches and tend to fall into two categories: those who say, "We tried it, and it didn't work," and those who say, "We simply don't have the resources to do those things." At least two fallacies lie behind holding up successful churches as models for other churches: equating structure with the essential nature of the church (wineskins versus wine) and the belief that the experience of one church can be replicated in a different one. Generally it can't, though helpful insights and ideas may sometimes be gained.

3. Michael S. Hamilton, "Willow Creek's Place in History," *Christianity Today* 44:13 (13 November 2000): 64.

4. Lyman Beecher Stowe, *Saints, Sinners and Beechers* (New York: Blue Ribbon, 1934), 371–74.

5. Carl F. George, *Prepare Your Church for the Future* (Tarrytown, N.Y.: Revell, 1991), especially section 2, "The Meta-Church Model"; Carl F. George with Warren Bird, *The Coming Church Revolution: Empowering Leaders for the Future* (Grand Rapids: Revell, 1994).

6. Jesus' parables (in Matthew 13, for example) are backed up by many Old Testament stories about God delighting to work through the few, the small, and the weak (Gideon's army of three hundred men, David and Goliath, the ambivalence about taking a census of Israel, even Daniel in the lion's den—in fact, Israel itself). This is part of the larger theme throughout Scripture that "God [chooses] the foolish things of the world to shame the wise; God [chooses] the weak things of the world to shame the strong" (1 Cor. 1:27).

7. Acts 1:15 mentions "about a hundred and twenty" believers, but otherwise Luke uses general language, such as in Acts 2:47, where it says the Lord "added to their number daily those who were being saved."

8. John Wesley's journals are full of references to church growth and decline, the reasons for it, and its relative significance. See, for example, Baker, *The Works of John Wesley*, vol. 23, *Journals and Diaries VI*, ed. W. Reginald Ward and Richard P. Heitzenrater (Nashville: Abingdon, 1995), 66–69, 83–84, 135–36, 209, 375–76.

9. Christian A. Schwarz, *Natural Church Development: A Guide to Eight Essential Qualities of Healthy Churches*, trans. Lynn McAdam, Lois Wollin, and Martin Wollin (Carol Stream, Ill.: ChurchSmart Resources, 1996), 47–48. Sociologists Rodney Stark and Roger Finke state flatly, "congregational size is inversely related to the average level of member commitment." Their research showed that "rates of participation decline with congregational size, and the sharpest declines occur when congregations exceed 50 members." Rodney Stark and Roger Finke, *Acts of Faith: Explaining the Human Side of Religion* (Berkeley, Calif.: University of California Press, 2000), 155.

10. Lynne and Bill Hybels, Rediscovering Church: The Story and Vision of Willow Creek Community Church (Grand Rapids: Zondervan, 1995). Willow Creek's success in building an "Acts 2 church" testifies to the power of the New Testament vision of the church. The main biblical basis of Willow Creek, according to Rediscovering Church, is Acts 2 and the Great Commission of Matthew 28:19–20. Largely missing from the vision, however, are some other key biblical themes. There is very little accent, for instance, on the kingdom of God or the Acts 13 model of the church. A fully biblical model of the church is much more than an "Acts 2 church."

11. Some megachurches provide deeper, more meaningful community than do smaller congregations (generally through networks of small groups), and many small congregations are dysfunctional. Nevertheless, statistics on congregational size seem to indicate that on average, community is more intense in smaller churches than in larger churches.

12. See Snyder, *Signs of the Spirit*, especially chapters 2 and 7, which explore in some detail the theoretical issues involved here.

13. See, for example, Robert and Julia Banks, *The Church Comes Home: A New Base for Community and Mission* (Sutherland, N.S.W., Australia: Albatross, 1989); Christian Smith, *Going to the Root: Nine Proposals for Radical Church Renewal* (Scottdale, Penn.: Herald, 1992); Lois Barrett, *Building the House Church* (Scottdale, Penn.: Herald, 1986); Bernard J. Lee and Michael A. Cowan, *Dangerous Memories: House Churches and Our American Story* (Kansas City: Sheed and Ward, 1986); and Del Birkey, *The House Church: A Model for Renewing the Church* (Scottdale, Penn.: Herald, 1988).

14. This is now widely recognized in much New Testament scholarship and research on the early church as a social movement. See, for example, Robert Banks, *Paul's Idea of Community*, rev. ed. (Peabody, Mass.: Hendrickson, 1994); Rodney Stark, *The Rise of Christianity: A Sociologist Reconsiders History* (Princeton, N.J.: Princeton University Press, 1996).

15. See, for example, the writings of Gene Edwards, such as *Revolution: The Story of the Early Church* (1987), *How to Meet in Homes* (1999), and *Acts in First-Person* (2000), which are all published by SeedSowers, Jacksonville, Florida. See also the many Internet websites devoted to house churches.

16. This point is argued extensively in Snyder, *The Problem of Wineskins* (Downers Grove, Ill.: InterVarsity Press, 1975), 139–48, and *Radical Renewal*, 149–57.

17. The Book of Proverbs provides much practical wisdom for business enterprise, and a number of authors have explored Jesus' "leadership principles." See, for example, David L. McKenna, *The Jesus Model* (Waco: Word, 1979).

## Chapter 5: The DNA of Church Structure: New Wineskins

1. Robert E. Coleman, *The Master Plan of Evangelism* (Grand Rapids: Revell, 1993).

2. Rodney Stark, *The Rise of Christianity;* Michael Green, *Evangelism in the Early Church* (Grand Rapids: Eerdmans, 1970).

3. See, for example, Richard M. Riss, *A Survey of Twentieth-Century Revival Movements in North America* (Peabody, Mass.: Hendrickson, 1988); Donald G. Bloesch, *Wellsprings of Renewal* (Grand Rapids: Eerdmans, 1974); Thomas P. Rausch, *Radical Christian Communities* (Collegeville, Minn.: Liturgical, 1990); J. Edwin Orr, *Campus Aflame: A History of Evangelical Awakenings in Collegiate Communities* (Wheaton: International Awakenings, 1994); John T. McNeill, *Modern Christian Movements* (Philadelphia: Westminster, 1954); as well as the extensive bibliography in Snyder, *Signs of the Spirit.*

4. W. A. Visser 't Hooft, *The Renewal of the Church* (London: SCM, 1956).

5. Marie-Dominique Chenu, *Nature, Man, and Society in the Twelfth Century* (Chicago: University of Chicago Press, 1968); Rausch, *Radical Christian Communities;* Patricia McNicholas, "A Study of the Charism of Angela Merici and a Comparison with the Ursuline Sisters of Youngstown and Cleveland" (D.Min. research paper, United Theological Seminary, 1990); Stephen Clark, *Unordained Elders and Renewal Communities* (New York: Paulist, 1976).

6. Since renewal movements stress the "new work" of the Spirit, they tend to infuse greater dynamic into the doctrine of God, balancing God's transcendence (ultimacy) with his immanence (intimacy) and in the process energizing ecclesiology.

7. For a fuller discussion of "the meaning of ecology and the ecology of meaning," see Snyder, *EarthCurrents*, 232–46.

8. Properly rooted in Scripture, the doctrine of the Trinity is more an ecological than a hierarchical reality, as will be discussed in a later chapter.

9. Thomas L Friedman, *The Lexus and the Olive Tree: Understanding Globalization*, rev. ed. (New York: Random House, 2000), 23–26.

10. Cisco Systems, Inc., *2000 Annual Report* (San Jose, Calif.: Cisco Systems, 2000), 4.

## Chapter 6: Genetic Material for Vital Churches

1. Ephesians 2:5–9; 4:7–12; 1 Corinthians 12:1–28.

2. Gregory Leffel, "Churches in the Mode of Mission: Toward a Missional Model of the Church," chapter 5 in Howard A. Snyder, ed., *Global Good News: Mission in a New Context* (Nashville: Abingdon, 2001), 65–95.

3. This threefold balance is further elaborated in Snyder, *Radical Renewal*, 117–37.

4. Schwarz, *Natural Church Development: A Guide to Eight Essential Qualities of Healthy Churches*. Although this book has been criticized by some church growth specialists, in part for its research methodology, we find its basic understanding of the church to be biblically and theologically sound. See also Christian A. Schwarz, *Paradigm Shift in the Church: How Natural Church Development Can Transform Theological Thinking* (Carol Stream, Ill.: ChurchSmart Resources, 1999).

5. Philip Jakob Spener, *Pia Desideria* (1675) (Philadelphia: Fortress, 1964); Snyder, *Signs of the Spirit*, 76–82.

6. John Wesley, *Explanatory Notes upon the New Testament*, 832.

7. A forthcoming useful resource for helping the church serve the poor is the World Vision/Zondervan Study Bible being published by World Vision U.S. and Zondervan.

8. Baker, *The Works of John Wesley*, vol. 19, *Journals and Diaries II, 1738–43*, ed. W. Reginald Ward and Richard P. Heitzenrater (Nashville: Abingdon, 1990), 46. Emphasis in the original.

9. Ibid.

10. Leslie R. Marston, *From Age to Age a Living Witness: A Historical Interpretation of Free Methodism's First Century* (Winona Lake, Ind.: Light and Life, 1960), 66.

11. Baker, *The Works of John Wesley*, vol. 20, *Journals and Diaries III, 1743–1754*, ed. W. Reginald Ward and Richard P. Heitzenrater (Nashville: Abingdon, 1991), 34.

12. Baker, *The Works of John Wesley*, vol. 9, *The Methodist Societies: History, Nature, and Design*, ed. Rupert E. Davies (Nashville: Abingdon, 1989), 262.

13. Resources on Wesley and early Methodism of particular significance for the form and structure of the church include D. Michael Henderson, *John Wesley's Class Meeting: A Model for Making Disciples* (Nappanee, Ind.: Evangel, 1997); Bernard Semmel, *The Methodist Revolution* (New York: Basic, 1973); Maldwyn Edwards, *John Wesley and the Eighteenth Century: A Study of His Social and Political Influence*, rev. ed. (London: Epworth, 1955); Richard P. Heitzenrater, *Wesley and the People Called Methodists* (Nashville: Abingdon, 1995); Snyder, *The Radical Wesley;* and Snyder, *Signs of the Spirit*, 183–242.

## Chapter 7: The DNA of Mission

1. William R. O'Brien, "Mission in the Valley of Postmodernity," in Snyder, *Global Good News*, 23.

2. Scripture quotations in this chapter are taken from the NRSV unless otherwise noted.

3. We use the term "Christocentric" theologically, not spatially. We make this point because some ecologists and postmodern writers have argued that given a proper understanding of ecology and of science, it is misleading to speak of anything as "the center" or "the foundation." Theologically, however, we all make something "central" and organize everything else "around" that "center."

4. Based on the NRSV of these passages, but substituting "cohere" for the phrase "hold together."

5. This presentation builds on, but goes beyond, Howard's book *EarthCurrents*, which surveys six emerging worldview options: global economics (as a worldview), quantum mystery, Gaia theory (which makes ecology central), theism, fate, and postmodernism.

6. From time to time some people have argued that *nothing* holds things together; life is incoherent, a chaos (see *EarthCurrents*, especially chapter 17). But most of us do in fact assume some principle of coherence in life and in the world, whether we think about it or not. In other words, we do assume "ecology" in the broadest sense.

7. Paul Hiebert points out that hierarchy is an essential element of the Indo-European myth that has profoundly shaped Western, Middle Eastern, and Indian worldviews. See Paul G. Hiebert, *Anthropological Reflections on Missiological Issues* (Grand Rapids: Baker, 1994), 204–11. It is a presupposition of Platonism and Neo-Platonism.

8. Trinity and hierarchy are fundamentally contrary notions. Yet some theologians have wed the two, trying to make them compatible. See for example the discussion in William J. Hill, The Three-Personal God: The Trinity as a Mystery of Salvation (Washington, D.C.: Catholic University of America Press, 1982), 40–50. Some evangelical theologians teach female subordination to males based on a misunderstanding of the relationship between God the Father and God the Son that in effect turns the Trinity into a hierarchy, as Gilbert Bilezikian points out in "Hermeneutical Bungee-Jumping: Subordination in the Godhead," appendix in Gilbert Bilezikian, *Community 101: Reclaiming the Church as Community of Oneness* (Grand Rapids: Zondervan, 1997), 187–202.

9. Louis Dumont, *Homo Hierarchicus: The Caste System and Its Implications* (London: Paladin, 1972), 104–105.

10. Riane Eisler distinguishes between "domination hierarchies" and "actualization hierarchies"; this corresponds roughly to the distinction here, though vertical hierarchies may be based on something more subtle than "force or the threat of force"—tradition,

mythology, or a religious ideal, for example. Riane Eisler, *The Chalice and the Blade: Our History, Our Future* (San Francisco: Harper and Row, 1987), 105–106.

11. This is consistent with the creation account in Genesis 1:26–28 where God says of the man and the woman together, jointly, "let them rule" or have dominion.

12. Gunton, *The Promise of Trinitarian Theology*, 60. Gunton argues that the mainly Greek notion of hierarchy combined with the Roman concept of law to produce what became the medieval ecclesiastical ideology and structure.

13. Jeffrey Burton Russell, *Medieval Civilization* (New York: John Wiley and Sons, 1968), 82, 510, 536.

14. The most notable example is Ephesians 4:11–12, which should be compared in the Greek, the Latin Vulgate, the KJV, and in various modern versions.

15. Arthur O. Lovejoy, *The Great Chain of Being: A Study in the History of an Idea* (1936; reprint, New York: Harper Torchbooks, 1960), 59. The origins of hierarchy are much more complex than can be summarized here, and as noted above seem to be grounded in the Indo-European Myth.

16. Lovejoy, *The Great Chain of Being*, 59.

17. Henri Daudin, quoted in Lovejoy, *The Great Chain of Being*, 61.

18. Quoted in "Ecology: The New Great Chain of Being," *Natural History*, December 1968, 8.

19. Alexander Pope, "An Essay on Man," in *Selected Works*, ed. Louis Kronenberger (New York: Modern Library, 1948), 104–105, 127–28. Pope's contemporary John Wesley pictured the created order *in its original state* similarly: "Every part was exactly suited to the others, and conducive to the good of the whole. There was 'a golden chain' (to use the expression of Plato) 'let down from the throne of God'—an exactly connected series of beings, from the highest to the lowest: from dead earth, through fossils, vegetables, animals, to man, created in the image of God, and designed to know, to love, and enjoy his Creator to all eternity." (Sermon 56, "God's Approbation of His Works," in Baker, *The Works of John Wesley*, vol. 2, *Sermons II*, ed. Albert Outler [Nashville: Abingdon, 1985], 396–97). Wesley's view is however less static than the traditional view because of his dynamically personal understanding of God and his strong stress on the image of God in men and women, making them "capable of God" (with the capacity for deep, transforming communion with God). Like most orthodox Christians, he viewed this original harmony as fundamentally distorted because of the fall.

20. See for example Denys Rutledge, *Cosmic Theology: The Ecclesiastical Hierarchy of Pseudo-Denys: An Introduction* (Staten Island, N.Y.: Alba, 1964).

21. Though we have traced the influence of the hierarchical idea in its Eurocentric form, hierarchy predates European civilization. It takes different forms in different cultures, and cultures have varied considerably in their degree of hierarchical structure. The caste system in India is one of the world's most elaborately developed hierarchies (see Dumont, *Homo Hierarchicus*), and ancient Chinese culture was quite hierarchical.

22. There was, of course, a long, mostly underground or marginal history of individuals and groups who challenged the whole concept of hierarchy. Many of these were radical Christian groups who found much of their inspiration in the account of the New Testament church and the example of Jesus.

## Chapter 8: Mission beyond Psychology and Ecology

1. The significance of the paradigmatic shift from psychology to ecology can be illustrated by comparing this list of psychological and emerging ecological terms:

| psychology | ecology |
|---|---|
| psychosocial | ecosocial |
| psychotherapy | ecotherapy |

psychoanalysis     ecoanalysis
psychopathic       ecopathic
psychohistory      ecohistory
psycho-theology    ecotheology

2. Theodore Roszak, *The Voice of the Earth* (New York: Simon and Schuster, 1992), 14.

3. See M. Douglas Meeks, *God the Economist: The Doctrine of God and Political Economy* (Minneapolis: Fortress, 1989).

4. "Ecology: The New Great Chain of Being," *Natural History*, (December 1968), 8.

## Chapter 9: In Christ: The Coherence of Mission

1. In terms of theories of truth, we are thus arguing not just for "coherence" but for "correspondence" (as discussed, for example, by Henry H. Knight III in *A Future for Truth: Evangelical Theology in a Postmodern World* [Nashville: Abingdon, 1997], 12).

2. G. K. Chesterton, *The Everlasting Man* (London: Hodder and Stoughton, 1927), 247.

3. John Wesley pictures this New Creation in suggestively ecological terms in some of his sermons, particularly "The General Deliverance" and "The New Creation."

4. Gunton, *The Promise of Trinitarian Theology*, 14. See also Colin Gunton, *Christ and Creation* (Grand Rapids: Eerdmans, 1992).

## Chapter 10: The Church Confronts Globalization

1. Benjamin Barber, "Jihad vs. McWorld," *The Atlantic Monthly*, March 1992, 53–63.

2. Jacques Ellul, *The Meaning of the City*, trans. Dennis Pardee (Grand Rapids: Eerdmans, 1970). *The Meaning of the City* is Ellul's theological counterpart to his influential book, *The Technological Society* (New York: Alfred A. Knopf, 1964).

3. Robert Gilpin argues that in important ways the world economy was actually more "globalized" a century ago than it is today. Robert Gilpin, *Global Political Economy: Understanding the International Economic Order* (Princeton, N.J.: Princeton University Press, 2001).

4. James Plueddeman, "SIM's Agenda for a Gracious Revolution," *International Bulletin of Missionary Research* 23 (1999): 153; Tom Sine, *Mustard Seed vs. McWorld: Reinventing Life and Faith for the Future* (Grand Rapids: Baker, 1999), 48.

5. "Commodity" is defined as "anything that is bought and sold; article of trade or commerce." Traditionally it has referred to material products such as grain, sugar, iron, and glass. Commodification today is turning a range of *life experiences* into "things" that can be bought and sold.

6. Jeremy Rifkin, *The Age of Access: The New Culture of Hypercapitalism Where All of Life Is a Paid-For Experience* (New York: Tarcher/Putnam, 2000), 7.

7. Ibid., 8.

8. Ibid., 10–12.

9. Ibid., 9.

10. Consider the key role of global commerce, including the "bodies and souls of men" (Rev. 18:13), in God's judgment on "Babylon," pictured in Revelation 18.

11. Rifkin, *Age of Access*, 12.

12. Robert Putnam, *Bowling Alone: The Collapse and Revival of American Community* (New York: Simon and Schuster, 2000).

13. The Internet was at first celebrated for being free and democratic, under no one's control, but it has become a major force for commodification and economic gain.

14. Erla Zwingle, "A World Together," *National Geographic* 196:2 (August 1999): 17.

15. Thomas Friedman makes the point that in some ways globalization *increases* the power of individuals and public-interest groups to bring about change by putting pres-

sure on the public image of global corporations. See Friedman, *The Lexus and the Olive Tree*.

16. Ron Westbury, "The Status of Christian Education in the Pentecostal Evangelistic Fellowship of Africa" (D.Min. document, Asbury Theological Seminary, 2000).

## Chapter 11: Gospel Globalization

1. A valuable resource on how Christians can respond positively and creatively to the challenges of globalization is Tom Sine's book, *Mustard Seed vs. McWorld*. This book gives dozens of practical suggestions and examples for Christian mission in this age of globalization.

2. Sine cites this data in *Mustard Seed vs. McWorld*, 108.

3. "Refugees and Others of Concern to UNHCR," <http://www.unhcr.ch/statist/98oview/ch1.htm> (2 August 2001).

4. See, for example, E. F. Schumacher, "Buddhist Economics," in *Small Is Beautiful* (New York: Harper, 1973).

5. Sine, *Mustard Seed vs. McWorld*, 111.

6. An excellent, thought-provoking resource is Christine D. Pohl, *Making Room: Recovering Hospitality as a Christian Tradition* (Grand Rapids: Eerdmans, 1999). Pohl shows how hospitality and community can be—and often have been—a bridge to mission, especially among the poor and marginalized.

7. Sine, *Mustard Seed vs. McWorld*, 107.

8. Ward and Heitzenrater, *Journals and Diaries II*, 46. From Wesley's decision on April 2, 1739, to preach the Gospel outdoors among the masses have come, directly or indirectly, some of the greatest evangelistic, missionary, and renewal movements of recent centuries, from British and American Methodism and the Holiness Movement and related denominations to present-day Pentecostalism (as documented, for example, in Synan, *The Holiness-Pentecostal Tradition*).

9. One useful and inspiring way to come to grasp this mission is to study what God says about "the nations," especially in the prophetic books of the Old Testament.

10. Did the Western church miss the boat two centuries ago? If Christian thinkers had "out-thought" Marx and Engels, dealing with their legitimate social and economic concerns in terms of the biblical vision of God's reign, might the twentieth century have been spared the horrors of Marxist totalitarian states?

11. In addition to many scattered references in Acts and other New Testament books, note especially the men and women listed in Romans 16 and how they are described as "workers" or "fellow workers" *(synergoi)*.

12. Wilbert Shenk, "Christian Mission and the Coming 'Clash of Civilizations,'" *Missiology* 28:3 (July 2000): 303.

13. Francis A. Schaeffer, *Pollution and the Death of Man: The Christian View of Ecology* (Wheaton: Tyndale, 1970), 66–68.

14. See Howard A. Snyder, "The Gospel as Global Good News," chapter 14 in *Global Good News*.

15. Quoted in "Looking Back . . . Looking Forward," *Mission Frontiers* 22:3 (June 2000): 10.

16. Shenk, "Christian Mission and the Coming 'Clash of Civilizations,'" 302. Emphasis in the original.

17. Quoted in "Looking Back . . . Looking Forward," 9.

18. This true story was told by the American missionary, but no more details can be given because of the sensitive nature of the work.

19. Ubolwan Mejudhon, "The Way of Meekness: Being Christian and Thai in the Thai Way" (Ph.D. diss., Asbury Theological Seminary, 1997). Nantachai Mejudhon, "Meekness:

A New Approach to Christian Witness to the Thai People" (Ph.D. diss., Asbury Theological Seminary, 1997).

## Chapter 12: The DNA of Public Discipleship

1. Theologians sometimes speak of God's grace as *prevenient* (preceding or going ahead of salvation), *converting*, and *sanctifying*. These are the three ways God's grace is experienced in the world. Prevenient grace is an unconditional benefit of the atonement (though it cost Jesus his life!), and in that sense appears to us as God's unconditional love. Converting and sanctifying grace, however, require the conditions of repentance, faith, and obedience.

2. Regarding this whole debate, see especially Ronald J. Sider, *Rich Christians in an Age of Hunger*, rev. ed. (Dallas: Word, 1990).

3. For further elaboration, see Snyder, *Liberating the Church*, 20–67, and *A Kingdom Manifesto* (Downers Grove, Ill.: InterVarsity Press, 1985; Eugene, Ore.: Wipf and Stock, 1997), 51–76 (republished in 2002 by Wipf and Stock as *Kingdom, Church, and World: Biblical Themes for Today*).

4. See, for example, Lawrence Goodwyn, *The Populist Moment: A Short History of the Agrarian Revolt in America* (New York: Oxford University Press, 1978); John D. Hicks, *The Populist Revolt: A History of the Farmers' Alliance and the People's Party* (1931; reprint, University of Nebraska Press, 1961); Norman Pollack, *The Populist Response to Industrial America* (New York: W. W. Norton, 1962); Richard Hofstadter, *The Age of Reform From Bryan to F.D.R.* (1955; reprint, New York: Vintage, 1960).

5. J. Philip Wogaman, *The Great Economic Debate: An Ethical Analysis* (Philadelphia: Westminster, 1977); Friedman, *The Lexus and the Olive Tree*.

6. The work of the Christian economist Herman Daly provides a good example here. See, for example, Herman Daly, ed., *Economics, Ecology, Ethics* (San Francisco: Freeman, 1980).

7. Evangelical Environmental Network, 10 East Lancaster Avenue, Wynnewood, PA, 19096.

8. For example, Loren Wilkinson, ed., *Earthkeeping: Christian Stewardship of Natural Resources* (Grand Rapids: Eerdmans, 1980); Edwin R. Squiers, ed., *The Environmental Crisis: The Ethical Dilemma* (Mancelona, Mich.: Au Sable Trails Institute of Environmental Studies, 1982); John B. Cobb Jr., *Sustainability: Economics, Ecology, and Justice* (Maryknoll, N.Y.: Orbis, 1992); Stan L. LaQuire, ed., *The Best Preaching on Earth: Sermons on Caring for Creation* (Valley Forge, Penn.: Judson, 1996); Dale and Sandy Larson, *While Creation Waits: A Christian Response to the Environmental Challenge* (Wheaton: Harold Shaw, 1992); John Houghton, *Global Warming: The Complete Briefing* (Oxford,: Lion, 1994); Calvin DeWitt, *Earth-Wise: A Biblical Response to Environmental Issues* (Grand Rapids: CRC, 1994), Calvin DeWitt and Ghillean Prance, eds., *Missionary Earthkeeping* (Macon, Ga.: Mercer University Press, 1992).

9. The genetic, complexity, and ecological models explored throughout this book help us understand some of the mystery of the power of prayer.

# SUBJECT INDEX

203

# Scripture Index